120 Walks
in Victoria

Tyrone T. Thomas

120 Walks
in Victoria
Including Family Walks

FIFTH EDITION

Tyrone T. Thomas

HILL OF CONTENT

MELBOURNE

First published 1975 under the title 100 Walks in Victoria
by Hill of Content Publishing Company Pty Ltd
86 Bourke Street Melbourne Australia

© Copyright Tyrone T. Thomas 1975

Reprinted 1975, 1976
Second (revised) edition 1976
Third (revised) edition 1977, published under new title,
120 Walks in Victoria; reprinted 1979
Fourth (revised) edition 1984; reprinted 1987
Fifth (revised) edition 1989; reprinted 1990, 1992

Cover photograph: Wonnangatta Valley (Walk 61 page 214)
Maps and drawings by author

Typeset by Midland Typesetters, Maryborough, Victoria
Printed in Singapore by Kyodo Printing Co. Ltd

National Library of Australia
Cataloguing-in-Publication data
Thomas, Tyrone T., 1939-   .
    120 Walks in Victoria

    5th ed.
    Bibliography.
    Includes index.
    ISBN 0 85572 187 1.

    1. Hiking—Victoria—Guide-books. 2. Walking—
    Victoria—Guide-books. 3. Victoria—Description and
    travel—1976—   —Guide-books. I. Title. II. Title:
    One hundred and twenty walks in Victoria. (Series: Hill
    of Content bushwalking series).

919.45′0463

CONTENTS

INTRODUCTION

This book contains information about one hundred and twenty walks in Victoria, including thirty walks suitable for families. The book is organized so that ready reference can be made to regions within Victoria. Within each region walks are graded easy family, easy, medium and hard. Most walks are circuits of one day's duration, or are planned so that public transport can be used to complete circuits. A number of selected walks, which the author considers to be some of the best in the State, are of overnight duration. They are included for those who want to try camping out. In many cases the suggested direction of the walk (clockwise or anti-clockwise) is for the benefit of walkers, so readers would do well to adhere to the recommendation.

It is hoped this book will induce people to go out walking, that it will help them to grow to love the Victorian bush and learn to care for it and themselves. Special sections deal with safety, mapping and navigation. The book is designed to suit all grades of walkers and should be a useful addition to other 'walk' books in this series.

Walks graded as ALPINE should not be undertaken during the snow season because the Victorian high country can prove dangerous when snowbound. Walks are also graded alphabetically 'A', 'B' or 'C', 'A' grade walks being those considered by the author to be the most interesting. The time taken will vary greatly depending on walker's experience, so track notes are listed in terms of distance rather than variable times.

All routes in this book have been personally walked by the author between January 1987 and October 1988.

Track notes were simultaneously checked with the field checking and updated, but it must be expected that changes may occur in some places with the passing of time. Every care has been taken in notes compilation, but no responsibility will be accepted for any inaccuracies or for any mishap that might arise through the use of this book. The author and publisher welcome advice of any errors or desirable changes in order to ensure that future editions of the book can be brought up to date.

Tyrone T. Thomas
South Yarra

BEARDED ORCHID

WALK LOCATIONS

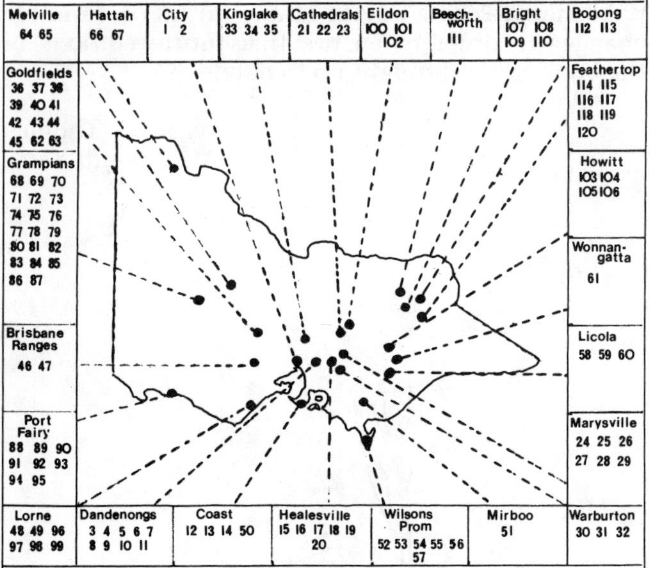

Melville 64 65	Hattah 66 67	City 1 2	Kinglake 33 34 35	Cathedrals 21 22 23	Eildon 100 101 102	Beech-worth 111	Bright 107 108 109 110	Bogong 112 113

Goldfields 36 37 38 39 40 41 42 43 44 45 62 63		Feathertop 114 115 116 117 118 119 120
Grampians 68 69 70 71 72 73 74 75 76 77 78 79 80 81 82 83 84 85 86 87		Howitt 103 104 105 106
		Wonnan-gatta 61
Brisbane Ranges 46 47		Licola 58 59 60
Port Fairy 88 89 90 91 92 93 94 95		Marysville 24 25 26 27 28 29

Lorne 48 49 96 97 98 99	Dandenongs 3 4 5 6 7 8 9 10 11	Coast 12 13 14 50	Healesville 15 16 17 18 19 20	Wilsons Prom 52 53 54 55 56 57	Mirboo 51	Warburton 30 31 32

EASY	MEDIUM	HARD
ONE DAY	**ONE DAY**	**ONE DAY**
1 2 3 4 5 6 9 10 13 14 15 16 19 24 25 27 28 29 30 31 33 34 40 41 43 44 46 47 48 50 51 52 53 54 58 63 64 66 67 69 70 74 75 76 79 80 81 84 88 89 90 91 92 93 94 96 100 101 107 109 110 111	7 8 11 12 18 26 35 36 37 38 39 42 49 62 65 68 71 77 78 82 87 98 99 102 108 114 115	17 21 32 45 83 85 86 106 112 117
OVERNIGHT	**OVERNIGHT**	**OVERNIGHT**
22 55 56 95 97 118	20 23 57 59 60 72 73 103 116 119	61 104 105 113 120

INDEX TO WALK SUGGESTIONS ACCORDING TO DISTRICTS

MELBOURNE REGION

Walk No.	Area	Walk grade	Walk km	Walk hours	Map No	Map page	Notes page
61	Wonnangatta Valley	hard overnight	36.4	14 (2 days)	42&43	217,219	214

WESTERN REGION

62	Mt Alexander	medium	10.5	3½	44	223	221
63	Maldon	easy	9.5	3	45	227	225
64	Melville Caves	family	5.0	2	46	231	229
65	Mt Kooyoora	medium	9.0	5	46	231	232
66	Hattah Lakes	easy	12.5	4	47	236	234
67	Lake Mournpall	easy	15.5	4½	47	236	237
68	Hollow Mountain	medium	2.5	2	48	242	239
69	Mt Stapylton	easy	5.5	2¼	48	242	241
70	Briggs Bluff	easy	10.5	4½	49	248	245
71	Mt Difficult	medium	6.5	4	49	248	247
72	Briggs Bluff-Mt Difficult	medium overnight	23.3	11	49	248	250
73	The Fortress	medium overnight	11.5	7	50	256	252
74	Cave of Hands	family	2.0	1½	50	256	255
75	Buandik-Red Cave	easy	5.0	2½	50	256	257
76	Calectasia Falls	easy	8.0	3½	51	260	259
77	Mt Rosea	medium	5.6	2¼	51	260	262
78	Mt Rosea Burma Tk.	medium	10.0	5	53	271	263
79	Boroka Lookout	easy	9.0	4	52	267	264
80	Sundial Peak	easy	3.5	1½	53	271	265
81	Sundial-The Pinnacle	family	4.5	2¼	52&53	267,271	268
82	Wonderland-The Pinnacle	medium	7.5	4	52	267	269
83	Wonderland	hard	16.8	7	52&53	267,271	272
84	Wonderland-Silverband	easy	6.5	3	53	271	274
85	Fyans Creek-Mt William	hard	16.5	7	54&55	276,278	275
86	Bomjinna-Mt William	hard	12.0	5	54&55	276,278	279
87	Mt Abrupt	medium	6.0	3	56	281	280
88	Mt Richmond	easy	5.5	1¾	57	285	282
89	Byaduk Caves	easy	3.0	2	58	288	284
90	Lake Surprise	easy	2.0	1	59	291	289
91	Mt Eccles	easy	8.0	3	59	291	292
92	Port Fairy	easy	5.5	2½	60	296	294

11

CLASSIFICATION OF WALKS
ACCORDING TO INTEREST

BEACH WALKS
12 Arthurs Seat
13 Sorrento
14 Cape Schanck
50 Cape Woolamai
52 Squeaky Beach
54 Oberon Bay
55 Sealers Cove
56 Waterloo Bay
57 Wilsons Prom.
95 Port Campbell
96 Lorne

HISTORICAL INTEREST WALKS
 1 Yarra River
13 Sorrento
63 Maldon
92 Port Fairy
111 Beechworth

WATERFALL WALKS
26 Steavenson Falls
29 Cumberland Falls
35 Murchison Falls
76 Calectasia Falls
97 Erskine Falls
98 Sheoak Falls
99 Kalimna Falls
107 Mount Buffalo

"PEAK BAGGING" WALKS
17 Mt St Leonard
32 Mt Donna Buang

59 Mt Wellington
86 Mt William
105 The Bluff
106 Mt Howitt
112 Mt Bogong
    (highest in Vic.)
114 The Twins
115 Mt Loch
117 Mt Feathertop (2nd
    highest in Vic.)
119 Mt Feathertop via
    N.W. Spur

CLIFFS & RUGGED TERRAIN WALKS
21 Cathedral Range
45 Lerderderg Gorge
68 Hollow Mountain
70 Briggs Bluff
71 Mt Difficult
72 Mt Difficult
73 The Fortress
79 Boroka Lookout
80 Sundial Peak
81 The Pinnacle
82 Wonderland
83 Wonderland
87 Mt Abrupt
103 The Bluff-
    Helicopter Spur
104 The Bluff-
    Mt Howitt
105 The Bluff
106 Mt Howitt
107 Mt Buffalo
113 Mt Bogong twice

14

CLASSIFICATION OF WALKS
ACCORDING TO SEASON

AUTUMN WALKS (MARCH, APRIL, MAY)
- 2 Melbourne parks
- 9 Mt Dandenong
- 11 Olinda Forest
- 30 Warburton
- 36 Mt Macedon
- 37 Willimigongon Creek
- 38 Hepburn Springs-Daylesford
- 43 Blackwood-Shaws Lake
- 109 Bright-Ovens River
- 110 Bright-Huggins Lookout

WINTER WALKS (JUNE, JULY, AUGUST)
- 39 Hepburn Springs
- 46 You Yangs
- 64 Melville Caves
- 65 Mt Kooyoora
- 66 Hattah Lakes
- 67 Lake Mournpall
- 100 Cook Point
- 102 Blowhard Spur
- 111 Beechworth

SPRING WALKS
(SEPTEMBER, OCTOBER, NOVEMBER)
- 2 Melbourne Parks
- 22 Cathedral Range
- 35 Murchison Falls
- 36 Mt Macedon
- 37 Willimigongon Creek
- 43 Blackwood-Shaws Lake
- 47 Anakie Gorge
- 49 Angahook Forest
- 69 Mt Stapylton
- 70 Briggs Bluff
- 71 Mt Difficult

SUMMER WALKS
(DECEMBER, JANUARY, FEBRUARY)

SAFETY AND COMMONSENSE
IN THE BUSH

Bushwalking is a very enjoyable recreation, and commonsense safety precautions will keep it that way. Be prepared for any problem that may arise.

First, plan your trip, leave details of your route in writing with some responsible person and report back on return. Always carry maps, compass, mirror, first aid kit, plenty of paper, warm, bright-coloured, waterproof clothing, whistle, matches in a waterproof container, candle, small sharp knife, torch and emergency rations of food. It is of the utmost importance that you should be able to read maps and use a compass.

Second, never try to rush a trip. Think before you act, watch your route on a map and recognize your limitations, especially with distance. A good walker can cover only about five kilometres each hour, in dense bush perhaps only two kilometres each hour. Always keep together when walking in a group and never walk in a party of less than three.

Third, if lost, STOP! Only move once you have very carefully thought things through. Remember that any movement is best made on ridges and spurs, not in scrub-choked gullies. You should be absolutely sure of directions and should leave a prominent note indicating your intentions and time of leaving. You should put on bright coloured and warm clothing. Once moving, constantly watch the compass, remain on as straight a line as possible and leave notes along the route. If you become tired, stop and rest. Do not over-exert yourself. Remember that severe physical and mental strain, plus cold, could mean death by exposure. Over the years far too many persons have died unnecessarily, or suffered serious injuries, mainly because they have not understood the seriousness of being caught unprepared in the bush, and then have not been able to cope with the situation. The accepted distress signal is three long whistles, cooees, mirror flashes, or any other signal repeated in threes every minute. Do not force yourself physically; rather, do things objectively and calmly with plenty of rest.

Fourth, when following suggested walk routes such as are recommended in this book and other publications, ensure that you obtain and use the recommended maps so that the maximum amount of information is available to you. Where more than one map of an area is available, it is advisable to use both. Maps frequently become outdated and this fact must be taken into account. The maps included in this book should be used in conjunction with other maps wherever possible.

Fifth, remember that care of the bushland itself is very important. Many walk routes are in declared National Parks and commonsense regulations must be respected. The bush and the life within it is often in a delicate state of ecological balance and, of necessity, your camp fire must be completely extinguished. Remember the slogan, 'The bigger the fire—the bigger the fool', and on no account light a fire on a high fire danger day.

Sixth, the camp fire is ideal for the disposal of most waste, but silver paper and other foils and cans will not destruct so readily. Wash all cans, remove both ends, flatten them, and carry them, along with any foil or glass, in a plastic bag to the nearest garbage bin. Many walking areas are frequented far more than you may realize and burial of rubbish will eventually create problems. Human waste should always be buried properly, away from streams and drinking water. Always wash downstream from the camp site and collect drinking water upstream from the camp site. Remember other people do not appreciate drinking your bath water.

Most walkers like to pitch their tents around a central camp fire but bad weather can drastically change the preference. When this happens an available hut or rock shelter in sandstone country can provide a welcome shelter in surroundings just as congenial. It is most important that huts used are respected, in return for the generosity of the owners in allowing bushwalkers to use them freely. They should always be left clean and with a good supply of firewood. Walkers who reach a hut or shelter first should not assume that they will be the only occupants for the night. Another party may come along later, probably feeling more tired than you through walking further, so you should move over, sleep on the floor, or do the best possible to share accommodation. It is always wise to carry your tent every trip you intend stopping overnight and not to rely on huts or rock shelters.

Camping in National Parks is frequently confined to certain areas and walkers should ensure that they are aware of those regulations. Some parks charge camping fees.

Seventh, flooding of streams, even days after heavy rains, can cause delays and even prevent walkers from continuing along their intended route. Some areas mentioned in these track notes are subject to flooding and walkers' discretion should be used.

Eighth, in the high country of the Victorian Alps, and occasionally in other districts suggested as walk venues in this publication, snow falls in winter. The high country being the State's highest, becomes completely snowbound and walks cannot be undertaken for a number of months of the year. This applies to a lesser extent in the mountains in many parts of Victoria.

Ninth, if you should be unlucky enough to be threatened by bushfire while walking do not panic. Do not run uphill, or run to try and outstrip a fire without giving some thought to the situation. Consider the area, the approach direction of the fire and the wind direction and velocity. In taking action remember that northern slopes are usually hot and dry and therefore a greater risk area. Fire tends to burn uphill and is usually most fierce on spurs and ridges. Choose the nearest open clear space, then quickly clean away all inflammable material, leaves, etc. Cover the body fully with clothing, preferably wool and wet if possible, even to the point of using urine to wet clothing if nothing else is available. Wear proper footwear, not thongs. Wet any towels and lie with face down in the clearing. Cover all exposed skin surfaces as radiant heat from fire kills, as well as flame. Do not be tempted to lift the head too much and so inhale smoke or get smoke in the eyes. The freshest air is right next to the ground surface.

Do not try to run through a fire front unless it is no wider than 3 m and no higher than 1.5 m. If you have a car parked *in an open spot* get into it and shut all windows, then lie low on the floor away from radiant heat. If possible clear all inflammable material from under and near the car, especially near the tyres. Do not chance driving in dense smoke.

If near a deep dam or deep flowing stream get right into the water. Avoid getting into shallow pools or water storages. Remember that concrete water tanks can explode and iron water tanks buckle and break open. Also, their water contents tend to boil in great heat. It is safer to use available water from shallow pools or doubtful storages to wet a clear patch of ground and clothing and then lie down as instructed above.

FIRST AID AT A GLANCE

It is essential that any emergency arising can be dealt with adequately. The St John Ambulance Association *First Aid Book* or an equivalent book should be carried by at least one member of every walking party.

The most likely troubles to be encountered are listed here for rapid reference as in many cases there is not time to do research in a full first aid book. In virtually all serious situations the patient needs to be rested and reassured, often whilst some other person obtains medical assistance. For this reason walk parties should never be less than three in number in any remote place. One person should stay with the patient whilst the other should go for aid.

COMPLAINT	TREATMENT
BLISTERS	Apply an adhesive foam patch; wear extra socks; if possible, do not break the blister thus increasing the risk of infection.
HEAT EXHAUSTION	Replenish body fluids with plenty of drinks of water or fruit juice and take a little salt if badly dehydrated. Rest in a cool place and fan the patient. Remove excess clothing from the patient.
ABDOMINAL DISORDERS, FEVERS	Rest is essential. Give patient plenty of liquid.
BURNS	Immediately immerse burn area in cold water to chill. Clean burn thoroughly, despite the pain, and apply a

clean bandage. Immobilize the burn area.

SPRAINS

Immobilize the area of the sprain and rest it. Immerse in cold water (stream etc.)

EXPOSURE TO COLD

Do not rub the skin, apply direct heat, or give alcohol as all cause blood to come to the skin surface, then to be returned to the heart, cooler. The body trunk and brain must be warmed. Insulate the entire body. Assuming the patient is conscious, give sugar in easily digested form, (e.g. sweetened condensed milk). Put patient in a sleeping bag, preferably with a warm person; cover bag with insulation, provide a wind break and pitch a tent over the patient. If breathing stops, apply mouth to mouth resuscitation. Only move to a warmer place if in doing so the patient is in no way physically exerted. Avoid patient standing as fainting will follow. The recognizable signs of the onset of exposure are: pallor and shivering, listlessness, slurred speech, poor vision, irrational and violent behaviour, collapse. *It is wet cold particularly that kills.*

SNAKE BITE

Most bites are of a minor nature and not all snakes are venomous. It is, however, wise to treat all bites as if a danger. Many persons have a disproportionate fear of the bite of a snake so need reassurance and rest. The majority of bites are to the limbs rather than the body trunk so first aid is easier. The need is to restrict venom movement in the body, therefore a broad bandage should be firmly applied to any limb bite area or pressure kept on bites to the body trunk. The bite area should be kept immobilized with pressure applied by bandage or pad until antiveneme is received from a doctor. Immobilization can best be achieved by binding a splint to any limb bite area. Old first aid methods of cutting the bite and of washing venom off skin are not recommended. Cutting upsets the patient and the venom can be tested to identify a snake species. Bring transport to the patient or carry the person to maximize rest. If patient deteriorates to unconsciousness, apply mouth to mouth resuscitation and artificial respiration until medical aid is given.

EQUIPMENT AND FOOD
SUGGESTIONS FOR WALKS

SAFETY EQUIPMENT
Maps, compass, small mirror, paper, whistle, matches in a waterproof container, sharp knife, small candle, small torch, textacolour or similar marker, first aid reference book, first aid kit containing bandages, Bandaids, adhesive foam, antiseptic, aspirin, safety pins, safety clothing consisting of warm trousers and pullover, thick wool socks, bright-coloured shirt or blouse and bright-coloured parka. Safety food rations should consist of nourishing concentrated foods plus a little bulky food like dried fruits, chocolate, nuts, fruits and seed bars and brown rice.

OTHER EQUIPMENT
Overnight walks: tent, tent pegs, tent guys, good quality sleeping bag, plastic groundsheet, a newspaper, toilet items and a billy.

All walks: shirt or blouse (wool for winter), shorts, jeans, handkerchief, walking or gym-boots, mug, bowl, cutlery, small towel, lightweight bathers for summer, waterbag (Japara type with zip top), water bottle (aluminium or plastic), can opener and pack.

FOOD
In addition to emergency rations which should be used only in an emergency, the following foods should be carried in quantities dictated by the number of days that the walk will occupy: nuts, dried fruits, chocolate, fruit and seed bars, hard-boiled eggs, packet or cube soups, fruit drink powders, brown rice and rice packet preparations, fresh fruit, honey, wholemeal bread, Vegemite, salami, fruit cake, coffee, tea or other hot drink, bacon, carrot, packet mashed potato and some muesli or porridge. Cans should only

be carried by persons accustomed to carrying heavy packs, and empty cans should be washed and carried out of walk areas to garbage disposal bins.

WEIGHT
The most important consideration when carrying an overnight pack is the combined weight of the contents, and if you carry no more than is stated in this list of equipment and food suggestions you should not encounter trouble. However, far too many persons include that little extra item or two, or overestimate the quantity of food that they can possibly eat and so suffer the consequences when they have to climb a hill bearing 'a ton of bricks'.

OBTAINING BASIC EQUIPMENT
The purchase of a pack, tent, or sleeping bag frequently constitutes a major problem for the newcomer to bushwalking circles. Elementary logic is all that is involved in the decision.

Packs; Comfort, weight and price to be considered; try the pack on in the shop after asking the shop assistant to load it. Generally speaking, for overnight walks, unframed packs are not popular, but framed packs are. Do not buy a pack that feels uncomfortable from the outset. Try to keep the weight down when deciding on the purchase but also ensure the pack is very strong.

Tents; Comfort, weight and price again to be considered. As a general rule nylon tents are wonderfully light but they are so closely woven that condensation inside them is so great that you might just as well be out in the rain! On the other hand Japara and similar type tents are quite heavy and leak if their inside is touched while it is raining.

The logical decision, therefore, is to do one of two things and in both cases the cost of the tent soars. But then you do need to be comfortable.

(1) Buy a nylon type tent and a fly which extends well out beyond each end of the tent and also have large air vents inserted in either end of the tent. Use the fly every night.

KOOKABURRA

(2) Buy a Japara type tent and a fly of nylon to go over it on wet nights only. The fly need not be very big.

Whichever alternative you decide upon, try to keep the weight down.

Sleeping Bags; Comfort, weight and price again to be considered. Far too many people do not think logically when purchasing a bag. They settle for a cheap bag, lie awake in it all night due to the cold, then defeat the whole purpose of their walking trip by being too tired next day to enjoy walking. Remember, you will spend many hours in that bag either blissfully sleeping or lying awake half frozen. The more warmth that you can achieve in a bag the better, and as a general rule the more you pay for one, the more warmth. Comfort is therefore the primary consideration in a bag choice. Weight and price are secondary.

MAPPING AND NAVIGATION

Navigation procedures are best learned from experience in the field using map and compass. This is sometimes difficult to arrange if one does not have a friend who can teach in the field.

Usually, excellent opportunities exist to learn navigation when walking with a bushwalking club. Clubs help walkers gain safety, advice, experience and companionship. Usually, their organized walks are led by experienced leaders, often with transport arranged. Enquiries of a general nature and those concerning the various clubs can be made through the Federation of Walking Clubs based in Melbourne.

This publication provides a map of the immediate area of every walk suggestion. To some extent they will assist with navigation, but to rely entirely upon these maps would be unwise. (For example, the walker might travel off the map coverage if lost). It is strongly recommended, therefore, that every endeavour be made to purchase Government or other maps before setting out on these trips.

One important point with which all walkers should be familiar is that magnetic north is presently eleven degrees east of true north in Victoria.

Certain maps are suggested in this book, but other maps are on sale and could usefully supplement information. These maps are available in the bigger cities at the appropriate sales outlets of Government Departments and at larger book shops and shops catering for bushwalkers' needs.

RECOMMENDED ADDITIONAL MAPS

Walk Number	Map
1	—
2	—
3	Melways Melbourne Street Directory
4	—
5	—
6	Melways Melbourne Street Directory
7	Melways Melbourne Street Directory
8	—
9	—
10	Melways Melbourne Street Directory
11	Melways Melbourne Street Directory
12	Vicmap 1:25,000 Dromana
13	Vicmap 1:25,000 Rye Special and 1:25,000 Queenscliff
14	—
15	National Mapping 1:100,000 Healesville
16	National Mapping 1:100,000 Healesville
17	National Mapping 1:100,000 Healesville
18	National Mapping 1:100,000 Healesville
19	National Mapping 1:100,000 Healesville
20	National Mapping 1:100,000 Healesville
21	National Mapping 1:100,000 Alexandra
22	National Mapping 1:100,000 Alexandra
23	National Mapping 1:100,000 Alexandra
24	National Mapping 1:100,000 Healesville
25	National Mapping 1:100,000 Healesville
26	National Mapping 1:100,000 Healesville
27	—
28	—
29	—
30	National Mapping 1:100,000 Healesville
31	—
32	National Mapping 1:100,000 Healesville
33	—
34	—
35	National Mapping 1:100,000 Yea

Walk Number	Map
36	National Mapping 1:100,000 Woodend
37	National Mapping 1:100,000 Woodend
38	National Mapping 1:100,000 Castlemaine
39	National Mapping 1:100,000 Castlemaine
40	National Mapping 1:100,000 Castlemaine
41	National Mapping 1:100,000 Castlemaine
42	National Mapping 1:100,000 Castlemaine
43	National Mapping 1:100,000 Castlemaine
44	National Mapping 1:100,000 Bacchus Marsh
45	National Mapping 1:100,000 Bacchus Marsh
46	National Mapping 1:100,000 Bacchus Marsh
47	National Mapping 1:100,000 Bacchus Marsh
48	National Mapping 1:100,000 Geelong
49	National Mapping 1:100,000 Geelong
50	—
51	National Mapping 1:100,000 Moe
52	National Mapping 1:100,000 Wilsons Promontory
53	National Mapping 1:100,000 Wilsons Promontory
54	National Mapping 1:100,000 Wilsons Promontory
55	National Mapping 1:100,000 Wilsons Promontory
56	National Mapping 1:100,000 Wilsons Promontory
57	National Mapping 1:100,000 Wilsons Promontory
58	—
59	—
60	—
61	—
62	National Mapping 1:100,000 Bendigo
63	National Mapping 1:100,000 Bendigo
64	—
65	—
66	—
67	—
68	National Mapping 1:100,000 Horsham
69	National Mapping 1:100,000 Horsham
70	National Mapping 1:100,000 Horsham
71	National Mapping 1:100,000 Horsham & 1:100,000 Grampians

Walk Number	Map
72	National Mapping 1:100,000 Horsham & 1:100,000 Grampians
73	National Mapping 1:100,000 Grampians
74	National Mapping 1:100,000 Grampians
75	National Mapping 1:100,000 Grampians
76	National Mapping 1:100,000 Grampians
77	National Mapping 1:100,000 Ararat
78	National Mapping 1:100,000 Ararat
79	National Mapping 1:100,000 Ararat
80	National Mapping 1:100,000 Ararat
81	National Mapping 1:100,000 Ararat
82	National Mapping 1:100,000 Ararat
83	National Mapping 1:100,000 Ararat
84	National Mapping 1:100,000 Ararat
85	National Mapping 1:100,000 Ararat
86	National Mapping 1:100,000 Ararat
87	National Mapping 1:100,000 Hamilton
88	National Mapping 1:100,000 Nelson
89	National Mapping 1:100,000 Coleraine
90	National Mapping 1:100,000 Portland
91	National Mapping 1:100,000 Portland
92	National Mapping 1:100,000 Warrnambool
93	National Mapping 1:100,000 Warrnambool
94	National Mapping 1:100,000 Warrnambool
95	National Mapping 1:100,000 Mortlake-Port Campbell
96	National Mapping 1:100,000 Colac-Otway
97	National Mapping 1:100,000 Colac-Otway
98	National Mapping 1:100,000 Colac-Otway
99	National Mapping 1:100,000 Colac-Otway
100	National Mapping 1:100,000 Alexandra
101	National Mapping 1:100,000 Alexandra
102	National Mapping 1:100,000 Alexandra
103	—
104	—
105	—
106	—
107	National Mapping 1:100,000 Buffalo
108	National Mapping 1:100,000 Buffalo

Walk Number	Map
109	National Mapping 1:100,000 Buffalo
110	National Mapping 1:100,000 Buffalo
111	National Mapping 1:100,000 Albury
112	National Mapping 1:100,000 Bogong
113	National Mapping 1:100,000 Bogong
114	—
115	National Mapping 1:100,000 Bogong
116	National Mapping 1:100,000 Bogong
117	National Mapping 1:100,000 Bogong
118	National Mapping 1:100,000 Bogong
119	National Mapping 1:100,000 Bogong
120	National Mapping 1:100,000 Bogong

CELMISIA
SNOW DAISY

FAMILY WALKS ADVICE

Thirty walks that cater especially for families have been included in this book. It is stressed that parents or party leaders attempting these trips should at no time leave the children unattended as becoming lost is a very unhappy experience for a child. It must be emphasized that any walking along roads should be done *facing the oncoming traffic*, that children should be instructed not to wander away from the party and if they do become separated or lost, to *wait where they are* until help arrives. It is also important that children be instructed not to drink from streams without supervision and not to eat tempting looking berries in the bush. Many leaves, fruits, berries and fungi, if not actually poisonous, can cause acute discomfort.

The areas selected are in the more commonly frequented places where usually tracks and signs are quite clear. This is not to be taken as an indication that adult supervision can be relaxed or that walkers can dispense with recommended maps. It is unwise to take babies on walks exposing them to the hot sun and wind.

By using a little extra care and avoiding placing children in dangerous situations, great family enjoyment can be had. The bush is full of wonders and what better way is there to give children fresh air, exercise and a first-hand knowledge of the wonder that is the Australian bush?

MAP   LEGEND

ALL   MEASUREMENTS   METRIC

MAIN ROAD	═══
MINOR ROAD	≈≈≈≈
JEEP TRACK	4wd
FOOT TRACK	─ ─ ─ ─
ROUTE	. . . .
RAILWAY	+++++
MAJOR SUMMIT	▲
CONTOUR	─50─
CLIFFS & QUARRY	ᴛᴛᴛᴛ ⌁
STREAM & WATERFALL	◄─
WATER FOR DRINKING	w
BUILDING	■
LAVATORY	wc
BRIDGE	br
LOOKOUT	L'out
BARRIER OR GATE	bar =╪=
PICNIC AREA	PG
BARE ROCK AREA	⬚⬚⬚
CAVE ENTRY	o
RIDGE / SADDLE / KNOB	··╫···o····

MELBOURNE REGION

1   MARVELLOUS MELBOURNE'S RIVER YARRA

Melbourne is a unique city in that it developed as one of the world's few Victorian era cities and consequently has splendid Victorian boulevards and lavish building styles. Its main early development occurred under boom conditions following the discovery of gold in Victoria. One of the world's best botanic gardens was established and the amount of parkland set aside for the city of Melbourne was quite exceptional. Another aspect of Melbourne's early development was that it had its river straightened, widened and beautified. Today the Yarra is one of the city's main features. This walk suggestion is to take a 'history walk' from inner suburban Hawthorn Railway Station to Flinders Street Station in the city, in order to see the beauty of some of 'Marvellous Melbourne' as it became known in the 1880s. A train could be used to complete a circuit for ease of transport. Hawthorn Station itself is quite historic and has been restored.

At the walk start the route leads through the St James Park area of Hawthorn so that an appreciation of the Victorian era buildings is gained. In 1847 Sir James Palmer, M.L.C., doctor and merchant, began to buy all the land south of Burwood Road and west of Yarra Street bounded by the Yarra River. He was one of Hawthorn's earliest settlers. He was Mayor of Melbourne in 1845 and operated a toll punt across the river from Richmond. In the middle of his land he built a large house from bluestone, completing it by about 1850. He called it 'Burwood'. In 1870 it was sold to a Mr Coppin and the estate was divided up to create Isabella Grove and Shakespeare Grove. Later the property name was changed from 'Burwood' to 'Invergowrie' and the locality became known as

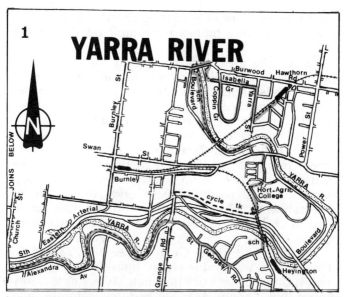

1 YARRA RIVER

the St James Park area. During the 1870s and 1880s many interesting homes were built on the former estate site.

To see the area, first walk from the south (city bound) side of the Hawthorn station along a footpath which leads along the south side of the railway to nearby Yarra Street. Turn right (north) on Yarra Street which formed the eastern boundary of Palmer's land. On the left there are four good examples of single storey Victorian houses at Nos. 22, 18, 16 and 12 Yarra Street. Just ahead on the right are three double storey houses at Nos. 9, 7 and 5 Yarra Street. They each occupy rather narrow blocks and No. 9 has an interesting small tower with a 'widows walk' on it. The three buildings are known as the Glucksburg group because of their unusual architecture.

Turn left up Isabella Grove to see Nos. 23 and 21. The former is a double storey house and the latter a most unusual red brick Italianate style, single storey house built about 1888. It features columns and formerly was a German Consulate. Next, back-track slightly to walk south along Shakespeare Grove. No. 1 on the corner is another large double storey house with a tower. Nos. 25 and 27 are single storey and Nos. 29, 31, 26 and 35 are each splendid double storey homes. Shakespeare Grove becomes Coppin Grove as it curves back north. No. 21 Coppin Grove, now called 'Invergowrie', is well preserved and is the former home of Sir James Palmer. On the west side of Coppin Street there are noteworthy homes at Nos. 12, 10 and 6. At No. 6, turn left down an easement opposite the west end of Isabella Grove and descend to the river bank and the Hawthorn Rowing Club buildings. Turn right (north) and follow the river bank the short distance to the Bridge Road Bridge. A foot track leads up to the east end of the bridge and just nearby is the former gatehouse of 'Burwood' ('Invergowrie') at No. 8 Burwood Road.

Cross the bridge to leave Hawthorn, then descend a foot track to the west bank of the river. At this point the city to Hawthorn bicycle track is reached and should be followed south (right) along the river bank. You need to *be aware* of bicycles as you proceed past Richmond High School to the Swan Street intersection with The Boulevard. Leave the bicycle track and cross Swan Street, then enter the front gate of the Burnley Horticultural College. Walk the college driveway to the front of the main buildings and adjacent Students' Union building, then head to the left to take a short walk in the college garden before walking out the east side entrance onto The Boulevard. As many plants are labelled the garden walk is most informative. Follow The Boulevard south-east (right) some 300m then turn right along a roadway through the Bartlett sporting complex until a rail bridge crosses the road. Pass under the bridge, turn right onto a path and use the path and bridge to cross the South-Eastern Arterial Road, the Yarra River and The Boulevard.

BLACK SWAN

Once across this long bridge, join Lansell Road Toorak just north of Heyington Station and beside St Kevins Junior College. Head west on Lansell Road until St Georges Road is intersected. Turn right and then follow St Georges Road to the Grange Road bridge. No. 76 St Georges Road is a big, magnificent, old mansion with a tower. Most other buildings in Lansell road and St Georges Road represent the general opulence of Toorak. From Grange Road

37

Bridge, the riverside bicycle track is rejoined. As you follow it along the south bank towards the city, Como Park is passed, as are the small but beautiful Darling Gardens of South Yarra. West of Punt Road Bridge the city skyline comes into view. Morell Bridge (1899) is nearby and has fine patterns on its masonry. Barbecue facilities exist beyond Morell Bridge and could be used for lunch or afternoon tea. A tempting alternative is to leave the riverside from the bridge and enter the Botanic Gardens. At the nearby gardens kiosk Devonshire teas and lunches are highly recommended. A short inspection of these world class

BLUE WREN

gardens could follow before returning to the river bank. The whole area has many deciduous trees which are at their best in autumn. Lastly, complete a final 1 km of the walk to Flinders Street Station by continuing along the bicycle track past rowing club buildings to Princes Bridge then cross the bridge to the station.

8.5 km; 4 hours; walk last reviewed September 1988; 'B' grade, easy walk; all on tracks; features Yarra River; rail transport available for access to walk; drinking water available at several drink fountains along route; walk suited to any season; *Melways Melbourne Street Directory* shows route as does Map No. 1, page 35.

2   THE BEST OF MELBOURNE'S PARKS

Melbourne is fortunate in having more parklands than most cities round the world. The city originally had a lot more parks but over the years large tracts have been used for 'development', for army purposes and for a host of sporting complexes and ancillary buildings. However, what is left is outstanding and walkers can certainly enjoy an excellent day in the parks. Many bushwalkers seem to adopt the attitude that they want bushland and to be away from the city for the day, to get away from the rush and bustle of the city and to hear birds and enjoy the serenity of the bush. The parks of Melbourne do provide serenity, birdlife, native bush, etc, but may be discovered only if one knows where to go and what to do. In fact, the parks can be conveniently seen by following a long string of them. For most of the year a suggested route is from south to north finishing at Royal Park Station. However, on 'beach days' the walk could be from north to south to Middle Park, with a short deviation included to Middle Park Beach via Armstrong Street in Middle Park. The day walk then includes Melbourne's world famous Botanic Gardens and some of the world's best elm trees stand in the Fitzroy Gardens. Most Melbourne people would be surprised to learn that the Fitzroy Gardens elms form the shape of a huge Union Jack when seen from the air. There are a host of surprises to be found so why not head out into the parks to find out for yourself why Victoria is known as the Garden State. Indeed Melbourne's parks leave much of our bushland looking drab and uninteresting in comparison.

Take the St Kilda light rail to Armstrong Street Middle Park or drive to the station area where car parking is not a problem and enter Albert Park on the east side of the railway. A sporting oval should be passed to its south (right) side by way of a bitumen path to reach Aughtie Drive. The south end of a golf

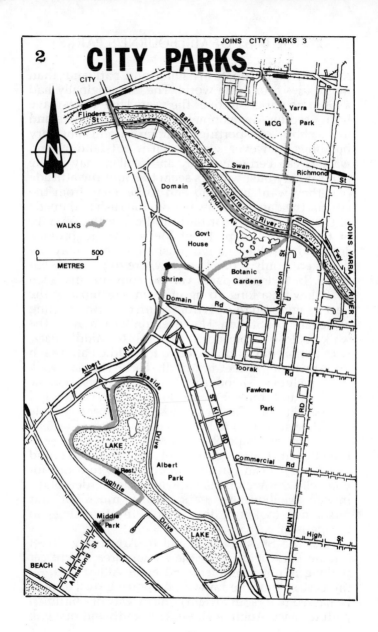

2 **CITY PARKS**

CITY

Flinders St

Batman Av

Yarra Park

MCG

Swan

Richmond St

Domain

Alexandra Av

Yarra River

WALKS

Govt House

0   500

METRES

Botanic Gardens

Anderson St

JOINS YARRA RIVER 1

Shrine

Domain   Rd

Albert   Rd

Lakeside

Toorak   Rd

Fawkner Park

St KILDA RD

LAKE

Rest.

Albert Park

Commercial   Rd

Aughtie

Drive

PUNT   RD

Middle Park

LAKE

High   St

BEACH

Armstrong   St

course should be skirted so that the western shore of Albert Park Lake is reached. It is only 400 m from the station to the lake shore. Views of the city and St Kilda Road skyline are excellent across the lake. Follow the shoreline path, left (north), for 1.8 km. Initially, Robs Carousel Restaurant is passed, then a number of boat sheds. When at the extreme northern end of the lake, walk across lawns to Albert Road. At this point Albert Park is left. The park is principally devoted to sporting venues including golf and a lot of water craft activities. It is a pleasant place to walk because of the lake, but its scenic beauty does not match that of other parks to be seen later in the day.

Walk just 400 m north-east on Albert Road which is one of Melbourne's lovely Victorian era tree-lined boulevards, then cross busy St Kilda Road, another broad boulevard, to enter The Domain. Near the intersection of Albert Road and St Kilda Road there are several interesting monuments, such as the South African War Memorial, a war horse trough, a fine fountain on the lawns as you enter The Domain and ahead is the Shrine of Remembrance, an architectural masterpiece. Go to the war memorial's north side and climb interior steps for a wonderful view of Melbourne. It is, in fact, a view which highlights parklands. Adjacent and eastwards of The Shrine is Birdwood Avenue, a delightful parkland drive. Follow it south-east (right) and within 200 m Governor Latrobe's historic house can be seen on the left side of the road. Another 100 m along Birdwood Avenue enter 'F' gate of The Botanic Gardens.

Walk any of the gardens' paths which lead downhill so that the central lake and kiosk are reached. The route you choose could be east, initially, through the Australian native plants section, then north to the kiosk or, in a more direct line, through exotic gardens perhaps including the magnificent rain forest of ferns, palms and tropical trees. As you enter the 'F' gate take a brochure from the holder and explore these gardens at leisure. They are said to be the third best

41

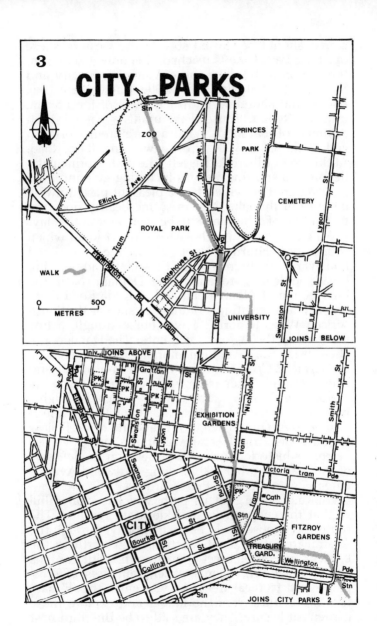

3

CITY PARKS

Stn
ZOO
PRINCES PARK
The Ave.
Pde
Elliott Ave.
CEMETERY
Lygon St
ROYAL PARK
Royal
Tram
WALK
Gatehouse St
Flemington Rd
0 500 METRES
St
UNIVERSITY
Swanston St

JOINS BELOW

Univ. JOINS ABOVE

Road Pde
Elizabeth
Grattan St
PK
PK
PK
Swanston St
Lygon St
Nicholson St
Smith St
EXHIBITION GARDENS
tram
PK
Spring
Victoria tram Pde
Stn
Cath
CITY
Bourke St
St
St
tram
St
FITZROY GARDENS
Collins St
TREASURY GARD.
Wellington Pde
Stn
Stn

JOINS CITY PARKS 2

42

anywhere in the world. Take full advantage of the opportunity to learn a few plant names, then perhaps enjoy a Devonshire Tea or lunch at the kiosk or on the lawns. The kiosk meals and teas are about Melbourne's best considering price and quality.

There are many birds near the kiosk which can be fed with bread, etc. At other parts of the gardens birdlife is amazing considering the proximity to the city centre. You do need to walk quietly, though. To leave the Botanic Gardens, walk a path from the kiosk to the 'A' gate at the north-east corner of the gardens at Alexandra Avenue and Anderson Street, South Yarra. Cross historic Morell Bridge (1899) over the Yarra River to continue into Yarra Park. To the left as you cross the bridge there are barbecue facilities as an alternative for lunch if desired. There is also a good view of the city and a fine riverscape as you cross the bridge.

A footpath can next be followed into Yarra Park after crossing busy Batman Avenue at traffic lights. The path leads north through parkland to nearby Swan Street then another path leads on a diagonal north-west past the Tennis Centre to a foot bridge over the main railway outlet from the city. Cross the foot bridge and walk around the east side of the Melbourne Cricket Ground.

Just to the right of the foot bridge is the re-located historic cabmans shelter formerly opposite the Windsor Hotel in the Parliament House precinct.

Walk north-west from the cricket ground on a path to the intersection of Wellington Parade and Clarendon Street East Melbourne. Cross Wellington Parade and enter Fitzroy Gardens next. Keep relatively near the south end of the gardens as you head westwards, but ensure you see both Captain Cook's Cottage and the superb displays of hot-house plants in the Conservatory. There is also a model Tudor village and a kiosk just a little further north. The aim is to cross Lansdowne Street, to walk west through the lovely Treasury Gardens next, and to reach Spring Street at the State Government Treasury Building. Walk along Spring Street past the front of Parliament House, then north on Nicholson Street for two blocks to Victoria Parade.

Enter Carlton Gardens from the Victoria Parade intersection and head north to the magnificent fountain and southern entrance to the Exhibition Buildings. This building could be described as the very epitome of the magnificence of 'Marvellous Melbourne' of the 1880s. Take a really good look at the architecture and the scale of the complex and imagine the work that went into it in those days of 'pick and shovel' work.

GRASS YELLOW BUTTERFLY

Go around the west end of the building to the north-west corner of the gardens. At this point Grattan Street Carlton leads off west and must be followed, regrettably, for a short period in an area of no parks. Did you know that the city founders set aside much of Carlton as a park? Somehow, however, the broad visions of parkland through both Parkville and Carlton ended up with only Royal Park being set aside. Walk Grattan Street for four blocks to cross Swanston Street, then continue west 300 m to the southern entrance of Melbourne University campus. It is then suggested you wander through the campus northwards until you reach Tin Alley, which is a narrow road aligned east-west and right across the campus.

Turn left (west) and walk out onto Royal Parade, yet another magnificent Victorian era boulevard. Turn north and proceed to the nearby traffic lights at Gatehouse Street, Parkville. Royal Park is then on the west side of the intersection. Enter the park. There is a most delightful native garden with labelled plant names and a central pond and a host of birds to be seen immediately.

Some 400 m north-north-west is the next objective—the historic Burke and Wills Memorial Cairn. Then, a further 400 m north-west is the main (Elliott Avenue) entrance to the Zoological Gardens. To finish the day you could visit the zoo and leave by the northern entrance to Royal Park Station, or you could walk round the north side of the zoo to the station. A train could then be taken back to Flinders Street City and the light rail used to reach Middle Park.

11.5 km; 4½ to 5 hours (or more, preferably); walk last reviewed September 1988; 'A' grade. easy walk; all on tracks, roads and lawns; features Botanic and Fitzroy Gardens plus Albert Park Lake; water for lunch at any of a number of drinking fountains along the route; rail transport best for access to walk start and end; trip can be easily short-cut if desired at several points; *Melways Melbourne Street Directory* refers as do Maps 2 and 3, pages 40 and 42.

3   ONE TREE HILL

This walk route in the Dandenong Ranges National Park is probably the closest fern gully and lookout walk to central Melbourne. It has been a favourite walk route for about a century and is still popular— a traditional walk for locals and visitors alike. The

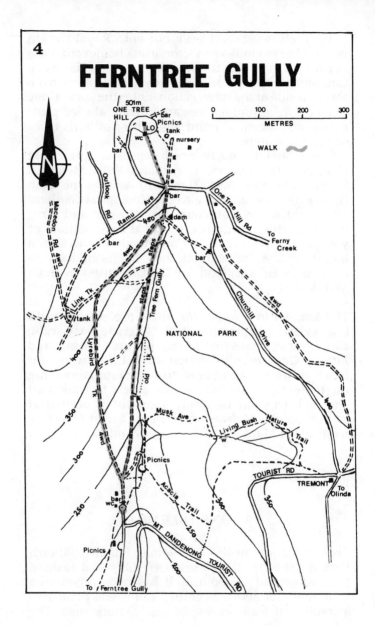

4

FERNTREE GULLY

route is known as the Tree Fern Gully Creek Trail and it leads from the Ferntree Gully main picnic area to One Tree Hill Lookout. Fine views of Melbourne can then be gained from a three deck lookout tower. The return walk can be varied by descending the Lyrebird Trail which virtually runs parallel to the Tree Fern Gully Creek Trail. However the variation is steep and can prove quite slippery especially in winter. Bushfire devastated the whole area in 1968, but so much regrowth has occurred that the casual visitor would hardly notice any damage.

From the extreme upper end of the picnic ground three tracks diverge simultaneously from a point on the western side of Tree Fern Gully. Take the central broad track which leads north close to the creek amid both rough and soft tree-ferns. After 200 m a track joins in from the right. Walk on 200 m further north up the gully, then the trail commences a steep climb up some 745 steps to emerge at a minor road intersection and fire dam. The steps rise through lovely ferns and over 200 m elevation is gained. They are known as 'The Thousand Steps'. Continue 200 m uphill on a minor road, then past a barrier onto the One Tree Hill Lookout Road. The spot is 2.25 km from the walk start. The One Tree Hill Lookout tower is 250 m north-west through open forest with a road and two foot-tracks leading to it. It is 500 m above sea level, and is adjacent to full picnic facilities including shelters and toilets. (Refurbishment of the old tower is likely to occur in 1988 or 1989 so the tower may be temporarily closed).

After lunch retrace the route to the fire dam and top of the many steps, then diverge right down steep Lyrebird Trail. The area has only small trees, the tall trees having been destroyed by past fires. Continue down Lyrebird Trail, south, back to the walk starting point 2 km away. The route is through forest and during the descent a minor jeep-track joins in from the left at first, then a second jeep-track slants off right soon after and, finally, a third and fourth track each join in on the left.

5 km; 2½ hours; (walk includes 745 steps). Walk last reviewed February 1988; 'C' grade, family walk; all on tracks; features One Tree Hill Lookout; transport available to near walk start by rail to Upper Ferntree Gully; water for lunch at lookout; walk suited to any time of the year but wet underfoot in winter; *Melways Melbourne Street Directory* refers as does Map 4, page 46.

**GREENHOOD
ORCHID**

4   FERNY CREEK

Sherbrooke Forest in the Dandenong Ranges National Park has many cool forest tracks amid its stately eucalypts, but one of the most beautiful places is along Sherbrooke Creek. The stream has foot-pads along much of its length. Mountain Ash (Eucalyptus Regnans) stands are particularly attractive in the area. It is good therefore to take a walk from the headwaters at the Mt. Dandenong Tourist Road and Sherbrooke Road junction, and head down-stream to Sherbrooke Falls then to return via the park edge. The falls are just a small cascade, but are a convenient turn-around point. There is also a picnic area adjacent to the falls which contains shelter, barbecue and toilets. If you are lucky a lyrebird may be seen.

From the road junction walk 400 m south along a foot-track parallel with the Mt. Dandenong Tourist Road initially, then into the forest further. After crossing a small creek veer left, rather than follow Moore Break (firebreak), then head 1.1 km along the south-west side of Sherbrooke Creek in damp forest. Turn left at a 'T' intersection of the tracks to cross Sherbrooke Creek then to reach some picnic tables and a barbecue at another junction. Turn right and go 200 m downstream to a track intersection. The Sherbrooke Falls Picnic Ground and falls are across the intersection. Lunch is suggested here.

To return, retrace the 200 m; cross back to the south bank side of Sherbrooke Creek then continue straight ahead uphill towards the Jacka Street entrance to Sherbrooke Forest. At the entrance 400 m distant, turn right along Moore Break Track so as to walk the perimeter fire break route 1.3 km. The route passes some fine private gardens then rejoins the outward route. The final 400 m is a retrace of the walk start. A large picnic area and National Park Visitor Centre is planned for the Nicholas Paddock area across the road westwards.

4 km; 2 hours; walk last reviewed February 1988; 'B' grade, family walk; all on tracks; features Sherbrooke Forest; water for lunch at falls; transport available to Ferny Creek by bus from Upper Ferntree Gully station; *Melways Melbourne Street Directory* refers as does Map 5, page 50.

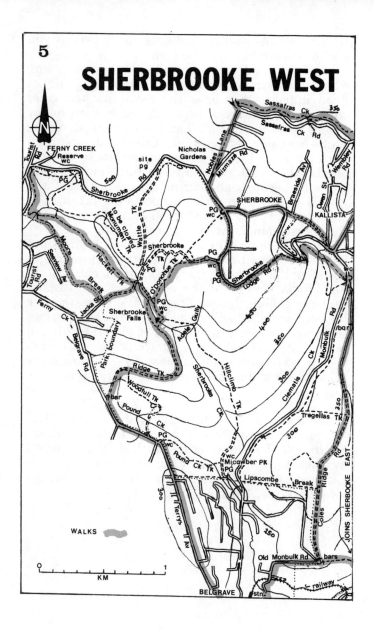

5
SHERBROOKE WEST

5 SASSAFRAS CREEK

The margins of Sherbrooke Forest near Sherbrooke itself, and Sassafras Creek provide delightful walking amid forest and ferns. A circuit walk can be completed incorporating both the forest and the creek without passing much residential area private gardens; those that are passed, in fact enhance the walk.

Start walking at the Kallista shops, up sealed Sherbrooke Road for 100 m, and then diverge right onto Owen Street. From the junction head left uphill steeply on Old Sherbrooke Road (an easement track) which rejoins Sherbrooke Road after 500 m. Follow Sherbrooke Road past famous George Tindale Memorial Gardens (open to the public), other magnificent gardens and the Sherbrooke Store, to Sherbrooke Forest within another 500 m. Sherbrooke Picnic Ground is on the left and could be a convenient lunch or picnic spot. Next, continue on Sherbrooke Road 300 m, then turn right into Nobles Lane. It soon becomes an easement with a rough track. Walk down it for 700 m directly north-north-east and avoid side roads off right during the descent. At the bottom of Nobles Lane hill, meet Sassafras Creek Road and walk 100 m to the left to cross Sassafras Creek and join into the Dandenong Ranges Walking Track. The ferny pad leads downstream for 1 km to join Boucher Road then Perrins Creek Road just 100 m short of its junction with Sassafras Creek Road. Beagleys Bridge Picnic Ground is set beside the creek at the junction, and would be an alternative lunch or picnic spot amid its tree-ferns and sturdy eucalypts.

Finally, walk Sassafras Creek Road uphill southwards onto the main Kallista to Monbulk Road, then continue south up the main road to Kallista shops and the end of the walk. It is 900 m from Beagleys Bridge picnic area to the shops.

4.3 km, 2½ hours; walk last reviewed September 1988; 'B' grade, family walk; all on tracks; features

Sherbrooke area private gardens and Sassafras Creek; water for lunch at picnic area; transport available to Kallista walk start weekdays and Saturday mornings by bus from Belgrave station; walk suited to any time of the year; *Melways Melbourne Street Directory* refers as do Maps 5 and 6, pages 50 and 54.

**WOOD WHITE
BUTTERFLY**

6   KALLISTA-MONBULK CREEK-COLES RIDGE

Sherbrooke Forest, part of the Dandenong Ranges National Park, contains areas which are, despite proximity to Melbourne, relatively unvisited. This walk suggestion passes through the quiet eastern sector of the park. It starts and finishes at Grants Picnic Ground 200 m south of Kallista.

To the north (Kallista side) of the car park a foot-track leads into forest eastwards and is known as the Lyrebird Walk. It also marks the start of the Hardy's Gully Nature Trail. Walk 100 m then take either fork of the nature trail for 300 m to where the forks rejoin. Next, continue east through the headwaters of Hardy's Gully, then fork right onto a broad foot-track called Neumann Road some 800 m from the walk start.

Head south on Neumann Road to ascend a ridge

and to reach a grassy clearing being managed to encourage wallabies. Some 2.2 km from the walk start, and just before meeting a further large clearing being revegetated with eucalypts, turn right (south) onto Paddy's Road which is a jeep-track. It leads downhill south-south-east towards Selby. Descend the track for 1.5 km, to cross Hardy's Creek just before its confluence with Monbulk Creek, to reach a small clearing known as Jack the Miners. It has a fireplace, good water and is a suitable lunch place. Ferns, wattles and giant Mountain ash trees grow throughout the area.

From Jack the Miners, walk west uphill on Welch Track rather than cross Monbulk Creek southwards on the continuation of Paddy's Road. After 800 m, a fairly steep sometimes slippery climb and more forest, reach Coles Ridge Road and two road barriers. Turn right and climb northwards on the minor Coles Ridge Road, keeping several houses on the left and forest on the right. Continue heading north on the road for 2.5 km through forest, avoiding three tracks off left and passing a road barrier at the 2 km stage. One section to the right of the road, formerly a pine plantation, was logged in 1987-88 and is now revegetating. Views eastwards result from the clearing.

7 km; 4 hours; walk last reviewed September 1988; 'B' grade, family walk; all on tracks; features Sherbrooke Forest; transport to Kallista available weekdays and Saturday mornings by bus from Belgrave station; water for lunch at picnic area; walk suited to any time of the year but wet underfoot in winter; Map, 'Sherbrooke Forest' Conservation Forests and Lands and Map 6, page 54.

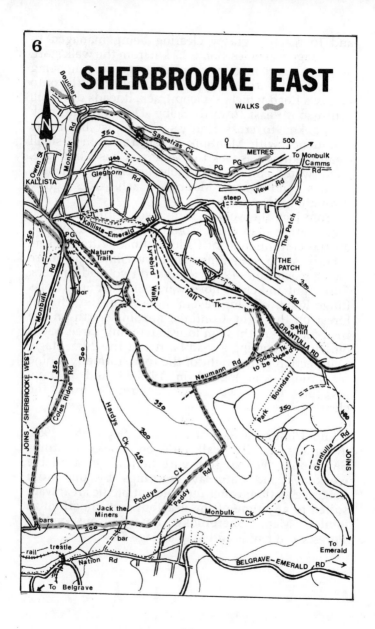

SHERBROOKE EAST

6

WALKS

Boucher

Monbulk Rd

350

Sassafras Ck

0   500
METRES

PG   PG

To Monbulk
Camms Rd

Owen St

KALLISTA

400

Gleghorn Rd

View Rd

steep

The Patch Rd

350

Kallista-Emerald Rd

PG

wc

Nature Trail

THE PATCH

Lyrebird Walk

300

350

400

Hall Tk

bar

bar

Selby Hill

GRANTULLA RD

Monbulk Rd

bar

JOINS SHERBROOKE WEST

Coles Ridge Rd

350

500

Neumann Rd

Foden Tk
to be closed

Park Boundary

350

400

Grantulla Rd

JOINS

Hardys

Ck

350

300

250

Paddys

Ck

Paddy Rd

Jack the
Miners

bars

260

bar

Monbulk Ck

To
Emerald

rail trestle

Nation Rd

BELGRAVE—EMERALD RD

To Belgrave

54

7   MENZIES CREEK-KALLISTA-BELGRAVE

The *Puffing Billy* Preservation Society has ensured that wonderful little steam train's future by modifying its route. It is now able to continue to puff up and down its narrow gauge railway through the Dandenong Ranges. It provides historical interest, a novelty for children, an excellent tourist attraction and an excellent transport system for walkers. Why not support the good work of the society by riding the quaint little train to Menzies Creek to the start of this suggested walk route. A steam museum at Menzies Creek provides added interest, although plans are afoot to relocate this museum to Lakeside in the future. The train does not operate on some days, so check times.

From Menzies Creek station, follow School Road west for 600 m on the south side of the railway line, to reach a level crossing, then go on for 1.3 km north-west then north, joining the main Belgrave to Emerald Road. Head across the main road onto Grantulla Road, passing Hermons Saddle Picnic Area on the left side of the road. After only 100 m the Jacksons Hill Road, straight ahead uphill to the north, should be taken. After 1 km, join Ridge Road, turn left (north-west) and walk 200 m to rejoin Grantulla Road. Follow Grantulla Road north-west for 1 km to the top of a small hill. There is a small car park at this point. Turn left onto Foden Track to enter the Dandenong Ranges National Park and walk south-west 300 m through forest to join onto Neumann Road—a park management road. There have been moves to close Foden Track. If this occurs it will be necessary to keep walking Grantulla Road for 300 m to join Neumann Road. This soon becomes a broad foot-track as you follow it westwards, passing a clearing which is being revegetated with eucalypts and managed to encourage wallabies. Avoid a left side jeep-track towards Selby within 500 m and proceed a further 1 km along the ridge, then down into the headwaters

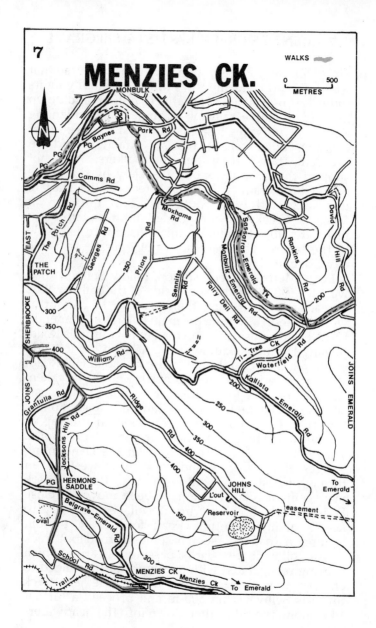

MENZIES CK.

7

WALKS

0 — 500
METRES

N

MONBULK

PG
PG Baynes
Park Rd
PG
PG
Camms Rd
PG
Moxhams Rd
The Patch Rd
Georges Rd
Priors Rd
Sennitts Rd
Fairy Dell Rd
Sassafras–Emerald Tk
Monbulk – Emerald Rd
Rankins Rd
David Hill Rd
THE PATCH
250
SHERBROOKE EAST
300
350
400
William Rd
Ti-Tree Ck
Waterfield Rd
Kallista – Emerald Rd
200
JOINS EMERALD
Grantulla Rd
Jacksons Hill Rd
Ridge Rd
250
300
350
400
JOINS EMERALD
PG
HERMONS SADDLE
oval
Belgrave–Emerald Rd
L'out
JOHNS HILL
Reservoir
easement
To Emerald
School Rd
rail
300
350
400
200
MENZIES CK
Menzies Ck
To Emerald

56

of Hardy's Gully. A path from Cooks Corner then joins in from the right as you continue generally northwards.

About 250 m beyond the Cooks Corner track, take either of two track forks then, after 300 m, emerge in Grants Picnic area just south of Kallista.

Lunch is suggested at that spot.

Cross the Belgrave to Kallista main road after lunch and head down a foot track across the headwaters of Clematis Creek then, on the west bank, fork right and climb out of the fern gully for 700 m to join Sherbrooke Lodge Road then walk along the road for 500 m to reach O'Donohues Picnic Area. Sherbrooke Lodge Road marks the forest perimeter and several roadside private gardens add interest. O'Donohue Track then leads directly from the picnic area to Sherbrooke Falls and should be followed. The distance is 800 m through magnificent forest. Avoid three tracks off right as you proceed. You could then take a break at Sherbrooke Falls Picnic Area which is close by Sherbrooke Falls.

Toilets, a shelter and fireplace are within the area. At the falls, cross a bridge to the west bank, turn left and walk south, then west for 1.5 km to Terry's Avenue on a broad track. Avoid Woodfulls foot-track off left at one stage near some pine trees. Lastly, follow Terry's Avenue for 2.5 km south-east to Belgrave *Puffing Billy* Station.

13.0 km; 6½ hours; walk last reviewed September 1988; 'A' grade, medium walk; all on tracks; features Sherbrooke Forest; water for lunch at Grants Picnic Ground Kallista; Rail transport to Belgrave start of walk available; walk suited to any time of the year; Map 'Sherbrooke Forest' Conservation Forests and Lands and Maps 5, 6 and 7, pages 50, 54 and 56.

8   EMERALD-MONBULK-KALLISTA-BELGRAVE

This longer walk includes much of the Dandenong Ranges Walking Track through the more open parts of the hills near Emerald and Monbulk. It includes some of the rain forests round Kallista. Ideally, transport should be left at Belgrave and *Puffing Billy* or bus used to reach Emerald, although a car shuttle using two or more cars would suffice.

CORAL FUNGI

From Emerald Station walk north-west back along the main Belgrave Road 500 m to the Pinnocks Road, Clematis, level crossing. It is the second level crossing from Emerald. Follow Pinnocks Road north, then north-west, then turn north again down Telopea Road to reach the start of the Dandenong Ranges Walking Track 1.4 km from the rail line. The track follows Menzies Creek downstream for 1.3 km to Avards picnic ground where Caroline Crescent is crossed. Walk on north from the picnic ground, 800 m to cross Kallista-Emerald Road and on further downstream 2 km to Butterfield Reserve and picnic area for lunch. The pad features bellbirds, blackberries in season and views of open tracts of rolling hills. The picnic spot has barbecues, tables, toilets and creek water. (Sometimes the creek water is too muddy to use.) The spot is at the confluence of Menzies Creek and

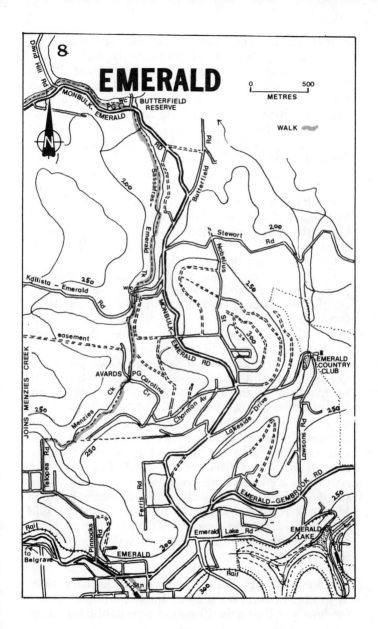

8

EMERALD

0   500
METRES

MONBULK. EMERALD

David Hill Rd

PG WC BUTTERFIELD RESERVE

WALK

Butterfield Rd

Sassafras - Emerald RD

200

Stewart Rd

200

Kallista - Emerald Rd

250

WC

Nobelius St

250

MONBULK EMERALD RD

300

EMERALD COUNTRY CLUB

easement

JOINS MENZIES CREEK

AVARDS PG Caroline Cr

Charman Av

Lakeside Drive

Lawsons Rd

250

Menzies Ck

250

250

EMERALD - GEMBROOK RD

250

Telopea Rd

Ferris Rd

Rail

Emerald Lake Rd

EMERALD LAKE

to Belgrave

Pinnocks Rd

EMERALD

300

Rail

Stn

300

Woori Yallock Creek and has a koala reserve adjacent to its east side. It is 6 km from the walk start.

After lunch, head west upstream along Woori Yallock Creek on the foot track for 800 m, then cross David Hill Road and go 700 m to a small cascade near the junction of Emerald-Monbulk Road and Rankins Road plus the confluence of Titree Creek and Sassafras Creek. The pad leads on west from Rankins Road on the north bank for 1.8 km then crosses to the south bank for 200 m before crossing Emerald-Monbulk Road and continuing west again on the south bank for 800 m. Moxhams Road, Monbulk, and Moxhams picnic area (tables only) is then reached. Cross the road and walk north-west 1 km to emerge from forest onto Baynes Park Road, Monbulk. Go left 300 m then enter Baynes Park.

Cross the park to its north side caravan parking area, then return to following the foot pad upstream, on the north bank initially, through the length of the caravan park, then across Monbulk Road 500 m from where Baynes Park was entered. Next, walk upstream 2.5 km to Beagleys Bridge following the ferny pad through each of Kensleys, Olympic, Kays, O'Donohues and Seabeck picnic grounds. Turn south up from the bridge for 100 m to join Monbulk Road. It should be followed south 800 m to Kallista shops. Enter Sherbrooke Forest (part of the Dandenong Ranges National Park) south of the shops. Go through Grants picnic area at the forest edge and then go southwards along Coles Ridge Road. Tall Mountain Ash trees are a feature in this area as are views from the ridge. Follow Coles Ridge south 2.5 km to join Old Monbulk Road at a barrier. Turn right (west) on Old Monbulk Road, and descend 500 m to *Puffing Billy*'s rail line, then continue on the road 300 m to Belgrave station.

18.5 km; 7 hours; walk last reviewed January 1988; 'B' grade, medium walk; all on tracks and roads; water for lunch at Butterfield Reserve unreliable; transport

to walk start at Belgrave available by rail; walk suited to any time of the year; *Map—Melways Melbourne Street Directory* and Maps 5, 6, 7 and 8, pages 50, 54, 56 and 59.

9 MOUNT DANDENONG

The Mount Dandenong summit, Mount Dandenong Arboretum, Olinda Falls and Kalorama Park are four points of interest in the Dandenong Ranges well worthy of a visit and a walk circuit. It is suggested that transport be left at Five Ways, Kalorama. The spot has good views of Silvan Reservoir and has each of Kalorama Park and Ellis-Geeves Picnic Area astride it.

At first you should walk 1.3 km south-west up Ridge Road to a car park and view overlooking Mount Dandenong Arboretum. There is a picnic area at this spot and opposite is a foot track leading up to the summit of Mount Dandenong 400 m distant. Take the foot track to see Melbourne and suburbs from the 633 m high peak then return to the arboretum. The summit has another picnic ground and restaurant on it. Back at the arboretum, head east down across lawns, among many lovely well-established exotic trees and, within 400 m, reach the main Mount Dandenong Tourist Road. Cross this main road and follow a small foot pad east down through Mechanics Reserve, following a ferny gully for 400 m until gravelled Farndons Road is reached.

Turn left and walk along the road for 200 m to join sealed Falls Road. Head to the right down Falls Road to the end of the asphalt surface 1 km distant where Olinda Falls Picnic Ground should be entered. This picnic area could be a good lunch spot. It has fireplaces, water, tables and toilets. From it you should

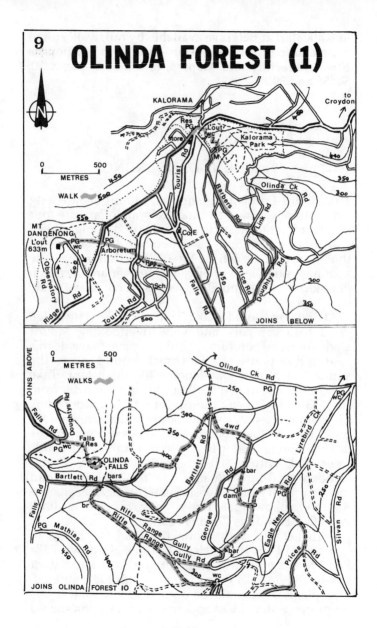

OLINDA FOREST (1)

9

take a side trip, 350 m each way, to small but pretty Olinda Falls. A good wide track leads south-east down to the falls and forms a small loop around the actual falls area. Tracks head off left and right just before the final steep descent to the falls and these side-tracks need to be avoided. The falls are within Olinda Forest and as such are surrounded by lush trees and ferns. Lyrebirds are frequently heard and seen.

Back at Olinda Falls Picnic Ground, follow gravelled Doughty's Road which skirts the western perimeter of the forest northwards. Descend this quiet forest road for 1 km, avoiding three roads off left (Price Road, Ernest Road and Outlook Drive), and then turn left up Barbers Road at a 'T' intersection. Barber's Road should be walked north-west up across Ernest Road-Link Road intersection and towards Five Ways, Kalorama, again. At a motel some 1.2 km up Barbers Road just 200 m short of Five Ways, turn right and enter Kalorama Park. The park contains picnic facilities, lawns, views and a nature trail. Pamphlets are available about the nature trail if you wish to include its short circuit to finish the day's walk. Afternoon Tea could be had using the picnic facilities or, alternatively, there is a shop at Five Ways selling Devonshire Teas.

7.2 km; 2½ hours; last reviewed February 1988, 'B' grade family walk; all on tracks, roads and lawns; features a large range of tree varieties and superb autumn tints in season plus a number of good picnic areas: tap water available for lunch at Olinda Falls picnic area; walk suited to any season; Maps— _Melways Melbourne Street Directory_ refers as does Map 9, page 62.

10 OLINDA FOREST

Olinda Forest vegetation varies considerably. The western fringe is high on the slopes of the ranges and therefore damp whilst the north-eastern section is much lower and drier. This walk suggestion is through the damper upper areas of ferns and wet sclerophyll forest.

Leave from Olinda Falls Picnic Ground southwards on the unsealed continuation of Falls Road for 500 m. Olinda Creek and its fern gully is crossed in the process. Turn left onto Bartlett Road and walk down it eastwards 500 m. Turn right down Rifle Range Gully Road and follow it for 1.3 km to Georges Road. The forest is particularly fine in the area and an old stone embankment is passed near the start of the gully. Bellbirds inhabit the latter section of the road route as the forest opens to some cleared land and picnic spots suitable for a lunch break.

Turn left onto Georges Road and meet a right side fork and barrier within 200 m on a small ridge. Next walk north-east down the ridge for 500 m on the side track to another junction. Turn left to cross a gully, go northwards past a small dam, then again meet the more major Georges Road at a barrier within 500 m. Double back left (south-west) and walk up Georges Road 400 m, diverge right and climb to meet gravelled Bartlett road on a spur. The latter sector involves a climb on a shortcut to avoid a hairpin bend.

Turn left and walk up Bartlett Road 500 m to rejoin the outward route then retrace Bartlett Road and Falls Road for the 1 km to Olinda Falls Picnic Ground.

6.2 km; 2½ hours; last reviewed February 1988; 'C' grade; easy walk; all on tracks; water available in Rifle Range Gully for lunch; walk suited to any time of year; Maps—*'Olinda State Forest'* Conservation Forests and Lands and Map 9, page 62.

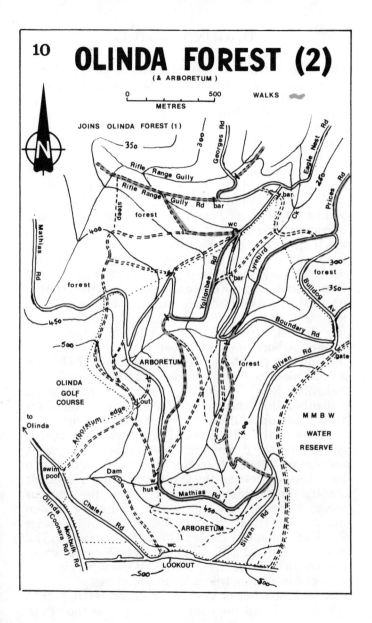

11   OLINDA FOREST

The Olinda State Forest and the adjacent Hamer Arboretum make an excellent place for a circuit walk which includes the variety of rain forest, ferns, dry forest with wild flowers, deciduous trees and views in the arboretum. Travel via Falls Road, Mount Dandenong, to the Olinda Falls picnic area to start the walk.

Walk south on the gravelled continuation of Falls Road across the gully of Olinda Creek to Bartlett Road turnoff, 500 m south of the picnic ground. Walk east 500 m into Olinda Forest down Bartlett Road to a barrier at Rifle Range Gully Road on the right. Pass the barrier and head down the gully road into lovely ferns and rain forest to follow Rifle Range Gully for 900 m. A very minor steep foot-track off right should be passed during the descent, then a right turn should be made to rise gradually on an angle away from the gully. After 300 m avoid a track joining in from the right and walk 300 m east to the edge of the Hamer Arboretum and a jeep track on a spur. At the junction you should be adjacent to a large clearing and picnic area. Head left downhill a few metres onto Yallanbee Road (near a toilet block). Turn right up Yallanbee Road and proceed 700 m as the road swings westwards up a hillside within the Arboretum.

Views of the Dividing Range appear as height is gained and the deciduous trees contrast well against the native forests. A minor jeep track should then be taken, off left as the road turns north. It leads among the deciduous trees to follow the contour across a creek gully and south, rising up to join gravelled Mathias Road in 900 m. Follow Mathias Road 150 m south to Red Dogs Hut for lunch. The hut has seating, a fireplace and good creek water. It is 4.4 km from the walk start and is in a most pleasant area of contrasting tree colours and views.

After lunch, follow Mathias Road east 900 m to turn left down a faint track on a small spur at the Silvan

Road junction. Walk 300 m down to near the edge of eucalypt forest, then go north downhill to continue north on either of two available tracks entering the eucalypt forest.

The pads rejoin after 500 m in a gully then, just 100 m further downhill, Boundary Road should be crossed and Prices Road followed on down the ferny gully. Walk Prices Road for 1.3 km, avoiding roads off left and right at the 800 m and 900 m stages, then turn north down a jeep track on a spur in dry forest. Within 400 m a barrier and Eagle Nest Road are reached. Follow the road north 200 m to a picnic area on the left.

FLY AGARIC
FUNGI

A track leads across a creek from the picnic area. Follow it west then south, and after 400 m turn right onto a pad down and across another creek. Walk north passing a small dam and on to Georges Road within a further 400 m. Head north on Georges Road 250 m to just past a small gully, then turn left (west) up a jeep track which stays near the gully initially, but then rises up into drier forest and to five ways on a ridge after 400 m. Take the ridge crest track south-west, rather than Bartlett Road, and climb steeply in an area which features wildflowers in spring. After 800 m and just beyond a small hillcrest, another jeep track joins in from the right then, 200 m further on, Bartlett Road is rejoined, almost opposite Rifle Range Gully Road. At this point rejoin the outward route and retrace the 1 km to Olinda Falls picnic area.

11km, 4½ hours; walk last reviewed February 1988; 'B' grade, medium walk; all on tracks and roads; features Hamer Arboretum; water for lunch available at Red Dogs Hut; walk suited to any time of the year, but best in autumn; *Map: Olinda State Forest* **Conservation Forests and Lands and Maps 9 and 10, pages 62 and 65.**

12   ARTHURS SEAT

This walk on the Mornington Peninsula at Dromana is one that provides variety of interest. Beaches are included as well as Arthurs Seat and Seawinds. The suggested start to the walk is 1 km west of the Dromana shops via the Nepean Highway, in the area of the Latrobe Parade, Foote Street intersection with the Nepean Highway. This spot is adjacent to the bayside foreshore reserve.

At first head onto the beachfront, then commence to walk west (left). A 2.5 km stretch of beach walking follows until the Eastern Lighthouse at McCrae is reached. Leave the beach 100 m before the lighthouse and cross the Nepean Highway into Beverley Road. If it is a weekend, public holiday, or school holiday, a short detour should be included next rather than to simply walk up the length of Beverley Road to the Mornington Peninsula Freeway foot underpass. The detour is to historic McCrae Homestead, which is open to the public on certain days only, or by specific appointment. The homestead is in Charles Street, but cannot be seen much from the street. If including the detour, turn left off Beverley Road into Burrell Street, then right into Charles Street which is the first street east of Beverley Road. At the south

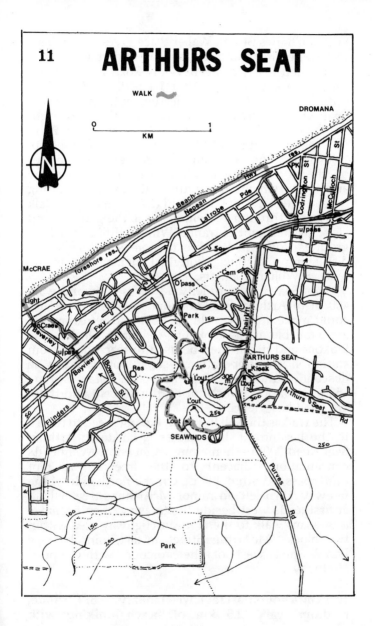

end of Charles Street, Waller Place gives access back to Beverley Road and the freeway underpass.

Turn left (east) along Bayview Road after passing under the freeway and after 1 km diverge off right onto a gravelled roadway leading into the Arthurs Seat parkland area. At this road junction turn right up Two Bays Walking Track which winds for 2 km up the mountainside to the rear entrance of 'Seawinds'. Boneseed, an African plant, proliferates on the slopes. Seawinds was once a private home and there remains the traditional garden extending to many hectares of lawns and deciduous trees. Walk eastwards through Seawinds to see the gardens and leave by the front entrance. Whilst within Seawinds grounds you will be able to note some sculpture displaying a distinct aboriginal theme. This is the work of William Ricketts.

From Seawinds turn left on Purves Road and walk 400 m to Arthurs Seat Lookout. Adjacent parkland could make a pleasant lunch spot and refreshments are available at the lookout. A chairlift services the lookout and it can then be used to reach its bottom station. If it is inoperative, a steep foot track can be descended under the lift for the 800 m distance. Some 150 m elevation is lost during the descent and there are good bay views.

The walk is then all but over, but you need to return to the beachfront. Best access is on down Arthurs Seat Road 200 m, then along Palmerston Avenue, its continuation adjacent to the freeway. A foot underpass is within 400 m. On the north side of the freeway, turn left on minor McArthur Street which at first leads west beside the freeway, then becomes a pleasant walk to the Nepean Highway area within two blocks. McArthur Street, in fact, joins Latrobe Parade just west of the junction with Nepean Highway.

10.5 km; 4 hours; last reviewed January 1988; 'C' grade, medium walk; 2.5 km of beach walking with

remainder on tracks and roads; features Arthurs Seat views; water for lunch at Arthurs Seat; walk suited to any season; bus transport to Dromana available along Nepean Highway; *Map: Melways Melbourne Street Directory* and Map 11, page 69.

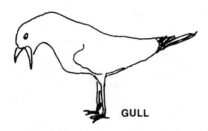

GULL

13   SORRENTO-KOONYA BEACH

A walk at Sorrento including the Port Phillip Bay (front beaches) and the Bass Strait (back or ocean beaches) includes not only coastal interest features but also places of great historical interest. Sorrento has long been a resort area, especially in bygone days when steamers brought thousands of Melbourne people across the bay to the town's splendid hotels and guest houses. The commercial area of Sorrento still has many of these historic and grand buildings and there is also a museum providing extra interest.

It is suggested that walkers go to Blairgowrie and the intersection of the Nepean Highway and Hughes Road where there are picnic facilities fronting the bayside beach and a suitable car park. A picnic could be included at this point either before setting off or upon return from the walk.

At first, walk the sandy beach north 400 m to its end then head up a foot track just near where a cliffline commences. This short track meets another track almost immediately. Turn right and walk along a short path past a lookout to the graves of early settlers, said to have belonged to the first Victorian settlement in 1803. Next, retrace the path to join Leggett Way, a short road which in turn links onto the Nepean Highway. Follow the side of the highway north-west for 200 m, then walk into a park area fronting another beach. Except in times of very rough sea you can then follow the beach and short sector of cliff base north-west for over 2 km to reach the main Sorrento pier. A minor road bypasses the cliff sector as an alternative. The pier was the focus of the resort in earlier days. Head up the Esplanade, north-west still, to enter nearby Sorrento Park, and after a quick look at this fine park head onto the adjacent Hotham Road frontage to see the grand Sorrento Hotel. Just to the right is the Nepean Highway again and you should join it to head south and turn south-west on Ocean Beach Road which is the main street. There are a number of interesting historic buildings to see in the main street. When Melbourne Road intersection is reached, you should veer left to see the museum.

Ocean Beach Road should then be walked south-west past Whitehall Guest House and into the Cape Schanck Coastal Park which is part of the National Parks system. Some 1 km from the museum Sorrento Back Beach and the park office should be reached. In the old days a tram operated from the front beach pier to this back beach. Today all that remains to indicate the historical background is a rotunda lookout replica known as Coppins Lookout. Coppin instigated much of the former development. A return trip climb to the lookout would be worthwhile.

At the south-east end of the main car park area a foot track leads off south-east and should be followed. It leads to St Pauls Beach and Diamond Bay, 1.8 km away. Roads reach the track and coast at both St Pauls Beach and Diamond Bay. Viewpoints of the coast are a feature of the track route, including

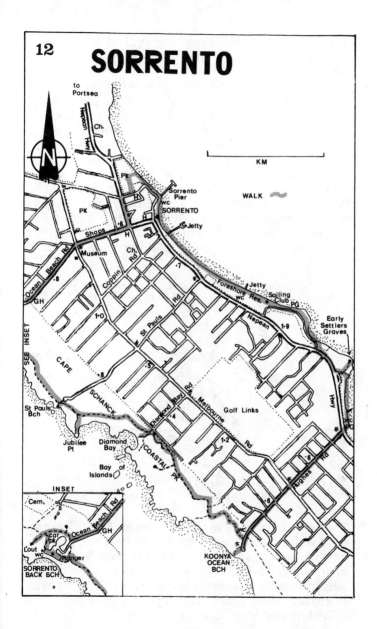

SORRENTO

to Portsea

Ch.

Pk

PK

KM

WALK

Sorrento Pier
wc
SORRENTO
Jetty

Shops
H
Museum
Ch.
Rd
Coppin
Ocean Beach Rd
GH
·8
1·0
St Pauls
Rd
·7
Foreshore Res.
wc
Jetty
Sailing
Club PG
Early
Settlers
Graves

Nepean
1·9

CAPE
·8
·5
SCHANCK
St Pauls
Bch
Jubilee
Pt
Diamond Bay Rd
·4
Diamond
Bay
Bay of
Islands
COASTAL PK
Melbourne
Rd
Golf Links
1·2
·6
Hughes Rd
·6
·6
Hwy
wc

INSET
Cem.
Ocean Beach Rd
GH
Car
pk
L'out
wc
Ranger
SORRENTO
BACK BCH

KOONYA
OCEAN
BCH

one at Jubilee Point. From the end of the road at Diamond Bay, ensure that you take the short side trip to see Diamond Bay and perhaps the adjacent Bay of Islands. The main route then is south-east again from the end of the Diamond Bay Road along what is known as Life Saving Track for 1.2 km to Koonya Beach car park and toilet. Coastal scrub prevails along most of this stretch. At Koonya Beach a short track leads from the car park to the beach area opposite the end of Hughes Road. The final walk stage is a 1.2 km stretch north-east along Hughes Road to the front beach. There is a store midway which could be convenient for drinks etc. on a hot day at the end of the circuit walk. Hughes Road, whilst within a residential area, is a quiet road bordered by much tea tree.

BANKSIA

10 km; 3¼ hours; last reviewed January 1988; 'B' grade, easy walk; all on tracks, roads and beaches; features bayside and ocean beaches; water for lunch at several picnic areas en route; walk suited to any season but best in summer; transport to area available by Nepean Highway bus; Map: Melways Melbourne Street Directory and Map 12, page 73.

14   CAPE SCHANCK

The Cape Schanck area of the Mornington Peninsula features high basalt rock cliffs at the cape and along Bushrangers Bay. An excellent walk route in a coastal park leads from the Rosebud to Flinders Road to Bushrangers Bay, then along the basalt clifftops to the Cape Schanck lighthouse vicinity. Additionally there is a fine beach at the bay, midway to the cape.

Start the walk at a car park 2.6 km south-east of the Cape Schanck Road turn-off along the Rosebud to Flinders Road. The spot is just west of Main Creek in a farming locality. Head off south-west on a good foot track through a park entry then along the slopes high above the west bank of Main Creek. Coast Banksias (Banksia Integrifolia), up to 10 m high, are prevalent and especially beautiful. They occur right from the walk start and have characteristic white coloration on the back of their leaves and large cylindrical flowers. Honeyeaters frequent the Banksia trees in large numbers and there are many robins, wrens and wattle birds too. There are fine views down Main Creek valley and to the surrounding rolling farmlands. The track contours along not far from a park boundary fence and in 2.5 km reaches a track junction.

The junction is above a good sandy beach on Bushrangers Bay and from it there are good views of basalt cliffs around the bay. A large rock stack known as The Elephant exists just off a small point at the southern end of the beach. Walkers would do well to descend to the beach, 200 m distant, and investigate the many lovely rock pools, The Elephant itself and a large arch of rock just around the small point at The Elephant. It is necessary to wade the shallow mouth of Main Creek to get to most of the beach area. Swimming could be dangerous as there are a lot of rocks and strong currents. There have been a number of volcanic basalt lava flows in the past causing layers of rock and these have been heavily eroded by the sea.

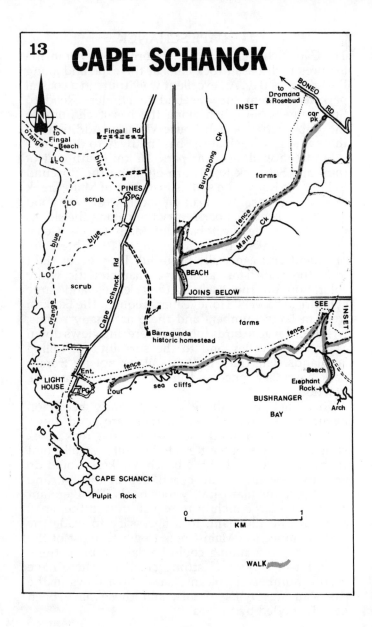

13 CAPE SCHANCK

to Fingal Beach

Orange

Fingal Rd

LO

blue

blue

PINES
PG

scrub

LO

blue

LO

blue

scrub

Orange

Cape Schanck Rd

Barragunda
historic homestead

Ent.

fence

LIGHT
HOUSE

PG

L'out

sea cliffs

CAPE SCHANCK

Pulpit Rock

INSET

to
Dromana
& Rosebud

BONEO RD

car
pk

Burrabong Ck

farms

fence

Main Ck

BEACH

JOINS BELOW

farms

fence

SEE

INSET

Beach

Elephant
Rock

Arch

BUSHRANGER

BAY

0				1

KM

WALK

Continue the walk, west, along the clifftop track after seeing the beach. From the junction (Peg No. 12), there are a number of pegs marking points of interest of a nature walk. At first the track leads down to nearby Burrabong Creek as the creek nears the sea in a steep-sided gully. The creek has a lot of Woolly Tea-tree growing near it and there is a bridge to be crossed. A wooden platform gives access to the creek water, but it would be unwise to drink the water as it flows off farmland just upstream. Next, the track leads up steps to emerge from scrub and cross some former farmland now being managed to be covered with native plants. The farm adjacent is on hummocky country sculptured by wind erosion in past dry eons. It is the Barragunda farm property, which dates from 1866 and which has a large homestead built of local limestone.

Further west on the track, a lookout gives better than normal views of the coastal cliffs. The exposed horizontal bedding of the cliffs is noticeable; then, nearer Cape Schanck Lighthouse, there is a second lookout known as Cape Schanck Lookout, and it is on a knob near Peg No. 1 of the nature walk. There is also a seat at the spot. Views are very good of both Bushrangers Bay and of nearby Cape Schanck with its off-shore rock stack known as Pulpit Rock. The stack is an excellent example of a volcanic plug formation. The track leads on west into car parks and the lighthouse area, and it is suggested that the lookout be your turn-around point as it is some 5 km from the walk start. Whilst Cape Schanck itself has more walking possibilities, the area is heavily developed with car parking, boardwalks and fences to prevent erosion. Retrace the 5 km back, using the same tracks but perhaps omitting the beach side track.

11 km; 4 hours; walk last reviewed February 1987; 'A' grade, family walk; all on tracks; features coastal cliff and beach scenery; carry water for lunch; walk suited to any season; *Maps: Melways Melbourne*

15   FERNSHAW-MORLEY'S TRACK

Fernshaw is now the site of a beautiful picnic area
in the midst of the Maroondah Reservoir catchment
area east of Healesville. Once a thriving tourist town
existed at the spot, but it was burned down. The
picnic grounds are an exceptionally pleasant place
in autumn when the many deciduous trees are
highlighed among the stands of stately mountain ash
in the valley. Additionally, two of the better places
in Victoria to see both ground and tree ferns are along
Morley's Creek and the Watts River, which both flow
through Fernshaw.

It is suggested that you commence to walk up a
foot track as it leaves the north-east end of the picnic
area and follow the track for about 3.5 km through
the Watts River Valley. Some 1.5 km from the picnic
area, the track crosses Morley's Creek and thereafter
skirts the north bank of the Watts River until it finally
ascends rapidly up to a place called Carter's Gap.
However it is suggested that you turn back rather
than start the climbing and retrace the route.

As the track is entirely within the water catchment
it is imperative that you remain on it and avoid the
side tracks which are appropriately signposted 'No
Entry'. The track, which is known as Morley's Track,
is a gazetted walking track as defined in the M.M.B.W.
Act and it is well defined and easy to follow.

A lunch spot could be chosen virtually at any point
or along the river bank and the Fernshaw Picnic
Ground could be used to advantage for a barbeque
to finish the day.

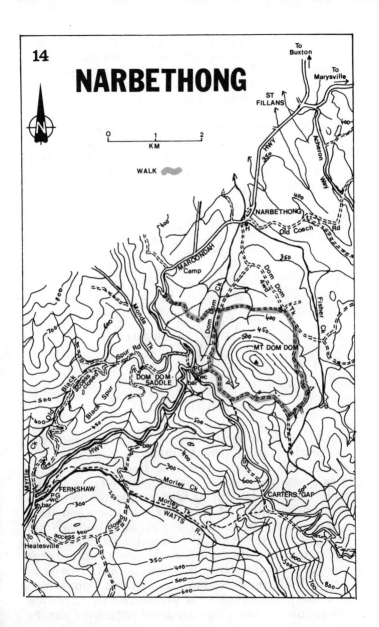

During the walk the eucalypts of the valley, and indeed throughout all of the Black Spur area beyond Healesville, will draw attention. Extensive replanting after a 1939 wildfire has resulted in the trees presently being at their prime and vigorously growing.

7km; 2½ hours; walk last reviewed February 1987; 'B' grade, family walk; all on tracks; walk suited to all seasons but wet underfoot in winter; *Maps: Vicmap 1:25,000 Marysville and 1:25,000 Monda* **refer as does Map 14, page 79.**

THORNBILL

16   NARBETHONG

Dom Dom Saddle on the Great Dividing Range can be reached along the Maroondah Highway. The saddle, 509 m above sea level, has a grassy picnic area and a view north whilst being surrounded by lush forests. As the saddle is approached from Melbourne, splendid stands of mountain ash trees and ferns are to be seen, but what is perhaps not realized so much is the remarkable change in vegetation on the northern slopes of the range compared to the damp southerly aspect. This walk circuit leads right around Mount Dom Dom which is a sharp little peak near the saddle. By circuiting the mountain the entire range of vegetation can be seen. A picnic lunch in the picnic area on the Dom Dom Saddle is also included.

It is suggested that the walk start 2.4 km north of Dom Dom Saddle on the northern slopes of the range. There is a sharp bend at the spot and suitable space for parking vehicles. It is just near a property known as 'The Hermitage'. A jeep track (Hermitage Track) leads off south-east from the road bend. It should be followed for 1.6 km through pleasant forest to intersect with Dom Dom Road after crossing Dom Dom Creek. Turn right up Dom Dom Road. After 1.3 km and a final steep ascent past a small pine plantation on the right, the road swings west for 300 m into the Dom Dom Saddle picnic area.

After lunch, retrace the 300 m, then continue ahead keeping right at the road junction. The route then leads to a saddle between the Dividing Range and Mount Dom Dom. It then contours around the southern slopes of Mount Dom Dom in very beautiful damp forest and where lyrebirds abound.

Avoid several minor logging sidetracks and keep left at a road fork some 2 km from Dom Dom Saddle, then follow the road as it swings north around Mount Dom Dom's eastern flank. The road gradually leaves the damp forest and passes into quite dry forest. Fisher Creek Road joins in from the right after 2 km then, just 300 m north, is a cross jeep track. Turn left and walk west 1.3 km, crossing a gully about midway. Dom Dom Creek Road is then approached. This latter section features a number of wildflowers, especially mauve tetratheca flowers. Lastly, cross Dom Dom Creek Road and retrace the 1.6 km to 'The Hermitage' corner and the main road, via Hermitage Track.

10.7 km; 4 hours; walk last reviewed February 1987; 'C' grade, easy walk; all on tracks and roads, carry water for lunch; walk suited to any season; *Maps: Vicmap 1:25,000 Marysville Sheet* refers as does Map 14, page 79.

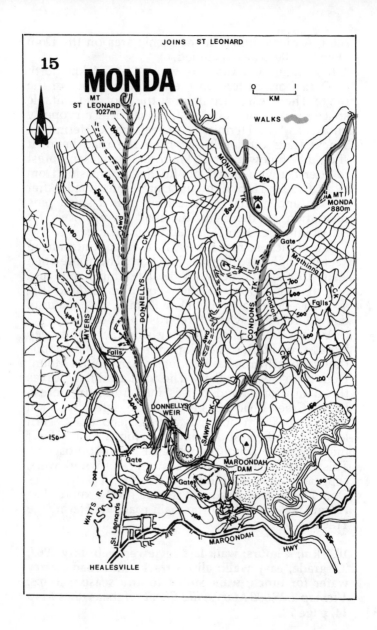

15
MONDA

MT ST LEONARD 1027m

WALKS

MT MONDA 880m

MONDA TK

CONDONS TK

DONNELLYS CK

MYERS CK

Mathinna CK

Fglls

Falls

DONNELLYS WEIR

SAWPIT CK

MAROONDAH DAM

Gate

WATTS R.

St Leonards Rd

MAROONDAH HWY

HEALESVILLE

82

17   HEALESVILLE-MOUNT ST LEONARD-CONDONS TRACK

The wet sclerophyll forests on the southern slopes of the Great Dividing Range at Healesville provide a beautiful, forest walk circuit for those walkers wanting a harder walk route. Mount St Leonard, 1028 m above sea level, is attained after a 920 m climb in elevation, so that those wanting a 'get fit trip' should be satisfied. The peak affords good views of the ranges and towards Melbourne. The whole circuit is either within or adjacent to the water catchment area of the Melbourne and Metropolitan Board of Works and the Board restricts access to the public on many jeep tracks which branch off the walk circuit.

Donnellys Weir Picnic Ground, within the catchment area, is the suggested place to start and finish the walk. The picnic area can be reached from Healesville shops via St Leonards Road. This road forks off the Maroondah Highway northwards near the east end of the shops. After 1.3 km, turn right onto Donnellys Weir Road and travel 700 m, then avoid a road off to the right and cross the small Watts River. Some 400 m further on, diverge left for another 700 m to a ford and gate. Normally the gate is open only on weekends and holidays to vehicles. It marks the entry to the weir area. It is best to leave transport beside the ford then walk 300 m north into the reserve, even if the gate is open. Within the reserve are fireplaces, toilets, tables and Donnellys Creek runs through it. Throughout most of the reserve there are large and beautiful conifer trees. The roadway continues up a hill to the west of the picnic area to act as a service road for the water catchment. Public vehicles are not permitted on this road and a further gate restricts entry to vehicles. Walkers, therefore, have a quiet minor road on which to climb.

Initially the road should be followed south to a sharp bend and spur crest 1 km from the ford and gate at the walk start. Next, head north as another road joins in from the left. The road ahead is known as No. 11 and it sidles up the east slopes of a small knob on the spur to a saddle. A horse trail can be walked as an alternative to the road for the short distance over the knob. The horse trail keeps to the crest and rejoins the road at the saddle. At the saddle, avoid road No. 23 off left, and shortly afterwards road No. 20 off right should be avoided.

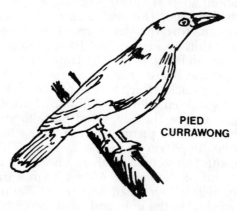

PIED CURRAWONG

As you continue up the spur road, along a firebreak, another section of horse trail exists and leads left, over a knob, and rejoins the road. However, this second section of horse trail is only worth following as an alternative for a few hundred meters, initially downhill and parallel to the road. After that it is too steep and requires a lot more climbing than the road route. About 6 km from the walk start, road No. 11 should be left as it leaves the spur and begins to sidle western slopes off left. Keep to the crest to climb more steeply on the horse trail. This section still follows along a firebreak.

After 2 km of steep ascent on this track, known as St Leonard Track, an access road to Mount St Leonard Fire Tower should be reached. During this latter ascent section the forest becomes increasingly more beautiful and lush. Once on the tower access road you need only walk up it for 200 m to be on the summit and at the tower base. Fit walkers should have taken about two hours, or two hours and fifteen minutes, for the 8 km walk so far. Good views and the end of the climb make the spot ideal for a lunch break. The tower is not normally open to the public, but some forestry officers have been known to invite walkers up the tower. Whether the tower is climbed or not you should get good views towards Melbourne and of much of the Dividing Range nearby.

From the peak follow a foot track north down the firebreak continuation on a spur to join onto the fire tower access road in 500 m. Walk this road (No. 10) 300 m northwards ahead to a gate and road junction. From the gateway, roads are open to public vehicles. Walk north still, on road No. 9 which soon turns east to a most delightful section of the walk along the firebreak. The trees are very lush and include many vigorous immature trees and some beech trees. The area would be a good alternative lunch place. Some 500 m from where road No. 9 was joined, avoid Quarry Track off left, then Tanglefoot Track off left 180 m later. Both are minor forest access roads. By now road No. 9 is following the crest of the Great Dividing Range. The forest remains very lush and lyrebirds can usually be heard in abundance, and even seen if you walk quietly. About 400 m from where Tanglefoot Track was passed, leave the road and diverge off right south-east along the firebreak continuation. Vehicles are prohibited on this section of firebreak and part of the area is fenced.

A minor range crest road can be used for the next 2 km before rejoining the road at a saddle after a pleasant descent.

Once back on the more major road No. 9, known also as Monda Track, avoid Hardys Creek Road off left at the saddle and proceed 3 km along the range top firebreak and road to a point where the road starts to turn north-east. At this bend, leave the road and walk through a gate onto jeep track No. 12.

This marks the start of Condons Track walking route through the water catchment area. Care is needed to locate the track ahead in some places so watch your position and timing. From the gateway follow the jeep track for just 400 m (five minutes), then fork left onto Condons foot track. The track is through bush and tall timber and the ground has been extensively scratched by lyrebirds and small animals. In parts the scratching is so widespread that it is difficult to decipher the track alignment. At first it keeps near a spur top, then begins to descend steeply south. Some 2.5 km from the gateway (on the Monda Track), the foot track joins onto the end of a minor road. It should take about forty-five minutes or more to reach this road as the descent is so steep.

**FUNGI
FAIRY RING**

Once on the road, follow it south. Shortly afterwards minor roads No. 22 and No. 21 fork in from the left and the way becomes a broader road leading south-west known as No. 17 road. At a bend, road No. 22 should be avoided as it forks off right. Echo Tunnel should next be met after a 2 km stretch of walking down the valley of Sawpit Creek. An aqueduct is just to the right of the road where Echo Tunnel ends. The tunnel and aqueduct carry water from nearby Maroondah Reservoir to Melbourne. Leave the road and walk along the south side of the aqueduct under some conifers, then onto another minor road which follows the aqueduct route. After

700 m of walking beside the aqueduct, pass through a gate, then turn left to rejoin your outward route just near Donnellys Weir entrance. It is then only 200 m south to the ford, gate and walk end.

21 km; 6½ hours; walk last reviewed January 1987; 'B' grade, hard walk; all on tracks and roads; features Mount St Leonard views and lyrebirds; water scarce and best carried; walk suited to any season; *Maps: Vicmap 1:25,000 Monda and 1:25,000 Maroondah* **refer as do Maps 15 and 16, pages 82 and 88.**

18   TANGLEFOOT TRACK-BLOCK FOUR ROAD

The Great Dividing Range in the Healesville district has long been a traditional walking area principally because of the fine forests on the range. This walk route is one of the traditional routes and lies wholly within forest. Sassafras, myrtle beech and ferns are interesting features. The walk starting point is reached from Healesville to Toolangi which is just west of conspicuous Mount St Leonard. Monda Road, a rough route from Toolangi to the peak should then be travelled south-east up the slopes for 1.5 km, round a sharp bend and on north up the slopes for another 2 km to the top of a main ridge and a gateway at a road junction north of the peak. A firebreak also passes along the ridge in the area. Travel the road along the firebreak for 700 m to the walk start at the junction of the Tanglefoot Track off left (north). It is just 200 m beyond the Quarry Road turnoff left. Tanglefoot Track has a road barrier across its start and is reserved for walkers only. The firebreak in the vicinity has long been a popular bush picnic area.

Head off north along Tanglefoot Track. The track features tall timber and ferns. It leads through good

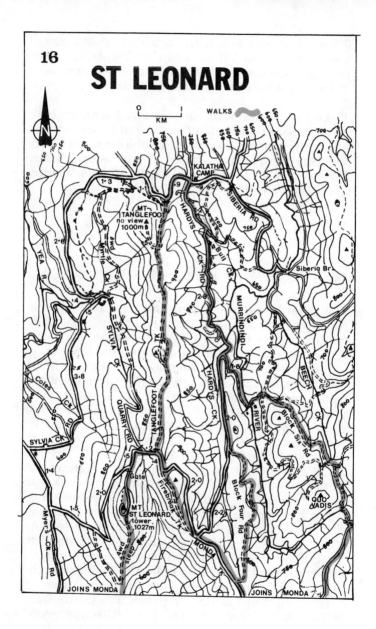

ST LEONARD

16

WALKS

KM

88

lyrebird haunts and north for 5.7 km. After 1.8 km the track divides temporarily and the right fork is the easiest in that it avoids a climb over a small hill. Some 4.5 km from the walk start, avoid a foot track off left 500 m to tree-covered Mount Tanglefoot. Thereafter the Tanglefoot Track ceases to remain fairly level and descends significantly through lovely ferny, beech and sassafras stands to reach Sylvia Creek Road and picnic area via another road barrier. Take a lunch break (no water or fires) then walk down the gravelled road to reach a road junction within 900 m at a spot known as Kalatha Camp. This spot once was a forestry camp.

MOTH

Hardys Creek Road, another forestry road, leads off south from Kalatha Camp and should be followed next. Head along the road for a total of 6 km to the junction of minor Block Four Road off left. Hardys Creek Road is a quiet road which winds around a number of gullies and crosses Hardys Creek at the 3.7 km stage. There are several minor forestry roads off left and right as you proceed along Hardys Creek Road, the most significant being the Block Six Road off left at the 4 km stage. There is a gradual uphill grade to the route after passing that intersection. You, in fact, rise about 70 m over a distance of 2 km then arrive at a small saddle. A 3 km stretch of most pleasant walking follows along Block Four Road amid more good stands of beech and ferns. Monda Track and the top of the Great Dividing Range is then regained, even though only another 40 m elevation is climbed. The remainder of the walk involves simply walking the crest of the Divide along the route of the firebreak. Monda Road is also followed for the first 1.4 km and the last 400 m of the total 3 km to the walk end. The firebreak has a foot track along it in the middle sector of this 3 km stretch and it passes over a hill, whereas the road diverges off round the northern slopes and is a longer route. There is a climb of 160 m elevation involved to pass over the hilltop.

18.5 km; 6 hours; last reviewed January 1988; 'C' grade, medium walk; all on tracks and roads; no water at lunch spot, but at several points during the afternoon walk; walk suited to any season; *Maps: Vicmap 1:25,000 Monda* refers as does Map 16, page 88.

19   UPPER MURRINDINDI-MONDA TRACK

North of Healesville and into the forests beyond Toolangi and Mount St Leonard, there are fine stands of forest especially in the headwaters of the upper Murrindindi River. A walk encompassing the watershed and part of the crest of the Great Dividing Range leads through much lush forest including myrtle beech and excellent fern gullies.

To commence this forest walk travel to Toolangi then up the Monda Road towards Mount St Leonard and on past the peak south-east along the Monda Road firebreak. Commence walking some 7.6 km from the start of Monda Road at a spot where Block Four Road (jeep track) leads off left into the forest.

At first you should walk along the Dividing Range for another 5 km following Monda Road and the firebreak which marks the northern limit of the M.M.B.W. water catchment. At one point the firebreak diverges away from the road temporarily to the right to pass over Mount Monda and it is more pleasant to walk the firebreak at this point. The 5 km stretch ends at a saddle where Block Six Road leads off left. Lunch could be eaten at the saddle on the grassy firebreak before you head down the northern slopes of the Divide on Block Six Road. If water is needed for lunch, it is present at the Murrindindi River 400 m down Block Six Road.

BIRD
ORCHID

After lunch follow the minor road north-north-west across the Murrindindi to a minor junction 1.6 km from the Divide crest. Keep left at the junction and after 300 m ignore A.P.M. Road off left so as to continue down Block Six Road for 2.1 km to the junction of Siberia Extension Road. Continue north-west 300 m, intersect A.P.M. Road at a saddle then head down and across the infant Murrindindi River within 500 m and on a further 1.5 km through areas of lovely ferns to reach Hardy Creek Road.

Follow Hardy Creek Road south 2 km rising about 70 m in elevation, then turn left onto Block Four Road at another wooded saddle. A final 3 km stretch along most pleasant Block Four Road completes the walk circuit. This latter sector includes many fine fern and myrtle stands.

16.4 km; 5½ hours; walk last reviewed January 1988; 'C' grade, easy walk; all on tracks and roads; water available for lunch from Murrindindi River; walk suited to any season; *Maps: Vicmap 1:25,000 Monda Sheet* **refers as do Maps 15 and 16, pages 82 and 88.**

20   UPPER MURRINDINDI-TANGLEFOOT TRACK

On the Great Dividing Range north of Healesville is an area well suited to bushwalkers wanting a couple of days in the bush close to Melbourne. Mount St Leonard and the surrounding fine stands of forest make an excellent venue for walkers such as youth groups and young scouts. The suggestion is to travel to Toolangi and up the Monda Road which road ascends the western flanks of Mount St Leonard for 3.5 km to the ridge top. At this point a firebreak passes along the ridge and a gateway restricts road access to the summit of Mount St Leonard on a side road southwards.

It is suggested that the walk begin with a side trip to Mount St Leonard without packs. To do this you need just pass through the gate southwards and climb to the summit lookout 800 m distant via the firebreak. There is an excellent view of Melbourne and the Dandenong Ranges from the peak.

Once back at the gateway, head off north along the road and firebreak for 700 m, passing Quarry Road off left at the 500 m stage. Tanglefoot Track leads off north beyond a road barrier at this spot and should be noted as it marks the return route the following day. At this spot there is a saddle and the firebreak is often used by people for bush picnics.

**BUTTERFLY
RINGED ZENICA**

To continue, for the rest of the day you need simply follow the firebreak along the Great Divide for 8 km to camp. At two points Monda Road diverges away from the firebreak and range crest. The first divergence is within 300 m of the Tanglefoot Track junction and the second divergence is at Mount Monda. The firebreak walk is very pleasant and there is a foot track to follow at points where the road is absent. The first 4.6 km involves heading south-east and the latter 3.4 km is north-east. Lunch could be at any point along the way, but there is no water supply. Camp is at the junction of Monda Road and Block Six Road in a saddle.

On the second day you need to follow Block Six Road across the Upper Murrindindi River and on north. After 1.6 km, avoid minor Black Range Track off right, and after a further 300 m, avoid A.P.M. Road off left. Continue downhill 2.1 km to where Siberia Extension Track slants in from the right and then on 300 m further to where A.P.M. Road is intersected at a saddle. On again 500 m to cross the infant Murrindindi River again, then on another 1.6 km to reach Hardys Creek Road. Turn north (right) down Hardys Creek Road and follow this quiet road through

MAGPIE

lovely ferny areas to Kalatha Camp 4 km away. There are several minor logging roads off left and right as you proceed to Kalatha Camp, (a former forestry camp).

Next head west up Sylvia Creek Road for 900 m, then diverge off the road onto minor Tanglefoot Track. It is on the left and has a picnic area and vehicular barrier across its start. Have lunch before continuing.

The first 1.2 km of Tanglefoot Track involves a climb of 100 m amid ferns, sassafras and beech trees. A track off right to Mount Tanglefoot should then be passed and the route levels out. Continue south for 4.5 km to rejoin Monda Track and the Divide crest firebreak, but midway veer left where Tanglefoot Track temporarily divides. (The right fork leads over a small hill and requires a climb.) Once at Monda Track, turn right and retrace 700 m of the previous day's walk to reach your destination.

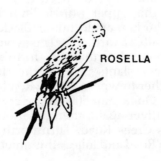

ROSELLA

28 km; 9 hours; two days walk, each day of 10.3 km, 3½ hours and 17.7 km, 5½ hours; walk last reviewed January 1988; 'C' grade, medium overnight walk; all on tracks and roads; features forests; carry water for lunch each day, water for camp from Upper Murrindindi River 400 m north of camp along Block Six Road; walk suited to any season, but occasional snow falls in winter; *Maps: Vicmap 1:25,000 Monda* refers as do Maps 15 and 16, pages 82 and 88.

21   SUGARLOAF-JAWBONES-
CATHEDRAL MOUNTAIN

Rock climbers frequent parts of the Cathedral Range just south of Taggerty on the Maroondah Highway, so it is perhaps the walker with a yen for rugged terrain who will enjoy this route most. While the walk is graded HARD in this book and includes the rock climbers' Sugarloaf Peak, it is still essentially a walk. However people have died from falls at the Sugarloaf so the inexperienced should be deterred.

Go to the 109 km peg from Melbourne along the Maroondah Highway and 2.6 km eastwards along sealed Cathedral Lane from near the peg. Turn right onto minor Little River Road just before the Little River is reached via Cathedral Lane. The walk start is then 2.9 km south-east along the minor road via a bridge over the Little River at the 1.2 km stage. Once across the bridge, pass a pine plantation and go along Little River Road south-south-east, following near the east bank of the river to the walk start at Neds Gully camp and picnic area. The picnic area is mainly across the river by footbridge.

Head off south from the picnic area on a foot track to Cooks Mill camp and picnic area some 2.7 km by way of the west bank. A pine plantation is passed as Cooks Mill is neared. Cerebus Road should then be followed west towards the range.

The road climbs for 1.2 km to a car park and pad turnoff to the Jawbones. Continue south up Cerebus Road another 3.4 km on a spur and within dry forest to reach Sugarloaf Saddle, camp and hut. This would be a suitable lunch spot, 7.3 km from the walk start and just before you climb the rugged Sugarloaf Peak. The cliffs of the peak can be seen nearby and indeed will have been evident as you climbed Cerebus Road to the saddle.

After lunch take the southernmost of two foot tracks which lead off to the peak. It is known as the canyon route and leads south-west uphill initially, then swings north-west and rises dramatically up the spine of the Sugarloaf. There is an awkward section of rock to be scaled and the canyon area is steep and a bit difficult, but with care and time the summit should be achieved without danger. However it is not a climb upon which to 'take Grandma'. There are a number of good hand-holds on the steep sloping rock ascent. The last few metres of climb is on a good track. The best views from 910 m Sugarloaf are from the top of the blade just north of the actual summit. Most of the Cathedral Range can be seen ahead and below, and you will be able to see that the walking ahead is not easy. The first section to be travelled is the most awkward. From the summit you will appreciate just how rugged this range is. As you begin to descend the blade it is necessary to keep as close as possible to the very crest until near the lower part of the blade, then a ramp must be descended on the left (west) side. Keep up near the ridge crest as much as possible thereafter. Some 3 km from the Sugarloaf summit, and after a lot of awkward rock hopping and time-consuming picking of the route, you should reach the Jawbones Saddle area. The spot is also known as The Farmyard and has been somewhat overcamped in the past. There is a clearing from which a track leads off the range east to Cerebus Road by

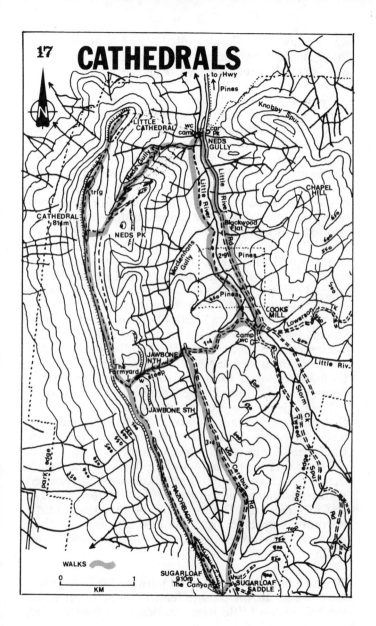

17 CATHEDRALS

N

to Hwy
Pines

Knobby Spur

LITTLE
CATHEDRAL

wc camp
car pk

NEDS
GULLY

Neds Gully

CHAPEL
HILL

trig

Little River

CATHEDRAL
816m

Blackwood
Flat

Rd

NEDS PK

2-9 Pines

MacLennans
Gully

Pines

COOKS
MILL

Lowersons

Tk

camp
wc

JAWBONE
NTH

The
Farmyard

Little Riv.

w. steep

1-4

JAWBONE STH

Storm Ck
Tweed

3-4

Cerebus Rd

Buck Spur

park edge

RAZORBACK

Rd

WALKS

0   1
KM

hut

SUGARLOAF
910m
The Canyon

SUGARLOAF
SADDLE

97

way of Jawbone Creek gully. Water is normally in that gully just 300 m from the clearing. The Farmyard was named after lyrebird calls resembling farm sounds.

Diverge left up a little onto the very crest of the range again and walk on north in forest. There are good views, to the west especially. Keep close to the crest. After nearly 1 km, a track sidles the eastern slopes and should be avoided in favour of remaining on the crest. The sidling track leads through a saddle between Cathedral Mountain and Neds Peak then descends to Neds Gully. At times the crest track does lie up to 20 m down the slopes, but in the main it is on the top and permits good views. Some 3.5 km from The Farmyard, the summit of Cathedral Mountain at 814 m elevation should be attained. By now the day will be getting late, and no doubt the rugged terrain will have made you tired, but there is still the descent off the range to complete.

Retrace some 600 m south along the crest to head steeply east down a track to a saddle between the Cathedral and Neds Peak. The saddle is only about 400 m from the tops. Neds Gully Walking Track can then be followed from the saddle north-eastwards down to Neds Gully Picnic Area some 2.5 m away.

The Little River is crossed by the footbridge at Neds Gully to reach the car park at the walk's end. The day's activities will have shown you the entire Cathedral Range—and what a beautiful range it is!

The main purpose of including this long, hard walk in this book is to satisfy the needs of more experienced walkers who may wish to get fit for that long holiday or Christmas trip. The route can be shortened if time becomes a problem or if the difficulty is more than desired. The short cut is from the Jawbones to Cooks Mill.

20 km; 8 hours; last reviewed January 1987; 'A' grade, hard walk; all on tracks; features Sugarloaf; water limited to the Little River basically so best carried;

walk suited to any season; *Maps: Algona Cathedral Range, Vicmap 1:25,000 Taggerty, 1:25,000 Margaret, 1:25,000 Buxton & 1:25,000 Rubicon* refer as does Map 17, page 97.

22   CATHEDRAL RANGES

The Cathedral Range provides excellent opportunities for camping at sites relatively close to Melbourne. The locality is especially suited to youth groups, scouts and guides. The range itself provides rugged walking with some challenge and a lot of interest. It is possible to camp on the range at a spot known as The Farmyard, but wood fires are not permitted on the range. It is suggested that this walk start from Neds Gully camping area and that camp be at The Farmyard, despite the campfire limitation. The Farmyard is a rather attractive spot and is quite convenient as a location in terms of making each day's walk more evenly matched. To reach the walk start at Neds Gully, take Cathedral Lane east from the Maroondah Highway for about 2.5 km, then Little River Road for 2.7 km south-east, crossing the Little River on a bridge in the process. Neds Gully camp area is beside the Little River.

From Neds Gully car park, walk along Little River Road south for 3 km, passing Blackwood Flat, then turning right to cross the Little River and enter the Cooks Mill site camp and picnic area for lunch. Some pine forest is passed during this riverside stretch of the walk. There is an alternative foot track connecting Neds Gully and Cooks Mill via the Little River West bank. Follow Cerebus Road west 1.2 km from Cooks Mill to a small car park on a ridge. This spot is adjacent to and just east of MacLennans Gully and there is a foot track off west across the gully and up to The

Farmyard via Jawbones Creek gully. It is a particularly steep 1 km climb to The Farmyard and the spring supplying water for camp is passed during the final ascent. It is therefore best to collect water on the way into camp. Establish tents and spend time along the cliff rim just west of camp to help fill in the day. A short walk south, along the range crest walking track and return, is a worthwhile option. (Sugarloaf Peak should be avoided by the inexperienced.)

On the second day the range top track should be followed north for 3.5 km to Cathedral Mountain itself. There are cliffs on the left for most of the way and the going is slow because of rocks underfoot. A track diverges off right following the contour, about 1 km north of The Farmyard and should be avoided. (It leads past Neds Peak and down to Neds Gully camp area). Keep on the crest of the range to see the views and rocky terrain of Cathedral Mountain, then retrace

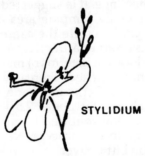

STYLIDIUM

some 600 m south along the crest to head steeply east down a track to a saddle between the main range and Neds Peak. The saddle is only about 400 m from the tops. Neds Gully Walking Track can then be followed from the saddle north-eastwards down to Neds Gully Picnic Area some 2.5 km away. Finally cross the Little River footbridge to the east bank and walk end.

11.2 km; 5 hours; 2 day walk each day of 5.2 km, 3 hours and 6 km, 2 hours respectively; walk last

reviewed January 1987; 'A' grade; easy overnight walk; all on tracks and roads; features rocky terrain and cliffs; water for camp from spring in upper Jawbones Creek, except in mid and late summer when water needs to be carried; suited to any season; *Maps: Algona 'Cathedral Range', Vicmap 1:25,000 Taggerty, 1:25,000 Margaret, 1:25,000 Buxton and 1:25,000 Rubicon* refer as does Map 17, page 97.

23   CATHEDRAL RANGES

Neds Gully camp area is an excellent bush camp site beside the Little River and within a convenient distance of Melbourne. It is therefore suggested for use during a two-day walk encompassing the whole of the Cathedral Range. Sugarloaf Peak is part of the circuit. People have died from falls on Sugarloaf so great care should be taken in that locality. The walk is best started from Sugarloaf Saddle, but visitors to the area will find the access road (Cerebus Road) closed to traffic from the north during wet weather. It is therefore best to approach Sugarloaf Saddle from the south (Marysville side) via Mount Margaret Road and Cerebus Road.

From the Sugarloaf Saddle two foot tracks lead off up steeply to nearby Sugarloaf Peak which is a rock climbers' venue. Both routes to the peak are awkward. One route is via The Canyon and the other via Wells Cave. The author personally favours the canyon route which is more direct, although it requires scaling sloping rock. This rock is not unduly difficult to negotiate. The Canyon, in fact, is nothing more than just a big groove between parallel rock spines. Once on top of Sugarloaf Peak the whole of the Cathedral Range can be seen extending out northwards. A true appreciation of the rugged terrain will be gained and views are quite impressive in all directions.

Next follow the foot track along the range crest. Progress will be slow and difficult at times. Some 3 km north of Sugarloaf you should reach the open grassy clearing known as The Farmyard. It is a camp site, but you should use it for lunch. It derived its name from lyrebirds imitating farmyard sounds.

After lunch, continue to keep to the crest of the range on a track to Cathedral Mountain itself. There are two foot tracks, which should be avoided, off right down to Neds Gully Camp 1 km and 2.9 km north of The Farmyard. Stay on the range crest track for the 3.5 km to Cathedral Mountain to see its rugged western cliff faces and views, then walk on north

MOUNTAIN HICKORY

another 1.3 km, still on the range crest tracks. This brings you to Little Cathedral which marks the northern abrupt end of the range. Just short of this peak another track diverges off right and should be avoided so that the fine views northwards from the peak are included. It is then necessary to retrace 1.9 km south along the range crest to head steeply east down a track to a saddle between the main range and Neds Peak, a distance of some 400 m. Neds Gully Walking Track can then be followed from the saddle north-eastwards down to Neds Gully Picnic Area some 2.5 km away. Camp can then be established.

On the second day head upstream along the Little River valley by way of the Little River Road. Pass Blackwood Flat and pine plantations to reach Cooks Mill site for an early lunch after just 3 km of walking for the morning. Time could be spent relaxing and enjoying the lovely camp and picnic area. (Little River Road enters Cooks Mill site on a bridge over the Little River after having followed the river's east bank.) There is an alternative foot track connecting Neds Gully and Cooks Mill via the Little River west bank.

After lunch, follow Cerebus Road west uphill 1.2 km, then south up a spur for 3.5 km back to Sugarloaf Saddle. During the ascent there are views of the near sheer cliff faces of Sugarloaf Peak on the right.

21 km; 9½ hours; 2 day walk, each day of 13.3 km, 6½ hours and 7.7 km, 3 hours respectively; last reviewed January 1987; 'A' grade, medium overnight walk; all on tracks and roads; features rocky cliffs; water for camp and lunch on second day from Little River and water for lunch on first day usually available from the headwaters of Jawbones Creek just east of The Farmyard. This supply can dry up by mid or late summer; walk suited to any season. Warning: Sugarloaf Peak is not suited to the inexperienced. *Maps: Algona 'Cathedral Ranges', Vicmap 1:25,000 Taggerty, 1:25,000 Margaret, 1:25,000 Buxton and 1:25,000 Rubicon refer as does Map 17, page 97.*

24   ISLAND HOP-TAGGERTY RIVER

Marysville has for many generations been a mountain resort with numerous delightful foot tracks through the bush. During recent years tracks have been upgraded and extended. One area opened up is in

18 Marysville (1)

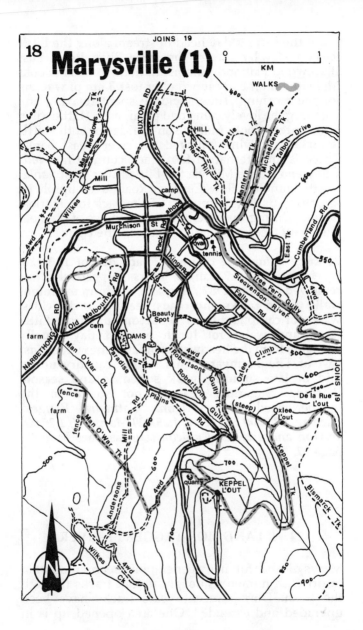

WALKS

the forests along the Taggerty River and north of the township. This walk suggestion starts and finishes at the Steavenson River bridge at the lower end of the main street of the town walking via ferny Michaeldene to the Taggerty River locality.

From the Steavenson River bridge walk east past a restaurant and up the start of Cumberland Road, to a saddle 500 m from the walk start.

Opposite, and on the saddle is a car park area and the start of the Michaeldene foot track. Walk this track downhill, northwards, crossing East Track after 400 m and continuing on down amongst tree ferns. A second pad then crosses Michaeldene Track. At this spot take a 100 m long side trip left to see the wishing well set amid ferns and on the stream. As you then continue on down Michaeldene you should next reach Trestle Track off left some 1.5 km from the Cumberland Road area. Marysville's links with the timber industry and old timber tramways can be seen at this junction in the form of a restored old timber tramway trestle. On again, some 2 km from Cumberland Road, cross Dickenson Track which is a four-wheel-drive track then, within 200 m, reach the Taggerty River at lovely Island Hop. Lunch is suggested here where the river divides and rejoins several times. There are small bridges connecting the islands.

A foot pad leads north-west downstream along the banks of the Taggerty River and it should be followed. About 500 m from Island Hop the track crosses to the north bank on a footbridge. The pad known as Vic Oak Track then leads on for 1 km to meet the main Buxton Road at its Taggerty River road bridge. Turn left along the road in an area of farms and golf links and where there are many fine deciduous trees, then walk 800 m along the roadside to Dickensons Track off left. The track is on the farmlands' margin and leads south-east into forest. Some 1.5 km along Dickensons Track turn right back onto Michaeldene Track for 500 m, then fork right onto Trestle Track.

Cross the stream and turn left off Trestle Track and follow Manfern Track up the gully for 1 km to meet East Track.

Turn left for just a few metres to rejoin Michaeldene Track, then retrace the 1 km back to the walk end at the Steavenson River bridge.

BUSH RAT

9 km; 3 hours; last reviewed January 1987; 'B' grade, easy walk; all on tracks; features Taggerty River; water for lunch from river at Island Hop; walk suited to any season; *Maps: Vicmap 1:25,000 Steavenson and 1:25,000 Margaret* refer as do Maps 18 and 19, pages 104 and 108.

25 MAN O'WAR TRACK-KEPPEL LOOKOUT

One of the better walks in the Marysville district is to Keppel Lookout using Man O'War Track and Robertson Gully Track. This routing is through quite varied bushland and can include Oxlee Lookout by taking a 400 m long return side trip. It is best to walk the circuit anticlockwise so as to descend very steep Oxlee Climb.

Start at the shops in Murchison Street (Main Street) and walk two blocks south on Pack Road to Kings Road. Go up to the west end of Kings Road where the Old Melbourne Road should be crossed and Man O'War Track starts. At this spot there is a view of some of the town. Follow Man O'War Track west round the contour of a hill, then south parallel to the main Narbethong Road to cross Old Melbourne Road again in 1.3 km. Keep on Man O'War Track which remains close to the east side of Narbethong Road for 200 m, then leads off south-east uphill. Shortly, a farm clearing should be seen off right as you climb further to a hill crest. Over the hill top, the pad forks off left away from the farmland and continues on up across Anderson Mill Road and onto the very ferny lower slopes of Mount Strickland. Some 2.5 km from where Old Melbourne Road was last crossed, turn left off the foot track end up a jeep track so that within another 600 m Paradise Plains Road is reached. Some 50 m uphill across the road is a track up to Keppel Lookout. Take this 500 m long climb to the lookout for a good view of Marysville. The ascent starts on a jeep track into an old quarry then becomes a steep foot track. Robertson Gully track joins in from the left as you climb. The lookout would be a good place for lunch. Keppels Track leads off south-east from the lookout and should be walked for 2 km round the head of Robertson Gully to meet the top end of Oxlee Climb track. Take the 400 m long return trip further along Keppels Track to see the view from rocky Oxlee Lookout before starting the steep descent of Oxlee Climb. The descent is only 700 m distance, but is quite time-consuming due to the steep grade. Robertson Gully Track is reached at the bottom of the main descent. Head on north, north-west, then north again along Robertson Gully Track to rejoin Kings Road after about 1.7 km. During this distance there are a number of foot and jeep tracks off right and left, all to be avoided. The first to be avoided

107

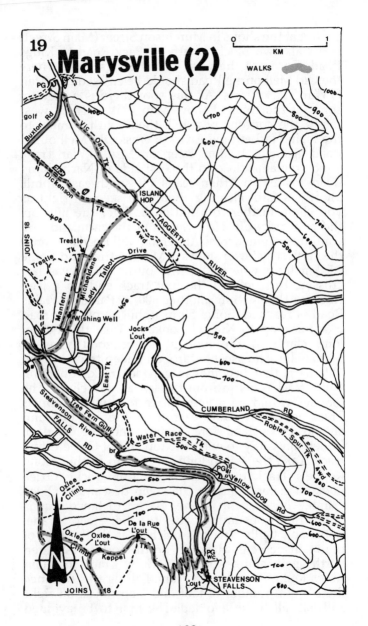

19 **Marysville (2)**

108

is the Oxlee Climb track continuation off right. Thereafter it is necessary to basically keep heading downhill in a north-west, then northerly, direction. At Kings Road, turn left and walk one block past some guest houses to Pack Road. It is then only two blocks to the right, down Pack Road, to reach the town centre again.

11.2 km; 4 hours; walk last reviewed January 1988; 'B' grade, easy walk; all on tracks and roads; features Keppel Lookout; carry water for lunch; walk suited to any season but a bit wet underfoot on Oxlee Climb in winter; *Maps: Vicmap 1:25,000 Marysville and 1:25,000 Steavenson* refer as does Map 18, page 104.

26 MARYSVILLE-STEAVENSON FALLS-KEPPEL LOOKOUT

South-east of Marysville are Steavenson Falls and three excellent viewpoints which overlook the town. They are all set amid lovely forest and tree and ground ferns really proliferate throughout the district. A well-maintained track system permits a circuit to be walked from the town that includes the falls and lookouts and many other features. While a relatively steep 200 m gain in altitude is necessary at one point, the route is still ideal for easy walking.

Lunch is recommended at the falls where water is always available. The Steavenson River has a catchment of about seventeen square kilometres above the falls.

Commence walking from the Steavenson River bridge at the bottom end of the town's main street and head up Cumberland Road to a saddle 500 m distant. Kirami foot track then needs to be followed downhill southwards to the river. At this point turn left (south-east) onto ferny Tree Fern Gully Track.

FUNGI

After 1.5 km, avoid a left fork jeep track uphill and cross the river at a bridge, then climb up to and cross Yellow Dog Road. Continue on the pad 1.3 km to join into the main Steavenson Falls tourist road. (At about the half-way point along the pad, a short track up from Yellow Dog Road should be avoided as it joins in from the left.) Head up the tourist road for 500 m to a car park and on another 300 m via a broad path into the falls. Sassafras, ferns and tall timber all feature well in the locality. The falls are about 80 m high and are flood-lit at night. Picnic facilities are available as are shelters.

Return to the car park after seeing the falls. A steep foot pad then should be taken from the car park for 1 km via seven hairpin bends to emerge on a plateau area about 200 m higher than the falls base. Continue

LYREBIRD

walking 400 m to De La Rue Lookout as the track broadens and for the first good view of Marysville town in the valley. Bismarck Track forks off south at the lookout and should be avoided.

Head 500 m west to a second viewpoint called Oxlee Lookout, pass Oxlee Climb track off right, and go south and west around the head of Robertson Gully for 2 km to Keppel Lookout. Most of the route is within dense rain forest. A road reaches the Keppel Lookout area from Marysville. It is just south of the lookout and should be avoided. Head on steeply downhill westwards for 250 m on the track, avoid a lesser track off left so as to double back down two hairpins into the ferny slopes of Robertson Gully. Some 500 m later a bend on Paradise Plains Road is reached.

At this road hairpin bend, head off right onto the continuation of Robertson Gully Track. It leads down across ferny Robertson Gully and on past the bottom end of the steep section of Oxlee Climb. Some 700 m from Robertson Gully Crossing and at a saddle, ignore a track off right. It is the continuation of Oxlee Climb. Instead, head on north-west, then north basically on Robertson Gully Track still, to join onto Kings Road after about 1.5 km. During the descent there are a number of foot and jeep tracks off right and left, all to be avoided. At Kings Road, turn left and walk one street block past some guest houses to Pack Road. It is then only two street blocks to the right down Pack Road, to reach the centre of town and the walk's end.

11.5 km; 4 hours; walk last reviewed January 1988; 'B' grade; medium walk; all on tracks and roads; features Steavenson Falls; good water for lunch at falls; walk suited to any season; *Maps: Vicmap 1:25,000 Marysville and 1:25,000 Steavenson* refer as do Maps 18 and 19, pages 104 and 108.

27   LAKE MOUNTAIN-
BERRY HIGGS PLAYGROUND

Lake Mountain, east of Marysville, is 1433 m above sea level and as such provides pleasant sub-alpine walking just over 100 km from Melbourne. A good circuit starts at Gerraty's Car Park in the Lake Mountain Alpine Reserve and includes the summit of the peak. The circuit could be undertaken as a snow walk in winter *by adults*, but extreme care should be taken, especially with navigation, and very warm clothing worn. Summer is the best season for walking to really appreciate this undulating plateau and mountain area.

From Gerraty's Car Park at the end of the main tourist road, walk south up a jeep track towards the summit of Lake Mountain, 1 km distant. Midway to the summit, the jeep track becomes a foot pad at a barrier and, just short of the peak, the foot track divides then rejoins on the top. Take the right fork to reach the summit so that you visit lovely Marysville Lookout. The summit has a trig point, is 100 m higher than Gerraty's Car Park and features some broad expanses of bare rock.

A foot track leads east-south-east and should be followed next. It leads 300 m through snow gums to an easterly viewpoint known as the Alps Lookout. The pad then leads on south through pleasant undulating areas of snowgums and tiny clearings of snow grass, then, 800 m from the Alps Lookout, another foot track from Lake Mountain summit joins in on the right.

Go south-west 100 m to emerge at Sherlocks Lookout which permits broad views west from open slopes featuring more bare rock. Walk west from Sherlocks Lookout down the pad which loses 110 m elevation within 1 km to reach the Snowy Hill roadside rest area and car park. Walk south from the car park about 100 m onto the main Lake Mountain tourist road, then Upper Taggerty Forestry Road forks

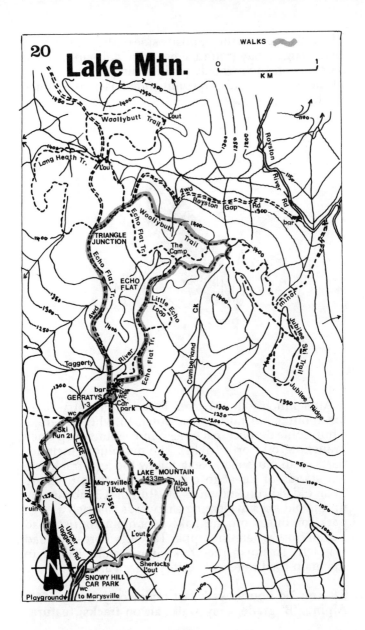

Lake Mtn.

WALKS

Woollybutt Trail

L'out

Royston River Rd

Long Heath Tr.

L'out

4wd

Royston Gap Rd

bar

Woollybutt Trail

TRIANGLE
JUNCTION

Echo Flat Tr.

The Camp

Echo Flat Tr.

ECHO
FLAT

Little Echo
Loop

Ck

Fleming

4wd

River

Jubilee Ski Trail

Taggerty

Echo Flat Tr.

Cumberland

Jubilee Ridge

bar

wc

GERRATYS
.3

Car park

wc

Ski
Run 21

LAKE

MTN

RD

LAKE MOUNTAIN
1433m

Marysville
L'out

Alps
L'out

ruin

N

Upper
Taggerty Rd

1.7

L'out

L'out

Sherlocks
L'out

SNOWY HILL
CAR PARK

wc

Playground

to Marysville

off north-west on the opposite side of the tourist road. Berry Higgs Playground, a beautiful sub-alpine grass slope, is on the low side of the main road just south of the junction and is recommended as a good lunch spot.

CALLISTEMON

After lunch follow Upper Taggerty Forestry Road for about 1 km north-west down to where there is a hut, some derelict machinery and a minor jeep track branching off north (right). The machinery includes parts of an old boiler. Next, follow the jeep track into tall stands of forest to cross a creek, then to climb to an old ski run known as Ski Run 21. Climb steeply up the old ski run clearing eastwards to reach a large park for buses on the Lake Mountain tourist road 1.2 km from where the Upper Taggerty Forestry Road was left. To finish the walk circuit, walk 300 m up the main road to reach Gerraty's Car Park.

5.8 km; 2½ hours; walk last reviewed January 1987; Alpine, 'B' grade, easy walk; all on tracks; features

Lake Mountain summit; carry water for lunch; walk suited to all seasons other than winter, but even a snow walk is feasible in winter; *Maps: Algona 'Lake Mountain Marysville & Mount Bullfight', Vicmap 1:25,000 Lake Mountain, 1:25,000 Steavenson, 1:25,000 Margaret and 1:25,000 Royston* refer as does Map 20, page 113.

28   ECHO FLAT

Echo Flat is fairly small, but abounds in true alpine vegetation and features several tiny alpine tarns. It is close to Lake Mountain and is snowbound each winter. Access is via Marysville and the Lake Mountain Road to Gerraty's Dugout Car Park which is the uppermost turntable serving Lake Mountain summit. Recently Lake Mountain and the Echo Flat area have had a number of cross-country ski trails established so that the trails and former tracks permit good walking when snow is absent.

From Gerraty's, start walking north-east past a barrier and up a jeep track towards Echo Flat. The jeep track starts on the west side of an amenities building and the information and first aid centre. Almost immediately after passing the barrier, a ski trail forks off left from the jeep track and it should be avoided. After 800 m of walking among snow gums you should emerge on Echo Flat. At the spot a ski trail intersects the jeep track. It is the same ski trail as the one seen at the barrier and it forms a loop. Walk north across Echo Flat on the jeep track avoiding two further ski trails off right as you proceed. A spot among beautiful snow gums known as The Camp should then be reached.

Two ski trails lead off left from The Camp and at this spot you are some 2 km from the walk start.

Continue on the jeep track (which has been named Jubilee Ski Trail). It leads east in snow gums, crosses tiny alpine clearings and generally remains on the alpine tops to reach another ski trail off left 600 m from The Camp. Turn left, walk about 300 m to a 'T' intersection of ski trails then go left (west) another 200 m to join Woolybutt Ski Trail. Proceed north-west through stands of Woolybutt trees and within 1 km the ski trail links to Royston Gap Road. Turn south-west (left) to walk 400 m on the road and Triangle Junction should be reached. The sector is slightly uphill and to the south-west. At the junction another minor road links in from the north and a further ski trail leads off west. It is then a 2 km walk south directly along the road back to Gerraty's Car Park and the end of the walk.

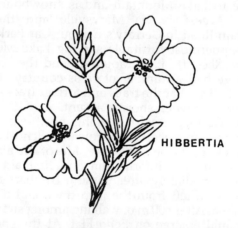

HIBBERTIA

6.5 km; 2½ hours; walk last reviewed January 1987; Alpine, 'B' grade; easy walk; all on tracks; features Echo Flat alpine area and tarns; carry water for lunch; walk suited to summer especially with winter quite unsuitable as area snowbound; *Maps: Algona 'Lake Mountain Marysville & Mt Bullfight' Vicmap 1:25,000 Royston and 1:25,000 Margaret* refer as does Map 20, page 113.

29 CUMBERLAND RESERVE

Mountain Ash is the tallest hardwood tree in the world and it is second only to the giant softwood Californian Redwood as the highest tree species in the world. Some 16 km east of Marysville Mountain Ash occurs in significant stands. Some trees estimated to have grown from seedlings after a fire 150 to 200 years ago are now past their prime, but they are the tallest known living trees in Victoria. Their age has meant that severe wind storms, particularly in 1959 and 1973, have snapped off their upper limbs, but one giant still reaches 84 m (275 feet) tall. Others are not far short of this height. The locality has been subject to logging since 1939 fires and it is obvious from stumps remaining that some felled trees would have far exceeded 84 m.

Messrs Cameron and Barton set up a sawmill, hence the name Cambarville which today marks a reserve picnic area and clearing in the bush. The bush today still is scarred by the logging operations to some extent, but one can appreciate the pristine qualities of the reserve and feel some sense of relative insignificance among these giants of nature. The Cumberland Reserve is established on a high plateau at the head of Armstrong Creek and streams flow off the plateau edge southwards creating further interest at Cora Lynn and Cumberland waterfalls.

Travel to Cambarville picnic area and head off on a circuit walk. The route is basically flat going and the track starts opposite toilets near the southern end of the clearing in the bush. The pad leads into damp forest north-westwards and soon crosses two small gullies. There are labels on some trees for educational purposes. Myrtle Beech trees and ferns are particularly beautiful and quite prolific. Within 800 m the 'big tree' should be reached. It has a girth of 5.2 m at 3 m above ground level, (far less girth than many stumps passed since leaving Cambarville clearing). Its present 84 m was 92 m before a wind

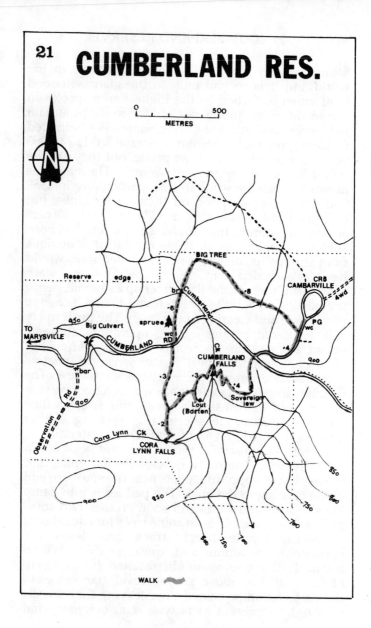

21 CUMBERLAND RES.

0 — 500
METRES

BIG TREE

Reserve   edge

CRB
CAMBARVILLE

4wd

br   Cumberland

•8

•6

950

Big Culvert

spruce

wc
RD

PG
wc

TO
MARYSVILLE

CUMBERLAND   RD

CUMBERLAND
FALLS

•4

900

bar

•3

•3

•4

900

Sovereign
iew

•2

Lout
(Barten

Observation

Rd

900

•2

Cora Lynn   Ck

CORA
LYNN FALLS

850

800

950

900

750

700

850

750   700

WALK

118

storm 'pruned' it in 1959.

The track should then be followed south across a bridge at very beautiful Cumberland Creek and on to Cumberland Road 600 m from the 'big tree'. Cross the road and walk downhill slightly southwards in an area of many silver wattles, blackwoods and myrtle beech trees plus, of course, more huge mountain ash trees. After 300 m and at a track junction, make a 400 m long return side trip to see most beautiful Cora Lynn Falls. The falls locality could be used as a pleasant lunch spot if desired. Then, after the side trip, go north-east 200 m to another 200 m side trip to Bartons Lookout for a view eastwards across the lower reaches of Cumberland Creek.

Some 300 m further north-east along the pad sees you at Cumberland Falls. This locality is very ferny and cool, but it is difficult to get a really good appreciation of the falls due to their relative inaccessability. Onwards again, the route leads past Sovereign View via a pad along a former water race constructed by early gold miners. The view is of the Armstrong Creek valley southwards. The track climbs a bit and leads north to the Cumberland Road again some 400 m from Cumberland Falls. Cross the road and walk up the 400 m long Cambarville access road to complete the circuit.

3.6 km; 1¼ hours; last reviewed January 1987; 'B' grade; easy walk; all on tracks; features tallest known trees in Victoria; water for lunch from creek at Cora Lynn Falls; walk suited to any season but snow is a possibility in winter *Maps: Vicmap 1:25,000 Lake Mountain* refers as does Map 21, page 118.

30   WARBURTON

Warburton has long been a most pleasant mountain resort town with walk possibilities in several directions. The Yarra River flows through the town and it is rewarding to walk the river banks and adjacent leafy parts of the township itself. At the western end of the town is a bridge to the north bank of the river and to golf links. The bridge is an ideal place from which to commence walking. Car parking, toilet facilities and a restaurant/shop are all at the spot.

Cross the bridge to the north bank, then walk along Dammans Road which is quiet and leads east near the riverside for a considerable distance. Picnic areas are passed and so is a footbridge back across the river to the main shopping area. Stay on the north side of the river and after 2.5 km you should reach the main road again, but well beyond the east end of the shops. Willows and ferns abound during the Dammans Road sector. Once back on the main road, cross it to a camping area, then follow the main camp ground road near the northern river bank to the east end of the camp ground. The way then continues as a foot track through riverside bushland to another picnic area between the main road and the river. This picnic area is some 4 km from the walk start. It would be a good place for lunch.

The pad continues south-east along the northern riverside but private property owners have extended their fences to the river. Stiles exist at some spots, but fences have to be negotiated at others. Better to forget the river bank walk unless you are agile and follow the main road for 1.4 km east until the main road crosses to the south bank on a bridge. Just 200 m east of the bridge turn right along a south bank road which leads south at first for 600 m then passes the Big Pats Creek Road turnoff and heads back towards the town. After another 700 m, diverge right along Riverside Road to stay near the river rather

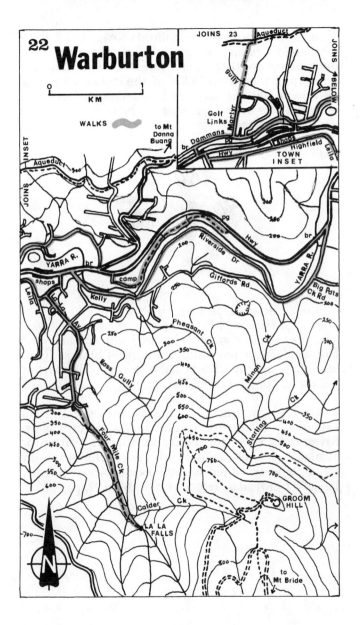

22 Warburton

WALKS

to Mt Donna Buang

JOINS 23
JOINS BELOW
JOINS INSET

Aqueduct
gully
Martyr
Golf Links
br Dammans
br
Highfield
shops
Leila
Highway HWY
TOWN INSET

Aqueduct
pg
Riverside Dr
Hwy
br
YARRA R.
camp
Giffords Rd
Big Pats Ck Rd
shops
Kelly
Leila
Av
Pheasant Ck
Ross Gully
Mingo Ck
Four Mile Ck
Starling
Calder Ck
LA LA FALLS
GROOM HILL
to Mt Bride

N

than to take more direct Giffords Road. Once these two roads rejoin, keep right at the next road divergence so that Kelly Street is followed into residential areas. Within 800 m, the main road should be rejoined at the west end of a bridge. Next turn left along the main road, then at the next corner turn left up Park Road.

FRINGED
HEATH
MYRTLE

Shortly afterwards turn right at the end of Park Road into Highfield Road after seeing some pleasant gardens and good views of Mount Donna Buang. Walk Highfield Road west and it becomes Station Road. Station Road then leads back to the walk starting point and completion of the circuit.

12 km; 3½ hours; last reviewed August 1987; 'B' grade easy walk; all on tracks and roads; features Yarra River; carry water for lunch; transport to Warburton available by occasional bus ex Melbourne and Lilydale; walk suited to any season; *Maps: Vicmap 1:25,000 Gladysdale* refers as does Map 22, page 121.

The mountain resort town of Warburton has, as one of its best walking attractions, a short walk to La La Falls via a foot pad along the west bank of Four Mile Creek. The falls are set amid tree and ground ferns near the headwaters of the creek and adjacent to the steep forested slopes of Groom Hill. The creek valley was ravaged by bushfire in 1983 but has since recovered substantially and even the lyrebirds appear to be returning. Mountain Ash trees are particularly susceptible to fire damage so you will notice that some spots on the slopes of Groom Hill now have stark dead mountain ash trunks evident, whilst all around these former lofty giants there is vigorous new growth.

GUM NUTS

From the Warburton shopping area La La Avenue leads south up the hillside through residential areas. Whilst walkers could use transport up La La Avenue, it is suggested that the distance be walked as there are many fine gardens to see as well as good views across the Yarra River valley to lofty Mount Donna Buang. One therefore tends to get a far better appreciation of the mountain resort character of Warburton.

From Main Street either Park Road or Highfield Road, then La La Avenue (which becomes Old Warburton Road) should be followed for 1.5 km out of town to where the avenue turns west for the first time. A minor road forks off left at that spot and there is a tiny car park where the foot track to the falls begins from the bend. The foot track should then be followed for 1.6 km along the west bank of Four Mile Creek to the falls. The falls, 15 m high, are fairly small but rather pleasant, especially on a hot day in summer when lunch beside them might be really appreciated. Return to Warburton using the same track and avenue.

6.2 km; 2½ hours; walk last reviewed October 1987; 'B' grade family walk; all on roads and track; bus transport to Warburton available; *Maps: Vicmap 1:25,000 Gladysdale* refers as does Map 22, page 121.

32   WARBURTON-MOUNT DONNA BUANG

Climbing Mount Donna Buang from Warburton is not easy. It involves climbing more than 1000 m through heavily timbered country. The foot track is quite steep and can be slippery even in mid summer. However if you want a training trip prior to heading off on a trek to the Himalayas or whatever, this is ideal. The walk starts and ends just east of the Warburton Golf Course and west of the town on the north bank of the Yarra River.

Walk up steep Martyr Road northwards on the east side of the links, to where the road turns east just over the top of a hill. Continue north from the road bend along a foot track across a gully and up past open paddocks. As forest is approached the track meets and turns east adjacent to a Melbourne and Metropolitan Board of Works aqueduct, then crosses the aqueduct and heads up steeply in the forest. Go on up the track until the main Warburton to Mount

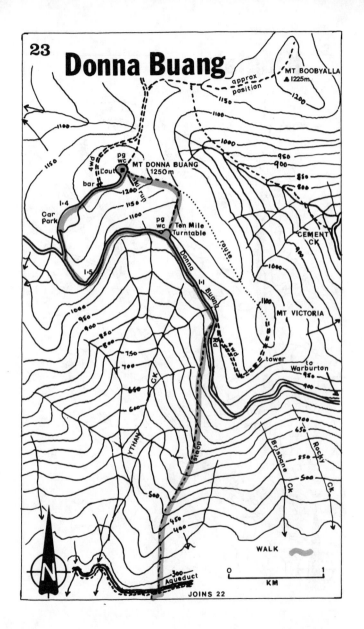

23 Donna Buang

MT BOOBYALLA ▲1225m

approx position

MT DONNA BUANG 1250m

pg wc
L'out
4wd
bar
1·4
Car Park
1·5

CEMENT CK

pg wc Ten Mile Turntable

route

Donna Buang Rd
1·1

MT VICTORIA

4wd
tower
to Warburton

YYTHAN CK

Steep

Brisbane Ck
Rocky Ck

WALK

N

0   KM   1

Aqueduct

JOINS 22

125

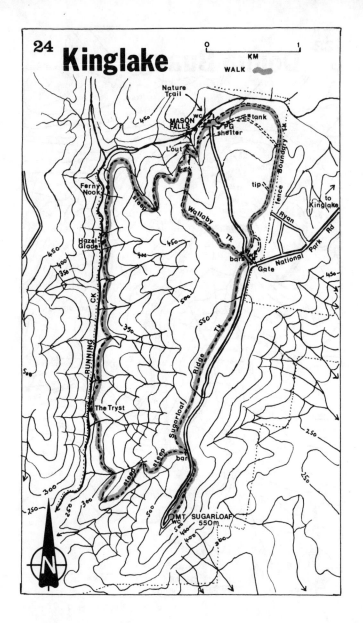

24 Kinglake

KM

WALK

Nature Trail

MASON FALLS

WC

tank

PG shelter

L'out

Ferny Nook

steep

Wallaby Tk

tip

fence

Boundary Tk

Ryan

to Kinglake

450

Hazel Glade

450

400

400

350

RUNNING CK

350

bars

Gate

National Park Rd

450

550 Tk

500

Ridge

The Tryst

Sugarloaf

250

300

steep

steep

bar

250

250

300

300

500

MT SUGARLOAF
550m

WC

450

400

350

250

N

Donna Buang sealed road is reached some 4 km (not 6 km as an old sign indicated) from Warburton.

Head up the road for 1.1 km to the large Ten Mile Turntable where there is a shelter and toilets, then walk east up the main tourist walking track from the turntable to the summit lookout on Mount Donna Buang about 1 km distant. The pad climbs onto a spur, then leads up that spur to the summit. Picnic facilities and a very high lookout tower create interest on the top.

For variety of scenery the return to Warburton could be varied slightly by following the main road down from the summit to Ten Mile Turntable. A 1.4 km stretch of road should be descended to the junction of the Healesville Road, which road leads off right. A further 1.5 km should then be descended to the turntable, and the rest of the walk would be a retrace of the earlier climb. This variation of route adds 1.9 km to the direct distance if you were to descend the foot track to the turntable instead of the road.

14 km; 5 hours; last reviewed March 1987; 'C' grade, hard walk, all on tracks and roads; water for lunch normally available at many places along way; walk suited to any season, but snow about in winter; *Maps: Vicmap 1:25,000 Gladysdale and 1:25,000 Donna Buang* **refers as do Maps 22 and 23, pages 121 and 125.**

33 KINGLAKE NATIONAL PARK

Along the forested slopes of the Great Dividing Range, north-east of Melbourne, lies the Kinglake National Park, a park noted for a broad variety of plant types, lovely Masons Falls and a pleasant lookout known as Mount Sugarloaf. Being on the southern slopes the area receives a reasonably high rainfall resulting in damp gullies, but the steepness of the terrain permits rapid rainfall runoff and leaves ridges rather dry. Vegetation is consequently of both the wet and dry forest types. In the gullies mountain grey gum, messmate, blanket-leaf, blackwood, silver wattle, musk daisy bush, hazel pomaderris, and ferns predominate, whilst on the higher reaches, red stringybark, broadleaf peppermint, grass trees, heaths, grevilleas and orchids proliferate. Masons Falls are perhaps the main point of interest and a large picnic area has been established near them. They descend in two stages totalling 45 m, the lower being a straight 20 m drop while just upstream is a further small cascade. Each is on Running Creek where the stream has cut through the edge of the ancient volcanic rock capping of the Kinglake area. A lookout exists just downstream of the main fall and good roads connect the park entrance with both the picnic ground and the other main attraction, Mount Sugarloaf, 3 km south of the entry. Mount Sugarloaf permits modest views towards Melbourne and Port Phillip. The park is also noted for lyrebirds and is also the home of rosellas, currawongs, thrushes, wombats, echidnas and black wallabies.

A 12.5 km circuit walk is possible within the park, including all the main features, but the park gate is closed each night so intending walkers should check closing times and allow sufficient walking time to return to their transport, or leave transport outside the entrance. Access to the suggested walk starting point at Mount Sugarloaf car park is from the Kinglake West to Kinglake Road, then 7.1 km along National Park Road entering the park at the 4.1 km stage. A small entry fee is payable. By starting at Mount Sugarloaf rather than elsewhere, the main picnic area is conveniently located in the area best suited for lunch midway through the circuit. Walking clockwise avoids an otherwise long climb up Running Creek Track.

From the lookout car park, follow a well-defined foot track north past some toilets and for a total of 850 m passing over two small knobs on the Sugarloaf Ridge, abutting the main roadway's east side at one stage then joining back onto the roadway. Next, walk 50 m north and turn left down a jeep track on the west side of the road. At this spot the Sugarloaf Ridge walking track also leads off. It marks the later return route. A barrier prevents vehicular access down the jeep track known as Running Creek Track, which descends steeply south-westwards through open forest then, at 'The Tryst', swings north to undulate up the east side of Running Creek in damp forest

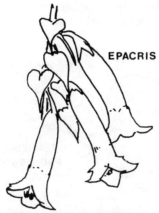

EPACRIS

conditions. Hazel Glade, a spot well endowed with the shrub hazel pomaderris, is passed and, soon after, Ferny Nook, noted for tree and ground ferns, is passed. The jeep track then climbs steeply and at a point about 6 km from where National Park Road was left, Wallaby Track forks off right. Turn left and walk 250 m north-east to the Masons Falls lookout, then follow an excellent foot track for 500 m past the top of Masons Falls and another small cascade further upstream and into a large picnic area with all facilities. A barbecue lunch might be appropriate in this pleasant tree-covered area.

Next, locate the start of Boundary Track, a foot track which leads further upstream beside Running Creek from near a toilet block in the lower sector of the picnic area. Then wander east in forest and swing south up a drier ridge, still on Boundary Track. Soon a jeep track from the picnic area joins in from the right and thereafter boundary Track is a jeep track as it leads for the 1.75 km from the picnic area to the park entrance and office. Opposite the park entry turn right along the Sugarloaf Ridge walking track. Follow this pad south along the dry forested ridge for 2.1 km to rejoin the National Park Road and the outward route just 900 m north of Mount Sugarloaf then, finally, either use the bitumen road or the foot track, to return along the last section to the car park.

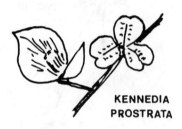

KENNEDIA PROSTRATA

Official park advice is to allow about four hours for actual walking time to complete the circuit but, like sign-posted distances in the park, the time seems a little over-stated for even fairly inexperienced walkers.

12.5 km; 3½ hours; walk last reviewed January 1987; 'C' grade, easy walk; all on tracks; water for lunch available at Masons Falls Picnic Area; walk suited to any time of the year; *Maps: Vicmap 1:25,000 Arthurs Creek, 1:25,000 Kinglake West, 1:25,000 Pheasant Creek and 1:25,000 Strathewan* refer as does Map 24, page 126.

The Kinglake section of the Great Dividing Range is of volcanic origin and has rich red soil which supports sturdy forest and thick undergrowth. At Masons Falls, however, the volcanic plateau gives way to the eroded valley of Running Creek and much steep country which marks the southern flank of the Great Dividing Range. In this steep country there is a very great range of vegetation types. The ridges and spurs support a dry type forest prolific with wildflowers and the gullies support damp forest and ferns.

This easy walk from the National Park gate includes dry type forest on a spur, damp forest and waterfalls, then a more open sector where the rich soils of the rangetop plateau have been farmed. Sawmillers once operated near Masons Falls but now there is a large picnic area in an attractive forest setting just near the falls. It is therefore good to use this picnic area for a lunch break. Barbecue, water, toilet facilities and shelters make the area an excellent place for the break. Masons Falls tumble some 45 m in total and consist of two main drops.

From the park entrance on National Park Road south of Kinglake, walk a few metres north-west on the sealed road towards Masons Falls then diverge left onto Wallaby Track, an old jeep track. This area supports the dry type forest including wattles and heaths as under-storey. Wallabies, echidnas and wombats frequent the locality. Some 1.5 km from the walk start, after descending a spur, you should reach a 'T' intersection and turn right (north). Within 250 m there is a lookout that gives a good view of Masons Falls and the damper type forest around the falls. From the lookout a track leads upstream after crossing a side gully then the track divides. The left fork nearest the creek is the more pleasant, but both forks lead into the nearby picnic area where lunch could be enjoyed. There is a very short nature walk adjacent to the creek and picnic area. The nature walk and other tracks in the vicinity lead through tall eucalypt forest with many trees, coral, fishbone and maidenhair ferns as part of the plant under-storey.

After a break head upstream on the Boundary Track fairly close to the stream bank. This track swings east then south along the park boundary fence and farms exist eastwards. Boundary track can be followed south back to the park entry gate and end of the walk. The return route from the picnic area to the gate is some 1.75 km. There is an alternative jeep track route but it is not as interesting and only shortens the distance by some 200 m.

4 km; 1½ hours; walk last reviewed August 1987; 'C' grade, family walk; all on tracks; water for lunch at Mason Falls picnic area; walk suited to any season; *Maps: Vicmap 1:25,000 Arthurs Creek, 1:25,000 Kinglake West, 1:25,000 Pheasant Creek and 1:25,000 Strathewan sheets* refer as does Map 24, page 126.

35   MURCHISON FALLS-
DIGGERS GULLY FALLS

Two falls well worth a visit during winter and spring, when there is usually a good volume of water, are Murchison and Diggers Gully Falls. Both are located on the northern slopes of the Great Dividing Range east of Kilmore. Murchison Falls are the highest at about 50 m. They are at the head of a gorge on Strath Creek. The district is also good for navigation exercise. Access is best via the Hume Freeway to the Sunday Creek—Clonbinane exit, east 10 km up Spur Road, and 3.1 km on Two Tees Road to No. 1 Forestry Camp picnic area, then north 2.8 km along Murchison Road, and south-east 1.1 km on Falls Road to Murchison Falls picnic area.

132

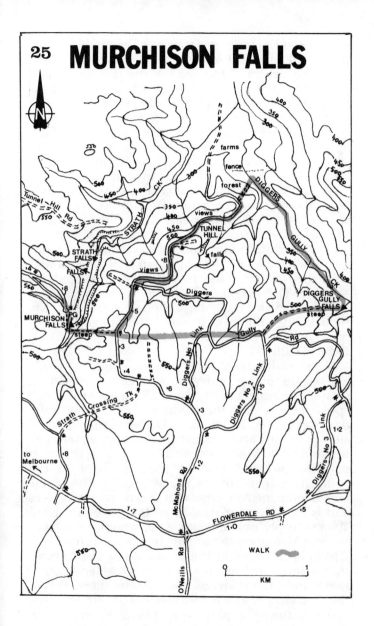

25 MURCHISON FALLS

Falls Road has one-way routings. Descend 142 steps to the falls just 250 m east of the picnic spot, then cross the stream at the head of the falls, and climb eastwards up a steep spur foot track. The pad is faint but remains on the very crest of the spur, then meets a road about 500 m from the falls. Cross the road, then scrub-bash on an 80° magnetic bearing through light scrub and dry forest. Since recent fires there are a few thickets of acacia to negotiate. After 900 m you should meet a road junction.

Continue across the junction area, still on the same bearing, and scrub-bash onwards to meet the same road again 500 m further eastwards. Veer left along the road and walk 300 m till it turns south-south-east at a small saddle. Next turn left onto a minor jeep track. Follow it, and in 600 m it becomes a foot pad, then descend the pad steeply on a spur for 450 m to Diggers Gully Falls for lunch. The spot is 3.5 km from the walk start. The falls are just to the right as the spur is descended and are some 30 m high. Another set of falls 10 m high are 200 m up Diggers Gully.

Next walk north-west down Diggers Gully streamside (or bed if dry) to a fence line bordering cleared land to the north, some 1.7 km from the lunch spot and just past the confluence of a main gully flowing in from the left. Both Diggers Gully and this side gully are about equal in size and water runs under rocks in their beds. A pad leads along the latter part of the west side of Diggers Gully to the confluence, then crosses the side gully. The whole area is renowned for kangaroos, has many acacia trees and is a good camp area. From the fence line, head 400 m steeply uphill, south-west, using a jeep track to meet McMahons Road which ascends Tunnel Hill. Old gold diggings in the area are not the features from which the Tunnel Hill name was derived, but rather from the underground streams there. Follow the road steeply uphill past views of the Strath Creek valley to the right, past Diggers Gully Road (off left) after 1.8 km, and back to the Murchison Falls Track in another 500 m. A rock cairn indicates the falls access pad. Finally, retrace the 500 m of spur track westerly descent to Murchison Falls and the further 250 m to the car park.

10.5 km; 4 hours; last reviewed March 1987; 'B' grade, medium walk but with some very steep sections; features Murchison Falls; creek water for lunch at several places; walk suited to any season; warning: good navigational ability essential as the route includes trackless light scrub; *Maps: Vicmap 1:25,000 Reedy Creek* as does Map 25, page 133.

36   MOUNT MACEDON

Mount Macedon, some 64 km north-west of Melbourne via the Calder Highway, has rich red volcanic soil combined with good rainfall induced by altitude, and this has enabled some of Australia's best private gardens to be established in the district. 'The Mount' has a long history as a mountain resort styled along Indian Hill Station lines. Hence visitors will note properties with Indian names such as Mandalay, Bangalore, Darjeeling and Bungl'hi. In the early days many wealthy families set up summer residences to escape the heat of Melbourne and a 'cottage' was also built for the Governor of the day. The village and most properties are situated within the crater of an ancient volcano. The crater wall is breached on its southern side by Turritable and Willimigongon Creeks which allows evening southerly breezes to enter and cool the crater area. The forested slopes, ferns and rushing streams have long been a real attraction. Three summits—Macedon, Camels Hump and Towrong mark the rim of the horseshoe-shaped crater.

135

In February 1983 (Ash Wednesday), a bushfire swept up the south-west slopes through the crater and over the summits, razing many houses and the village stores and churches but luckily most of the big gardens were not ruined. It seems the many deciduous trees cooled and even stopped the fierce fire in its tracks. Now, after a few years regrowth even the heavily damaged eucalypts are starting to look good again. The ferns have flourished and massive fire damage compensation has been ploughed back into properties to revitalise the district. The summit of Mount Macedon is still stark and will take some years yet to recover but elsewhere superb bushwalking is again possible. In autumn especially, the exotic deciduous trees, avenues and gardens are unforgettable. In late October and early November, at the height of spring, thousands of azaleas and rhododendrons bloom. During both seasons and in some instances throughout the year, private gardens are opened to the public, usually to aid charity, so it is an ideal plan that includes several of these gardens in a day's walk.

Commence this walk at the rebuilt village general store 'The Trading Post' and head up the Main Street past the Post Office and such fine properties as 'Cameron Lodge', 'Darjeeling', 'Forest Glade' and 'Sefton', to a spot where the Main Road turns sharply right 2 km from the walk start. The best of the gardens open to the public tend to be along this 2 km stretch. At the bend take the short rough roadway leading straight ahead north-north-west. The entrance and gate house to 'Duneira' is just at this turnoff. The property features a magnificent 400 m long tree-lined driveway. Continue 200 m past the gate, leaving the settled areas to enter the forests, then diverge right at a fork to walk up a forestry road. This roadway can be followed for 800 m up the valley of Turritable Creek to McDonald Reservoir. The location was a pine plantation before the 1983 fire and is now being revegetated with native forest as part of an overall

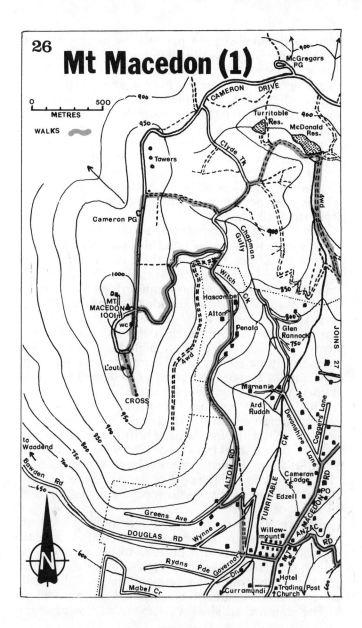

26 **Mt Macedon (1)**

137

plan to rationalize pine plantations in the district. At the reservoir, cross the retaining wall to head west 400 m in forest then, at a fork in the jeep track, go south (left) for another 400 m. You should then veer right for 100 m onto Clyde Track, a gravelled roadway. The road can then be followed south-west 400 m until just before reaching Chapman Gully from where a jeep track should be followed west uphill for 600 m to emerge at asphalted Cameron Drive. It is the main tourist road around the rim of the former crater. Cameron Picnic Ground is just 200 m to the left (south) and is the recommended lunch spot some 5.1 km from the walk start.

Cameron Drive should next be followed south for 1 km to the road end beyond the summit of Mount Macedon. A foot track can then be walked south 400 m to the famous Mount Macedon Cross set high on the southern end of the summit ridge. Views from The Cross on a clear day include all of the Port Phillip Bay region and even as far east as the Great Dividing Range in the Warburton district, well over 100 km away. The Cross is a 23 m high First World War memorial donated by a Mr William Cameron formerly of Cameron Lodge, after whom Cameron Drive was named. (He paid for the road also.)

The summit has been re-planted and is now regenerating well after a slow start, but a compensating factor for the fire damage is the view. Just north of The Cross, a short track leads 50 m west to a lookout point and small cairn. Early explorer Major Mitchell climbed and named the peak and the cairn recognizes the fact. Some snow gums grow on the slopes adjacent to the spot.

Retrace 600 m north to a rough forestry road off east (right) opposite the Mount Macedon summit cairn to start the return descent to the village. It is a long descent highlighting views, hence the reason for these track notes recommending that the walk be undertaken in an anti-clockwise direction.

The rough road should be followed downhill for

1 km through a former pine plantation area now being revegetated with native plants. Next turn right (south) at the 'T' intersection with Clyde Track so as to leave the forest area and enter the residential area. Immediately one is struck by the obvious post-fire resilience of many deciduous exotic trees—the prevailing atmosphere of the Track is that of a leafy country lane. Two large and beautiful properties, 'Alton' and 'Hascombe', are passed as Alton Road is descended. There are holly hedges, many rare trees and conifers well over 100 years old and, in autumn, maples are a real highlight. Shortly afterwards, near 'Penola', views of Melbourne commence and continue as the asphalted road is descended. Some 1.6 km down quiet Alton Road is the first of some hairpin bends.

PIGMY POSSUM

About 500 m later, at the third hairpin bend, walkers can take a short cut down a gravelled roadway for 400 m to reach the end of Alton Road at Douglas Road intersection. From there, walk east (left) on Douglas Road 300 m to reach Main Street and the end of the walk just 300 m south, (right turn).

11.3 km; 4½ hours plus time spent in gardens; last reviewed January 1988; 'B' grade; medium walk; all on tracks and roads; carry water for lunch; walk suited to any season but autumn and spring best; *Maps: Vicmap 1:25,000 Macedon* and Maps 26 and 27, pages 137 and 140.

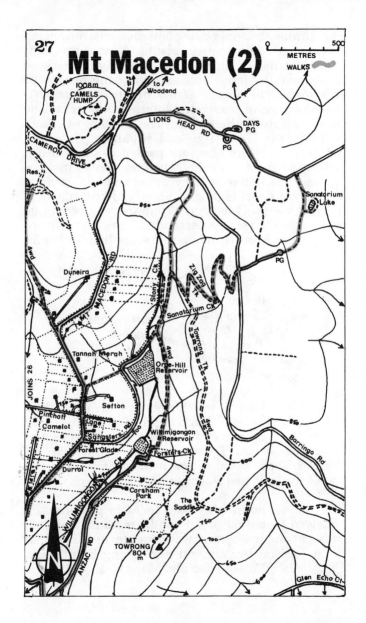

37   WILLIMIGONGON CREEK

At Mount Macedon a good walk is to the Sanatorium Lake area and return from the village. Willimigongon Creek valley is a highlight of this route. On the return leg it would be a good plan to include a visit to several large gardens on the Main Road. These gardens are open to the public at times, generally in spring and autumn. The walk route includes a good deal of walking within forests. Walk number 36 in this book should be read before attempting this route (No. 37) in order to gain a better appreciation of the district.

From the 'Trading Post' in the village head up the Main Road 400 m and turn right (east) onto gravelled Anzac Road. It leads down to cross Willimigongon Creek, negotiates a hairpin bend, then can be followed up the creek valley in forest to Willimigongon reservoir, 1.7 km from the Main Road. Anzac Road is a pleasant quiet road along which maples, alstromerias and many wildflowers grow. Some private gardens are to be seen, including 'Corsham Park' and the fern gully section of 'Forest Glade'.

At the reservoir Anzac Road becomes a jeep track and should be followed 900 m further up the valley past a second, newer reservoir (Orde-Hill) to a jeep track junction. Here, near the confluence of Stony Creek and Sanatorium Creek, once stood a sanatorium which was part of the early resort facilities of the mountain. Turn right, up the valley, diverge right within 150 m and continue for another 350 m to a hairpin bend in the jeep track.

The next part of the walk should be undertaken clockwise to avoid difficult location of a foot track. At the hairpin bend, go straight ahead onto a foot track to continue north up the Stony Creek valley. Within 700 m Barringo Road should be reached. Turn left at the road and go 700 m to the junction of Barringo Road, Lions Head Road and Mount Macedon Road, then double back east on Lions Head Road to walk the rangetops. Some 800 m onwards lunch is suggested at Days picnic area, about 5.7 km from the walk start.

After lunch head further east on Lions Head Road for 600 m to turn right onto a foot track down to Sanatorium Lake 300 m from the road. Former conifer plantations in the area have been logged and the location is being re-vegetated with native forest. The foot track actually divides to pass on either side of the small lake, then can be followed 400 m onwards south down to a most pleasant picnic ground among exotic trees. A break would be worthwhile before heading west out of the picnic area on a road for 400 m to cross Barringo Road, then descend Zig Zag Road 1.5 km back to Stony Creek valley. Towrong track leads off left during the descent and near the creek you need to head 500 m down the valley, retracing the earlier route so as to return to the former site of the sanatorium.

ECHIDNA

Next, take the right fork roadway past the north end of Orde-Hill Reservoir, using Sangsters Road. Taylor and Sangsters nursery last century existed to the right of the road and supplied Melbourne's Government House, Botanic Gardens and the great 1880s exhibition, plus many large Toorak and Mount Macedon gardens, with rare plants. Some rare huge oaks, monkey puzzle and other trees can still be seen. After just 400 m at a sharp bend in the road, leave the road and climb straight ahead on an easement track for 400 m to gain the Main Road. 'Sefton', Elders IXL convention centre is to the left of the easement.

Turn left down the Main Road and simply follow it 1.6 km to the walk's end. The leafy roadway passes such fine private gardens as 'Forest Glade', 'Durrol', 'Cameron Lodge' and, at the walks end, is 'Carramundi'. See as much of these gardens as possible. The small entry fee charged usually aids charities.

11.8 km; 5 hours (plus time spent in gardens); last reviewed September 1988; 'B' grade; medium walk; all on tracks and roads; carry water for lunch; walk suited to any season but best in spring and autumn; *Maps: Vicmap 1:25,000 Macedon* and Maps 26 and 27, pages 137 and 140.

38   HEPBURN SPRINGS-DAYLESFORD

The old gold mining town of Daylesford has substantial commercial and public buildings as evidence of its former prosperity. 1856-7 saw the main gold rush that created a big mining industry which subsided as gold finds were exhausted.

In 1837 Captain John Hepburn settled in the district near hot and cold mineral springs and while some of the springs were right at Daylesford, others were at the settlement which was named Hepburn Springs. It was to become a famous spa resort for tourists. Today, interesting and elaborate churches and buildings such as the post office, town hall, banks and stores, plus three lakes and the mineral springs, can be seen in a picturesque hillside setting. Sailors Creek Gully is adjacent in extensive bushland, and at Wombat Hill in Daylesford itself there are delightful historic botanic gardens and a high lookout tower from which to view the district. Daylesford is at the edge of volcanic country and fertile volcanic soil farmlands lie nearby.

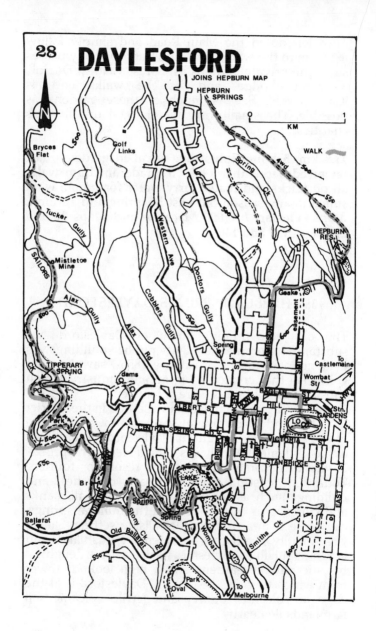

28 DAYLESFORD

JOINS HEPBURN MAP

HEPBURN SPRINGS

WALK

Bryces Flat

Golf Links

Tucker Gully

SAILORS

Mistletoe Mine

Ajax Gully

TIPPERARY SPRING

Park

To Ballarat

Br

Springs

Spring

Story Ck

Old Ballarat Rd

Western Ave

Cobblers Gully

Doctors Gully

Ajax Rd

dams

Spring

CENTRAL SPRING RD

ALBERT ST

LAKE

Wombat

MIDLAND HWY

Spring Ck

4wd

HEPBURN RES.

Geake

easement

Castlemaine

To Castlemaine

Wombat St

RAGLAN

HILL ST

Stn.

GARDENS

LOCH

VICTORIA

STANBRIDGE ST

EAST

Smiths Ck

Park Oval

To Melbourne

144

North of Hepburn Springs is one of the district's extinct volcanic peaks, complete with a significant crater. The peak dominates the countryside in that area. A walk circuit which includes both Daylesford, smaller Hepburn Springs and most of the district's principal attractions is thus possible. The walk starts and ends at Hepburn Springs at the main mineral springs area. The spot is near the north end of the main street, beside Spring Creek where there are mineral baths, kiosk and a mineral water bottling plant. There is a large car park where transport can be left.

Walk north from the entrance to the car park area, cross Castlemaine Road (Dry Diggings Road) and walk up Golden Springs Avenue northwards. Where the avenue turns right sharply, continue ahead down a foot track to Golden Spring in Womans Gully. The spring is 700 m from the walk start. The track should then be followed onwards downstream for 1.5 km, basically along the alignment of an old water race which skirts the eastern slopes of Spring Creek's gully. Liberty Spring is passed on the way, but it is about 100 m to the left of the main track down a side track to the stream bed. Blackberries tend to overgrow the tracks and may slow progress. The main track reaches a sealed road at Breakneck Gorge bridge. Cross Spring Creek on the road bridge and head west along another foot track along the south side of Spring Creek. Within 200 m the confluence of Spring Creek and Sailors Creek is neared.

From the confluence the streams flow as Jim Crow Creek. The next section of walking involves following a good foot pad south upstream along the east side of Sailors Creek to The Blowhole within a dry forest environment. The Blowhole is a tunnel made by miners to divert the stream from a loop in the creek course. This was done to open up the stream bed for mining. Further south along the stream, the track meets and crosses Bryces Flat Road at Bryces Flat, then continues past the former Mistletoe Mine area, across Ajax Gully and on to Tipperary Springs. The whole of this long streamside sector is within eucalypt forest. At Tipperary Springs there is a small park. The foot track actually joins the park access road some 200 m east of the spring. This park could be suitable for a late lunch.

CORREA

The foot track continues and should be followed still further along the east side of Sailors Creek, starting a few metres east of where the road was met as Tipperary Springs was neared. Soon the Midland Highway should be reached. Walk south on it for 250 m to a spot just short of a road bridge. A foot track then leads east along the slopes near the north bank of another creek and above an area previously bulldozed and cleared. By walking this pad you should soon reach, in turn, Sutton Spring, Wagga Spring and Central Spring. The latter has a kiosk nearby and is the main mineral spring at Daylesford. It is 1.1 km from the Midland Highway and just 100 m short of Lake Daylesford outlet.

From this outlet walk a pad round the western and northern lake shore for 700 m, then diverge left (north-east) up a track through pines for 250 m to join Bridport Street, Daylesford, which is aligned north-south. Turn right and walk the street as it swings east to become Ruthven Street and to join Vincent Street (Daylesford's main street). By following the main street north to the third street off right

(Albert Street), you see the best of the town's main street historic buildings. Turn east up Albert Street to its end nearby, then walk to the right into Camp Street. There are three fine church buildings adjacent to Camp Street, each of historic interest. Next turn left up Victoria Street and climb a hill which gives views of the town and picturesque Lake Daylesford. One street east, off left, is Daley Street. Pass it, then 100 m further uphill is the south-west pedestrian gate of the Wombat Hill Botanic Gardens.

A track within the gardens leads uphill from the gate. Keep to the highest track as you proceed and you will soon reach a small reservoir. East of it is a high concrete lookout tower which should be climbed for the view. From the tower the Mount Franklin volcanic peak can be seen to the north and, indeed, the whole district is in view.

PARROT
PEA

Afternoon tea could be in these lovely gardens.

Next take a foot track north-west from the tower base down to a roadway which forms a loop in the gardens and circuits the hilltop. Nearly opposite where the road is met, a foot track leads north down out of the gardens to link with Hill Street. Cross east-west aligned Hill Street and go north down short Wombat Street to east-west aligned Raglan Street. Turn left and walk one block, then turn right into Jamieson Street in a residential area. Walk north on Jamieson Street for 1 km, then turn right into Geake Street and walk it 600 m east as it deteriorates into a bush road. It then meets the upper reaches of Spring Creek. During the 600 m stretch to this creek, three roads diverge off left and should be avoided. Once across the creek, turn north as it descends to reach Hepburn Reservoir in 400 m. Cross the dam wall in a bush setting then meet another minor road near the north end of the wall on a small spur. Head up this road onto a ridge, then continue on it down a long spur within dry eucalypt forest for 2.2 km to reach Hepburn Springs Public Park area. Just near the confluence of Spring Creek and Welshmans Gully the bush road joins onto a more major road in the park. It is then only about 200 m downstream, along this more major road, to the car park and end of the walk circuit. You are now back at Locarno Spring in Hepburn Springs.

GNAT ORCHID

19.5 km; 6½ hours; last reviewed January 1987; 'B' grade, medium walk, all on tracks and roads; features spa areas and historic Daylesford; water for lunch from mineral springs (best to carry flavouring); walk suited to any season; *Maps: Vicmap 1:25,000 Daylesford and 1:25,000 Eganstown* refer as do Maps 28 and 29, pages 144 and 150.

Hepburn Springs is renowned for numerous mineral springs and a mineral water bath-house. It is a very small town with an old world atmosphere. The gold diggings and the early Scottish settlers' influence pervades. The village is just north of Daylesford and lies close to rich volcanic soils, but is itself in an area of poor soils. Dry forest, scrub and wildflowers predominate on the poor soils while farms dot the volcanic tops. One volcanic peak nearby is Mount Franklin and it has a pronounced crater in it. The peak, of course, is extinct, as are all Australian volcanoes, but it is very interesting and beautiful. Try this circuit walk which includes the spas, forests, farms and Mount Franklin. Kangaroos are common in the area too. A day of variety is assured.

The route starts and ends at the main spring known as Locarno Spring. Conspicuous sign-posting indicates the way to the springs which are close by the main street. On Spring Creek, near the Mineral Baths, is a kiosk and a mineral water bottling plant. Carry a mug—and perhaps some flavouring—and sample the water as you progress.

Leave transport in the Springs's car park and walk back north out of the entrance of the park. Cross the Castlemaine Road (Dry Diggings Road) and walk up Golden Spring Avenue. Where the avenue turns sharply right, continue ahead, then down a foot track to Golden Spring in Woman's Gully. This spring is only about 700 m from the walk start. The foot pad should then be followed downstream for another 1.5 km, basically along the alignment of an old water-race which skirts the eastern slopes of Spring Creek's gully. Liberty Spring is passed on the way. It is about 100 m to the left of the main track and is in the stream bed. Blackberries tend to overgrow the pad in places and progress may be slowed. The track reaches a main road at Breakneck Gorge bridge. Follow the main road north 700 m to the top of a spur, amid farmland,

HEPBURN

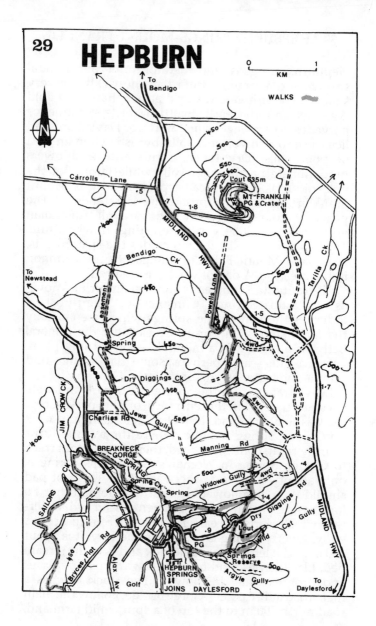

KM

WALKS

To Bendigo

To Newstead

Carrolls Lane

MIDLAND HWY

Bendigo Ck

Powells Lane

MT FRANKLIN
PG & Crater
L'out 635m

Tarilta Ck

Spring

Dry Diggings Ck

JIM CROW CK

Charlies Rd

Jews Gully

4wd

BREAKNECK
GORGE

Spring

Manning Rd

SAILORS Ck

Spring Ck

Spring

Widows Gully

4wd

Dry Diggings Rd

MIDLAND HWY

Bryces Flat Rd

Ajax Av

Golf

HEPBURN
SPRINGS

JOINS DAYLESFORD

L'out

PG

Wild

Cat Gully

Springs
Reserve

Argyle Gully

To Daylesford

then turn right (east) down an easement right beside a farmhouse. A minor road exists in the easement. After 300 m turn left down another easement and head down round a corner to a ford at Dry Diggings Creek. Turn north again and walk into the edge of some dry forest then reach Lithia Spring, about 1 km from the farmhouse. Lithia Spring appears to be sealed off, but the area is pleasant and grassy. Continue north on the minor road up over a spur and within 300 m meet the end of another fenced easement leading due north. Follow the minor road along this easement for 2.2 km out into farmlands and up to a T junction. Turn right for 500 m and

HONEYEATER

gradually climb to the Midland Highway, then veer right again to follow the highway 700 m south-east to the Mount Franklin Reserve access road off left. Mount Franklin is covered with pine trees and is surrounded by farms. Its crater is the next goal and the access road should be followed 1.8 km east, then through a breach in the crater wall. There is a picnic ground with full facilities on the floor of the crater and many beautiful deciduous trees make a good setting for a late lunch.

Next follow a foot track from the picnic ground up to the northern lip of the crater, then left around the lip to meet the end of a road. Follow the road for 200 m to a Forestry fire watch-tower, then on

151

back down to the picnic area thus completing an 800 m long circular walk. Return to the farmlands via the access road and, once back at the Midland Highway, follow it 1 km south-east, then diverge south along a quite minor road. Continue south for 1 km to leave farmland and reach the road end at the start of State Forest and the entrance to a property called *Hidden Valley*. Opposite the property gateway, a very minor jeep track veers off south-east into the forest. Use it as a rough guide to set a course south-east through scrub for 400 m to intersect a north-south aligned jeep track, then turn south on the jeep track for another 400 m until it begins to swing west.

ACACIA

Scrub-bash 400 m south-east again down across a gully and up to another jeep track on a ridge. Head east, then south-east, on the track 600 m, then scrub bash again 400 m south, across a gully and up to a good gravel road aligned east-west. Farmland should be on the right over the latter sector. Walk west 200 m up the road to the edge of the forest on the left (south) side of the road, then turn south again down a jeep track within the forest, and with farmland on the right. Keep heading south, avoiding two minor jeep tracks off left, then one off right; cross a gully, then climb to an east-west aligned jeep track on a ridge some 600 m from where the road was left. Next go 50 m west on this track, turn south down another track for 200 m into a gully. Head down the gully 200 m, then climb to bitumen Dry Diggings Road 300 m away via another track leading south. Cross this main road to Jacksons Lookout Tower, a steel tower just left of the main road. A view of Hepburn Springs is the reward for the climb.

Lastly, follow a broad foot track from the tower south down into Wild Cat Gully, then west back to Locarno Spring and the walk's end. It is only about 800 m from the lookout to the springs. A mineral bath may be a pleasant way to finish off the day.

18.3 km; 6½ hours; last reviewed January 1987; 'C' grade, medium walk; 95% roads and tracks 5% open forest floor walking; features Mount Franklin volcanic crater; water at crater for lunch; walk suited to any season but could prove hot in summer; *Maps: Vicmap 1:25,000 Daylesford and 1:25,000 Eganstown* refer as does Map 29, page 150.

40   HEPBURN SPRINGS

This short walk in the Hepburn Springs area includes mineral water springs plus Jacksons Lookout Tower. The spas are therefore an attraction, as is the view of the old health resort of Hepburn Springs from the lookout.

The walk starts and ends at the main springs picnic ground near the kiosk and mineral water baths. Track notes in this book to walks number 38 and 39 could be read to advantage before setting out on this route. The notes give a better appreciation of the district and its history as a health resort and as a gold rush district.

Head off back north out the entrance of the picnic area and car park to cross Castlemaine Road (Dry Diggings Road) and walk up Golden Spring Avenue.

Where the avenue turns sharp east (right) shortly afterwards, ignore a foot track off left down to Golden Spring in Womans Gully. Instead go east up the road which becomes a track. Some 1.2 km from the Golden Springs Avenue turn, you should reach a track off right uphill, out of the gully. Follow it up to Dry Diggings Road just 300 m away then cross this main road to Jacksons Lookout. It is a steel tower, the principal view being of Hepburn Springs.

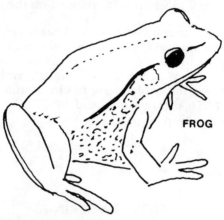

FROG

Next, ignore the broad direct track south down into Wild Cat Gully and follow a lesser but better route which leads to the same gully location but through more interesting terrain. Go south-east on this pad from the lookout and follow it for 1 km into and then down Wild Cat Gully. Thereafter a broad pad continues down the gully for some 400 m to the end of the walk circuit back at the picnic area and car park. A bath at the mineral springs baths may then be of interest or sampling the mineral water could be an attraction.

3.5 km; 1 hour; last reviewed January 1987; 'B' grade; easy walk; all on tracks; carry water; walk suited to any season; *Maps: Vicmap 1:25,000 Daylesford* and Map 29, page 150.

41   TIPPERARY SPRING

The mineral water springs of Hepburn Springs and Daylesford have long been a real attraction to the Central Highlands Region. This has resulted in a good network of walking tracks leading to the various mineral springs. One of the better short walks is to Tipperary Spring and return from Lake Daylesford. The lake is readily seen on the left (west) side of the main road as the town is entered from the Ballan (Melbourne) side. There are picnic facilities and paddle boat hire facilities at the lake and swimming is another option. The lake retaining wall is only about 100 m from the principal mineral spring at Daylesford. That spring (Central Spring) is beside Wombat Creek. Foot tracks lead from the retaining wall down both sides of the creek. It is therefore good to take a mug (and perhaps some flavouring) and walk to various mineral springs—Central Spring, Wagga Spring, Sutton Spring and more distant Tipperary Spring. One assumes the name of the latter reflects the influence of early Irish settlers present in gold rush days. Lunch could be taken at the Tipperary Spring Picnic Ground where there is, among other facilities, a shelter. The foot tracks at first lead downstream on Wombat Creek along both sides of the gully, then once Wombat Creek links into Sailors Creek the pads are on both sides of Sailors Creek as far as Tipperary Spring. An interesting track in fact continues for many kilometres downstream thereafter.

Before undertaking the walk it is suggested that track notes in this book to walks number 38 and 39 be read so as to learn more of the district and its fascinating history.

For the walk you need simply to follow a pad down one side of Wombat Creek to the Midland Highway, then on down one of the banks of Sailors Creek, later to return using the tracks on the opposite banks. Where the Midland Highway is reached it is best to use the highway itself for 250 m so as to avoid scrub when following the tracks on the north-east side of the watercourse.

The whole of the walk route is within pleasant, open forest which consists principally of eucalypts and acacias. In some areas the track follows the former route of gold mining water races. Therefore, in these areas, the track follows the contour closely, down the valley and in and out of side gullies. This results in very easy walking and a greater range of vegetation. Some of the side gullies are especially ferny whilst the more open parts tend to be good wildflower habitats.

5 km; 2 hours; last reviewed July 1988; 'B' grade; family walk; all on tracks; features mineral water springs; walk suited to any season; *Maps: Vicmap 1:25,000 Daylesford and 1:25,000 Eganstown* refer as does Map 28, page 144.

WILLY WAGTAIL

42   BLACKWOOD TUNNEL

The tiny town of Blackwood (pop. 100), is on the Great Dividing Range some 90 km north-west of Melbourne. In 1854 gold was found at nearby Golden Point on the Lerderderg River and the rush which followed founded the town in 1855. Alluvial gold panning occurred initially at the river and in adjacent tributary gullies; bigger quartz crushing mining was established later. Sizable gold nuggets were found and in late 1855 the population reached about 13000.

To obtain water for sluicing, parties clubbed together to have up to 150 km of water races constructed round the contours of the steep hillsides to their mine sites. The rush was short-lived and as early as 1856 the population dropped back to 3500. The Chinese diggers persisted longer than others in the streambeds despite river flooding, and found gold for many years thereafter. By the turn of the century the field seemed exhausted. At one stage a tunnel was excavated through a spur to divert the river and facilitate panning the streambed.

The Chinese are said to have discovered mineral springs on each side of the Lerderderg River and by 1888 a reserve was established at the springs. The springs then became a focus for tourists. One local family—the Shaws, who date from 1855 in the district—built a sizable dam now known as Shaws Lake. It was to hold water for their gold mining operations and all construction of the dam was done with pick, shovel and wheelbarrow. The lake became a swimming spot and is now the site of picnic facilities.

The Dividing Range round Blackwood is steeply eroded, relatively dry, country with poor soils, and the forested slopes feature fairly sparse eucalypt and acacia trees. The gullies, however, are damper and cooler with ferns and there are many rock pools along the Lerderderg.

During the gold rush most timber was stripped off the hills for mine timbers and firewood but the trees have regrown. Wombat State Forest covers much of the district and many access tracks lead through the forest. Good walking results from the combination of historic and natural interests. Some tracks follow the old water race lines and thus provide easy level walking. An excellent round walk is one which includes the mineral springs, Shaws Lake, the Tunnel and Byres Back Track. Byres was the name of a renowned early family and the track leads along a race downstream of Golden Point.

Travel to Blackwood then go east some 600 m to

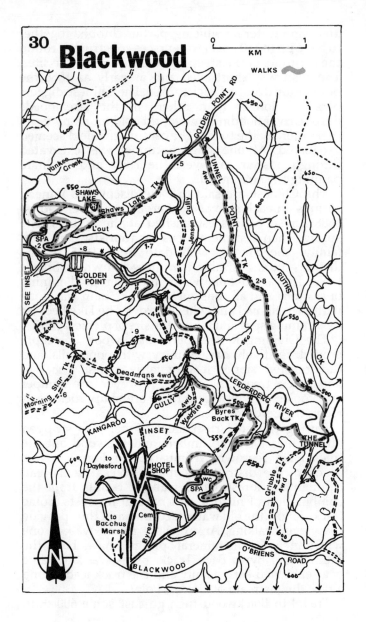

30 Blackwood

0 KM 1

WALKS

Yankee Creek

SHAWS LAKE
550
Shaws Lake Tk.
L'out
SPA .2
.8   br
GOLDEN POINT
SEE INSET
GOLDEN POINT RD
650
650
.5
TUNNEL POINT TK 4wd
Jensen Gully
1.7
1.0
650
600
.4
2.8
RUTHS
550
.9
550
.4
550
Deadmans 4wd
Morning Star Tk
.6
GULLY 4wd
Websters
Byres Back Tk
500
550
550
LERDERDERG RIVER
CK
500
THE TUNNEL
KANGAROO
600
INSET
to Daylesford
HOTEL & SHOP
br
wc
SPA
to Bacchus Marsh
Cem
Byres
BLACKWOOD
Gribble Tk 4wd
550
600
O'BRIENS ROAD
600
N

158

the mineral springs reserve. A small vehicle entry fee is charged to enter the pleasant reserve, which contains a kiosk, camp ground, picnic shelters and full facilities plus two springs. An arched concrete footbridge links the mineral springs on either side of the Lerderderg. The spring nearest the car park has a high level of soda and the spring across the river is high in iron content. They therefore taste very different. Rainwater seeps down through rock fissures to create the springs.

Start the walk from the north end of the concrete bridge (distant end), avoiding tracks along each direction of the river bank so that you begin to climb. Head to the right (north-east) to climb via a direct route to Shaws Lake 700 m distant. After the first 400 m the ridgetop is gained and you need to walk the spur crest for the 300 m to the lake. It is worthwhile crossing the dam wall to best appreciate this pleasant spot before returning to the Shaws Lake Track to continue up the spur eastwards. (A track from the mineral springs via the riverbank and Sweets Lookout joins in at Shaws Lake.) About 1 km up the spur from the lake you should reach Golden Point Road. The road can then be followed 500 m uphill to enable you to turn onto Tunnel Point Jeep Track and follow it for 2.8 km south-east along a ridge top to its end. The ridge is the Ruths Creek-Jensen Gully divide.

To this point the walk has been on dry tops in sparse forest where wildflowers are good in spring. Ahead, the vegetation changes. There is a defined foot track to follow as you proceed 500 m off Tunnel Point Track down a spur crest to the tunnel. Take care to swing south (right) from a small hilltop on the spur as you head to the tunnel. The tunnel is 5.5 km from the walk start and is a suitable lunch spot. A swim could be included if the weather is hot.

Gribble Track, a jeep track, descends to the tunnel and after lunch should be climbed westwards 200 m distance to where Byres Back Track is intersected. Turn right along this old water race line track to follow the contour of the steep hillsides. Cross Kangaroo Track jeep track and several normally dry gullies. Websters Track should then be intersected as Kangaroo Gully is neared after some 2.8 km of walking the water race line pad. At this point short-cut the contouring foot track by descending Websters Track,

IRONBARK

crossing Kangaroo Gully and climbing up the jeep track northwards to rejoin the contouring foot track area 400 m away. The track actually leads off a small right-side jeep track extension on a spur, then contours 900 m towards Golden Point. Midway along this next bushland section is an old miners' tunnel. At Golden Point the foot track links to a gravelled road which can then be followed for 1 km to the junction with Golden Point Road. Golden Point, the former hive of mining activity is now a sleepy little settlement featuring some interesting old exotic trees and shrubs. Follow Golden Point Road west through the settlement 1 km up to the mineral springs reserve entrance. Turn right downhill into the reserve to end the walk.

12 km; 3½ hours; last reviewed January 1988; 'C' grade medium walk; all on tracks and roadway; features springs, lake and tunnel; water for lunch from river; walk suited to any season; *Maps: Vicmap 1:25,000 Trentham* refers as does Map 30, page 158.

Mineral springs, the Lerderderg River, Shaws Lake and evidence of former gold rush days are all a feature of the tiny town of Blackwood. The springs were evidently discovered by Chinese on the goldfield, the river has good rock pools along its course, the lake, built for gold operations, is now the site of picnic facilities and the old goldfield water race lines and tracks provide good walking.

For general background information about the locality it may be helpful to read the track notes for walk number 42 before setting out on this short walk.

Travel to Blackwood some 90 km north-west of Melbourne then go east about 600 m to enter the town's Mineral Springs Reserve. A small vehicular entry fee is charged to offset costs in the provision of excellent picnic facilities, including shelters in the form of rotundas. There is also a kiosk and camp ground within the reserve. An arched concrete bridge links the two mineral springs which are set on either side of the infant Lerderderg River.

Start the walk by visiting the springs, crossing the river by footbridge in the process. Turn west (left) after the bridge is crossed to ascend a good foot track which swings up onto a broad spur. Continue up the lightly wooded spur as the track turns back east and leads directly to Shaws Lake 1.2 km from the walk start. The lake, near the spur crest, has picnic facilities which could be used for a lunch break if desired. It is worthwhile crossing the dam retaining wall to best appreciate the spot which was man made by the Shaw family using pick, shovel and wheelbarrow.

Just near the south end of the lake is a junction of tracks which can be used to return to the mineral springs via Sweets Lookout. The view point is only about 200 m south of the lake via the track which leads south-west on a spur crest. The Lerderderg River and the Golden Point area are in view from the lookout. A steep descent of the spur crest track follows, to reach the banks of the Lerderderg River some 700 m from Shaws Lake. Thereafter you need simply follow a track 900 m along an old water race line near the northern river bank to the concrete bridge at the mineral springs. The riverside walk is a cool ferny one.

2.8 km; 1 hour; last reviewed January 1988; 'C' grade easy walk; all on tracks; features mineral springs and Shaws Lake; carry water for lunch; walk suited to any season; *Maps: Vicmap 1:25,000 Trentham* refers as does Map 30, page 158.

GUM NUTS

44   LERDERDERG GORGE

One of the most rugged localities near Melbourne is the Lerderderg Gorge. Access is from the Bacchus Marsh to Gisborne Road then 6 km north-west to a car park known as Darley Ford.

Summertime walking is the best, when sandy beaches and good swimming holes usually add to the attraction and walking is easy when the river water level is low. The gorge has all but recovered from the 1983 bushfires which swept through the entire area.

A good foot track leads from Darley Ford car park along the north-east bank of the river following what was once an old water race used by gold miners. The entrances to some old tunnels can be seen to this day, despite the passing of some 130 years. There are rugged cliffs and steep ravines along both sides of the gorge.

This easy walk involves simply following the foot track from the car park for 1.75 km, then fording the river at a bend in the river where cliffs bar progress on the north-east side of the stream. Sometimes wet feet will result in crossing to the far bank but usually stepping stones assist progress. A sandy beach and deep swimming hole is at the bend so a swim might be attractive.

The suggestion is to go a further 1.25 km upstream to a second beach and swimming hole. A minor pad exists on the north-east bank and to reach it you need to ford the river a second time immediately after the bend. The pad leads all the way to the second beach but is very scrubby; generally it is easier to walk the river bed if the water level is sufficiently low.

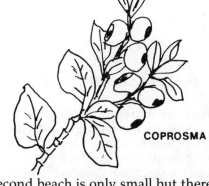

COPROSMA

The second beach is only small but there is a good swimming hole and area suited to camping. Again, the beach is near a sharp bend in the stream. The track disappears further upstream, so to go further involves scrub-bashing or river bed walking. By this stage there are a number of steep bluffs which abut the river and the gorge is some 250 m deep. Eagles and hawks are often seen, as are a great number of other birds.

It is suggested that this second beach be the turn around point and lunch break. As with much of the Lerderderg Gorge the area is fairly well timbered near the river and the slopes tend to be sparsely timbered. Near the river you should see a lot of tea tree, wattles, hazel and cassinia. The rocky bluffs and pools in the river bed, when dry in summer, make excellent subjects for photography.

After lunch you need to retrace the route back downstream to the Darley Ford car park, thus completing a most enjoyable trip even though the distance is quite short.

6 km; 2¾ hours; walk last reviewed March 1988; 'B' grade easy walk; mostly on foot tracks but with some river bed walking (the river is nearly always quite shallow); features rugged gorge; walk suited to any season but summer best; *Maps: Vicmap 1:25,000 Bullengarook* refers as does Map 31, page 165.

45 LERDERDERG GORGE

North of Bacchus Marsh is remarkable Lerderderg Gorge. It is perhaps the most rugged country near Melbourne. Geologists tell us that a fault line, aligned roughly north-south just west of the town, marks the edge of the so-called Ballarat Plateau, with all land west of the fault being considerably higher than Bacchus Marsh. Streams such as the Werribee River and the Lerderderg River have eroded deep gorges as they descend the fault escarpment, and the result is an area well suited to bushwalking with special points of geological interest and much scenic attraction.

In 1983 bushfires spoiled most of the Lerderderg Gorge but regrowth has been substantial and the

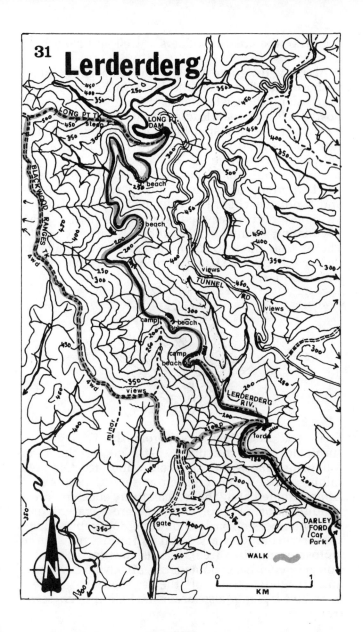

31 Lerderderg

LONG PT TK
Long pt tk
steep
LONG PT DAM
beach
beach
BLACKWOOD RANGES TK
4wd
views
TUNNEL RD
views
camp
beach
camp
beach
views
4wd
minor
LERDERDERG RIV.
fords
gate
DARLEY FORD Car Park

WALK

N

0   1
KM

appeal of the area to walkers is well and truly back again.

Access to the gorge is best from the Bacchus Marsh-Gisborne Road exit on the Western Freeway, then north along the Gisborne Road for 2.5 km to a sign-posted left fork road leading for 6 km north-west to a car turntable at a spot known as Darley Ford. The turntable is right beside the Lerderderg River at the entrance to the gorge.

Summertime holds the most appeal to walkers in the Lerderderg as there are many swimming holes and sandy beaches. The river bed is then also dry at times, and river bed walking is easier than negotiating somewhat scrubby streamside pads. There is no track to follow for more than half the distance between Darley Ford and the Long Point Diversion Dam

FERN

A good foot track leads from the Darley Ford turntable along the north-east bank of the river following what was once an old water race. Old gold mining tunnels can be seen at several points too. Almost immediately the typical sturdy eucalypt forest conditions of much of the gorge are apparent, and large numbers of birds should be noticeable. Along the riverbank walk you should see some leptospermum (tea-tree), acacias (wattles), clematis, hop goodenia, hazel pomaderris, prickly box, cassinia, and rhagodia (one of the saltbushes). A few introduced plants also occur, including even some fruit trees.

The track should be followed for 1.75 km to a ford at a sharp bend in the river. Cliffs on the right bank make it necessary to cross the ford on stepping stones then, within 100 m, to reford the river on more stones to reach again the north-east side. Occasionally the stream rises to a point where it is unavoidable to get wet feet when crossing, unless you climb over the very awkward rocky cliff section. Between the two fords is the first of many small sandy beaches which occur throughout the gorge, and a foot track leads west from the beach up a steep spur to the crest of the Blackwood Range which is actually the western rim of the gorge. This scrubby track should be noted as it is the suggested return route of the walk. By this stage the gorge is about 250 m deep and rocky bluffs make the walk most interesting. For ease of navigation in the Long Point area the walk should be undertaken in an anti-clockwise direction from this spot.

Walk for another 1.25 km to a second beach, still on the same north-east side of the river. The streamside pad is poor and progress will be slow unless you can walk on the river bed. This second beach is only small, but there is a good swimming hole and a spot suited to camping. Again, the beach is near a sharp bend in the stream. Continue around the bend.

The track disappears as more bluffs abut the river. In this area it is necessary to ford the river to reach another spot used for camping, thereafter to scrub-bash through quite light scrub along the banks.

Some 800 m upstream is a bluff which forces travel on the south-east bank to a major camping spot at the mouth of a tributary stream. Walking further upstream becomes more difficult, but is rather wild and beautiful. It is suggested that this camp area be your lunch spot.

The morning's distance is 3.8 km, rather short, but conditions make walking slow and also, if the day is hot, a swim in one of the several big pools would be ideal. However you need to quicken the pace in the afternoon as there is some 13.5 km further to walk.

After lunch head upstream to the area of the Long Point Diversion Dam which channels water to Lake Merrimu. For most of the 4 km there is no track and light scrub must be negotiated. There are a further four places where bluffs abut the water's edge and fording is forced, but for ease of walking it is best to ford many more times and wet feet are a certainty. In parts minor pads exist and should be followed wherever possible, but always the stream bank should be within a few metres. A further two beaches exist before the dam, and the upper beach is just 400 m short of the dam. This beach is attractive and is a camp site also. It is on the north bank in a spot where

HARDENBERGIA

the river runs east-west and has a well defined saddle 200 m north. The saddle is on the Long Point Spur. Another rocky and interesting saddle also exists south across the river from the beach. The dam area can be approached but walkers are warned that water can at times be released causing the river level to rise rapidly.

There is a scrubby foot track (Long Point Track) from the dam wall west to the top of the gorge rim 1.7 km away and 340 m higher. This track can be joined in the Long Point Spur saddle 200 m north of the beach; it will avoid the dam vicinity, yet still provide a view of the dam from the high spur crest. It is suggested you make the steep climb up to the gorge rim to join the Blackwood Ranges Track, a minor jeep track. A cairn exists at the junction. Turn south and follow the jeep track for 3.6 km along the gorge rim and through sparse, stunted, dry sclerophyll forest indicative of the poor and denuded soil.

The tops support mainly heaths, pultenaea (bush peas), monotoca scoparia (prickly broom heath), acacia aspera (rough wattle) and hakea, plus the stunted eucalypts. Hakea is particularly common about 3 km south along the jeep track. After 3.6 km a minor jeep track should be avoided. It leads off south as the main route turns east, and superb views emerge northwards up the Lerderderg Valley. The really wild nature of the area, and the tangle of interlocking spurs, can be fully appreciated.

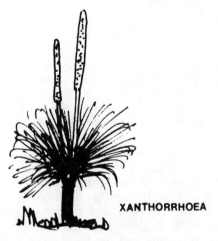

XANTHORRHOEA

At the 4 km stage is a bend and the start of a poorly defined route back down to the river northwards. Avoid this route and turn south, still on the tops, for 650 m to a saddle and jeep track fork. The right fork leads to Swan Road and should be avoided. The left fork climbs onto a small knob, 100 m distant, then just a few metres south of the top, a foot track leads off east, steeply down to the Lerderderg River.

Take this track, which is quite scrubby, and descend 300 m over a distance of 1.3 km back down to the first riverside beach and first ford out from Darley Ford. Ford the river, turn south-east, and retrace 1.75 km of the outward route along the excellent contouring riverside pad to the car park.

17.3 km; 8½ hours; walk last reviewed March 1988; 'B' grade hard walk; about 5 km of trackless light scrub or riverbed walking involved; features rugged gorge; walk suited to any season but summer best; *Maps: Vicmap 1:25,000 Bullengarook* and Map 31, page 165.

46   YOU YANGS

The You Yangs Forest Park provides surprisingly good walking amid rocks and excellent views. The park features a number of small but rugged peaks which rise from the plains between Melbourne and Geelong, the highest of which is Flinders Peak at 343 m elevation.

Access from Melbourne is best via Little River and from Geelong via Lara Lake. There is a Ranger Station and park entrance on the southern boundary of the reserve. Drive from the entrance 2.5 km up Turntable Drive to a main car park and picnic area on a spur to start the walk. Bushfire damage from January 1985 is fast disappearing and, in fact, distant views are improved. Young wattles are now very prolific.

First, climb the tourist track for 1.5 km north to the summit of Flinders Peak for good views of all the forest park, Geelong and Port Phillip Bay. A plaque at the summit tells of Matthew Flinders' ascent of the peak in May 1802 to survey the area.

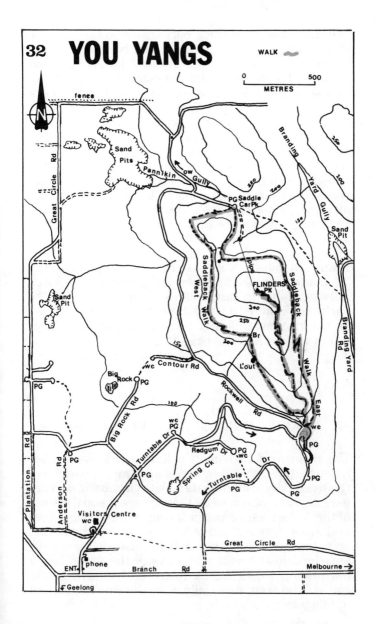

32 YOU YANGS

WALK

0 — 500
METRES

fence

N

Great Circle Rd

Sand Pits

Pannikin

ow Gully

PG Saddle Car Pk

Branding

Yard Gully

250

200

200

Sand Pit

150

150

Saddleback West Walk

FLINDERS PK

Saddleback

East

Walk

Sand Pit

Br

300

250

200

L'out

we

PG

Branding Yard Rd

wc Contour Rd

Big Rock PG

Rockwell Rd

150

PG

Big Rock Rd

100

we PG

Turntable Dr

Redgum Dr

PG wc

Dr

PG

Plantation Rd

Anderson Rd

PG

PG

Spring Ck

Turntable

PG

PG

PG

Visitors Centre
wc

ENT

phone

Great Circle Rd

Branch Rd

Melbourne →

Geelong

171

Retrace the good track back down to the car park then begin to walk a circuit which basically follows the contour and skirts right round Flinders Peak and back south to the walk starting point. The 4 km circuit also skirts a small hill just north-west of Flinders Peak and passes through another car park known as the Saddle Car Park. The circuit can be walked clockwise or anti-clockwise. You will see an African low-growing shrub with yellow flowers, 'Boneseed', and no doubt will be amazed to see how much is has overrun the hillsides. Attempts to control it spreading are under way. However, to compensate for the lack of plant interest during the walk, there are plenty of birds including eagles, rock formations and, of course, the views.

7 km; 2¼ hours; walk last reviewed October 1988; 'B' grade, easy walk; all on tracks; water for lunch only available in picnic areas in other areas of the park; walk suited to any time of the year, but can be hot in summer; *Maps: Vicmap 1:25,000 You Yangs* refers as does Map 32, page 171.

47   ANAKIE GORGE-STONY CREEK RESERVOIR

The main road between Geelong and Ballan passes through the interesting Brisbane Ranges, which are relatively dry and forested with ironbark, stringy bark, box and acacia trees. Orchids are the real feature of the district, especially in spring, and banksia, hakea and grass trees are also of interest. Birds are plentiful and the whole district has a history intricately entwined in the gold rush days of the 1860s. Many old mining shafts, tailing heaps and miners' tracks can still be seen, especially near the tiny settlement of Steiglitz.

Acknowledging all these attractions, the Brisbane Ranges National Park was formed and included an interesting gorge called Anakie Gorge. This gorge is actually one of several similar gorges which cut through the eastern escarpment of the ranges along a geological faultline. The following walk route remains within the bounds of the National Park and commences and ends at a delightful picnic area known as Anakie Gorge Picnic Area which harbours some koalas. To reach the spot, either fork right off Geelong-Ballan Road onto Anakie-Bacchus Marsh Road, then go 3.4 km to a left turn into the picnic area, or travel south on Bacchus Marsh-Anakie Road for 3.5 km after crossing the Little River, then turn right. The side road into the spot is just 800 m long.

After leaving the picnic area, the gorge is entered almost immediately. It is not 'grand' or even outstanding, but has many rocky bluffs, pleasant bushland, and contains Stony Creek. The good track (for walkers only), crosses and recrosses the creek as it heads upstream. A very old pipeline and system of stone walls run right through the gorge.

About 1 km from the picnic ground, and after five creek crossings, a turnoff should be seen indicating a steep minor track up to the ridgetops. The track (Nelsons) leads up south-east on a spur. Small track markers on trees facilitate navigation and on the higher slopes grass trees become quite prolific. The pad then leads around some tops, swinging south-west close to a fence line.

Stay to the right of the fence and within the park rather than cutting across private farmland, then about 1.5 km up from Stony Creek meet a gate.

Next follow a jeep track west, away from the gate for 1.5 km, avoiding minor jeep track forks off left. The area is lightly forested and in spring supports wildflowers, and there are some kangaroos in the locality. The jeep track joins into a gravelled road, but a few metres before the junction a minor jeep track forks off right, and a few metres further north

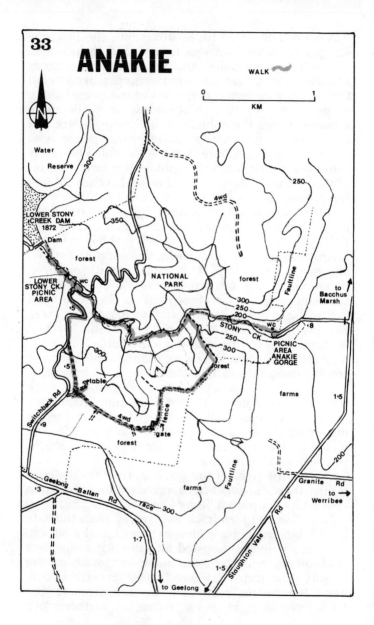

33 ANAKIE

WALK

Water Reserve

LOWER STONY CREEK DAM 1872

forest

Dam

LOWER STONY CK-PICNIC AREA

·5

NATIONAL PARK

forest

300
250
200

STONY CK

wc

·8

300

250

PICNIC AREA ANAKIE GORGE

·5

300

table

4wd

forest

farms

1·5

Switchback Rd

·9

fence

gate

forest

farms

Faultline

Geelong –Ballan Rd

·3

race

300

Granite Rd

to Werribee

200

·4

1·7

1·5

Staughton Vale Rd

to Geelong

250

350

4wd

Faultline

to Bacchus Marsh

0   1
KM

a pad leads off right to a pleasant view of the Stony
Creek valley and Lower Dam. There are a picnic table
and seats at the spot, so the minor deviation is well
warranted. Next, rather than follow the gravelled
road, take the minor jeep track which in that area
is parallel and virtually adjacent to its east side, and
head downhill northwards. After 500 m rejoin the
gravelled road and follow it down via a hairpin bend
into the Lower Stony Creek Picnic Ground beside
the Creek, a further 500 m distance.

**ACACIA
PRICKLY MOSES**

Lower Stony Creek Reservoir was built more than
110 years ago and is part of the Geelong water supply.
It is located 1 km up stream, and an old pipeline
and good track lead from the picnic area to the dam
wall via the creek's south bank. This return trip is
highly recommended before Stony Creek is followed
back downstream and through Anakie Gorge to the
trip's end. The whole of this section of Stony Creek's
valley is well forested and very pleasant. The distance
from the reservoir to the walk's end is 3.5 km, of
which the last 1 km is a retrace of the outward route.

**9.5 km; 3½ hours; walk last reviewed October 1988;
'C' grade, family walk; all on tracks; water scarce with
creek water not usually suitable for drinking for
lunch; walk suited to any time of the year; *Maps:
Vicmap 1:25,000 Staughton Vale and 1:25,000 Eclipse
Creek* refer as does Map 33, page 174.**

Within the Angahook Park at Aireys Inlet on the Great Ocean Road is a wooded gorge worthy of exploration. Ironbark, a tree of the eucalypt type, is widespread and the gorge takes its name from the stands of the tree. The wooded nature of the gorge makes it a cool, pleasant place for a walk on a hot day and a swim at nearby beaches is also an attraction.

Much of the park contains drier type forest prolific with wildflowers, but within the gorge ferns flourish in damp, moist conditions. The park was badly burned in February 1983 but has now recovered well, so the gorge shows little evidence of the fire.

To reach the start of the walk, travel Bambra Road from Aireys Inlet for 2.3 km northwards then westwards 400 m to a picnic area on the north side of the road. At the western end of the picnic ground tracks lead off up the valley of a small stream. The northernmost of the tracks should be taken. It is close to the creek.

Just 300 m from the picnic area there is a divergence of tracks. Take the left fork to remain on the south bank of the creek. The pad can then be readily followed upstream for another 1.7 km at an easy gradient, crossing and re-crossing the creek until the pad doubles back eastwards then returns along the southern creek slopes higher up the hillside. A return distance of 2 km includes areas which tend to be drier than the gorge floor and therefore wildflowers are more common. At three spots along the way you need to avoid diverging right up to nearby Bambra Road.

4 km; 1½ hours; walk last reviewed February 1987; 'C' grade; family walk; all on tracks; carry water; walk suited to any season; *Maps: Vicmap 1:25,000 Aireys Inlet* refers as does Map 34, page 177.

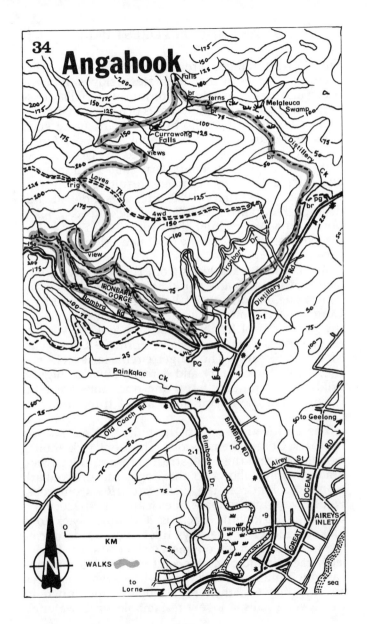

The Otway Ranges are different to most other Victorian ranges in that their steep slopes abut the ocean and give rise to rugged terrain, waterfalls, dense vegetation and many panoramas of a coast that ranks as one of the best in the State. A particuarly good walk in the district is at Angahook Park near Aireys Inlet. It is renowned as a forested area containing waterfalls, a gorge, lookouts, fern gullies, wildflowers and picnic facilities. Damage resulting from Ash Wednesday, February 1983, fires has now all but disappeared. Travel Distillery Creek Road 2.3 km north from Aireys Inlet then turn left to go 400 m west to a picnic area on the right hand side of Bambra Road.

A good foot track leads from the north-west end of the picnic area and marks the start of two circuit walks, one a short route (Walk No 48) into Ironbark Gorge and the other a longer route which includes the north rim of Ironbark Gorge, a lookout view of Aireys Inlet, Currawong Falls, Ferntree Grove and Melaleuca Swamp. The longer circuit far excells the short circuit for beauty and is recommended highly. Wildflowers, ironbark forest and open tops are extra features and the circuit takes about three hours to complete.

The pad leads west up the gully 300 m towards Ironbark Gorge, then divides. The right fork should be followed and the small stream crossed, then a well graded climb follows to the north rim of Ironbark Gorge, 1.5 km from the picnic area. Rock outcrops, wildflowers and ironbark trees feature in the locality. Continue up on the track as it doubles back to a lookout and view of Aireys Inlet, then heads north-west to a trig point on the crest of a spur. Love's jeep track should be crossed at this spot. Head north-east downhill across open tops with views, grass trees and wildflowers, then round bends and down to Currawong Falls, a lovely reasonable sized waterfall surrounded by superb displays of red heath in season. Further on down the pad a small cascade should be passed, then Tree Fern Grove crossed and, as the pad contours around the slopes of Tree Fern Gully,

MELALEUCA

Melaleuca Swamp should be reached. It is in the gully to the left. Walk on east to the area of a track junction. Keep right at the junction to head south-west downstream along Distillery Creek valley, crossing a minor road then forking right 800 m later at a foot track junction. This right-hand track joins the picnic area and walk circuit and ends within 500 m after crossing a minor road midway.

10 km; 3 hours; last reviewed February 1987; 'B' grade, medium walk; all on tracks; carry water; walk suited to any season; *Maps: Vicmap 1:25,000 Aireys Inlet* refers as does Map 34, page 177.

SOUTH EASTERN REGION

50   CAPE WOOLAMAI

At the eastern end of Phillip Island is a rugged headland of pink granite. Adjoining is a dune area with Woolamai Surf Beach to the south and quiet Safety Beach to the north. The whole extremity of the island is protected as a faunal reserve. It contains large rookeries of Short-tailed Shearwaters (Muttonbirds). These remarkable migratory birds each year fly a fantastic circuit of the Pacific, first to New Zealand, then around the western Pacific all the way to the Aleutian Islands of Alaska, along the west coast of North America, then across the Pacific and down Australia's east coast. The flight takes place after the breeding season. A single egg is laid in October, the parents alternate sitting on the egg till hatching occurs in January. The bird's lifespan is normally about twenty years and they come back to Phillip Island each year for the breeding season. A walk to the rookeries and headland is most interesting in the season, especially about January and February. The reserve has a foot track system which should not be left at all: burrows of the muttonbirds abound and easily collapse if walked upon, thus killing the fluffy chicks and adults. Be careful not to frighten birds. The reserve is also worth a visit because of its good views and interesting cliffs. These are especially fine from a position occupied by a small gas-operated ship warning light on the very crest of the 112 m high headland.

From the Phillip Island Bridge travel west to Woolamai Beach Road off south, then start the walk as soon as the ocean beach front is reached. There is a car park at the spot among sand dunes.

Walk south-east along the surf beach for 1 km to

WOOLAMAI

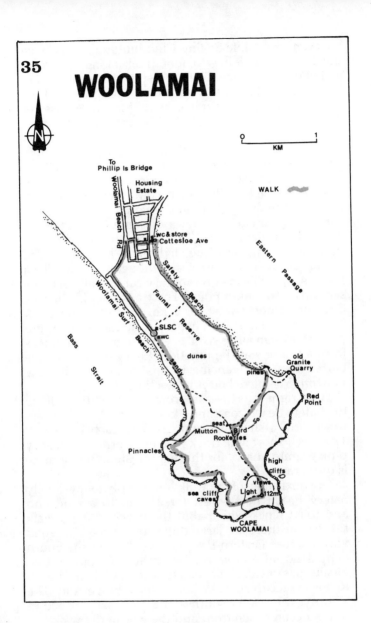

N

0   KM   1

To
Phillip Is Bridge

Housing
Estate

WALK

Woolamai Beach Rd

wc & store
Cottesloe Ave

Eastern   Passage

Safety   Beach

Faunal

Reserve

SLSC
swc

Woolamai Surf   Beach

Bass

Strait

sandy

dunes

old
Granite
Quarry

pines

Red
Point

seat
Mutton
Rookeries

Bird

Pinnacles

high
cliffs

sea cliff
caves

views
Light   112m

CAPE
WOOLAMAI

Woolamai Surf Life Saving Club building, then leave the beach and follow a foot track along the coast just above the beach. The track starts between a toilet block and the beach and continues through sand dune country being regenerated with Marram Grass for dune stabilization. (There has been some talk of re-locating the surf club building). Some 700 m from the surf club, the track divides and dunes are left. Take the cliff rim track to the right and after 800 m you should see sea-cliff formations which are known as The Pinnacles. The track continues around cliff tops climbing higher and higher past several viewpoints, including views of some large caves at the base of some cliffs. The track then reaches the small shipping warning light 1.5 km from The Pinnacles area. Mount Dandenong, the Strzelecki Ranges and Wilsons Promontary can usually each be seen from this high point. The track should then be descended north-west for 1 km to a seat and track intersection. Banksias, sheoaks, wattles, tea tree and paper bark can all be seen as you progress. The tracks form a triangle at the junction. Revegetation of once barren tops is advancing in this locality so that the muttonbirds have better protection.

Turn right (north-east) from the seat to walk to the Safety Beach coastline 1 km distant. A few cypress trees form a sheltered spot as the beach is neared. There is a short side track (800 m return) to a nearby pink granite quarry for those interested. Pink granite is quite rare.

The next stage of the walk is to simply follow lovely Safety Beach north-west for 2.5 km to a road end and toilet block which abut the beach. As you walk this sector there are large dunes to the left and good views across Eastern Passage to cliffs and the South Gippsland hills. From the beach head inland for two blocks, past a store/milk bar, to reach Woolamai Beach Road via Cottesloe Avenue, Vista Drive and The Cranny, then walk south along the road for 500 m to the ocean beach front and the end of the walk.

9.4 km; 3 hours; walk last reviewed August 1987; 'B' grade; family walk; all on tracks, beaches and roads; features Muttonbird rookeries; carry water for lunch; walk suited to any season but summer best especially if birds are to be seen; *Maps: Vicmap 1:25,000 Phillip Island Special* refers as does Map 35, page 181.

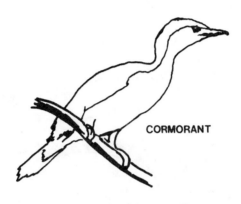

CORMORANT

51   STRZELECKI STATE FOREST

In the South Gippsland Strzelecki Ranges 3 km north of Mirboo North along the Thorpdale Road is the start of the Lyrebird Forest walk. It is a walk in relatively dry type forest for South Gippsland but includes a pleasant sector downstream along the side of the Little Morwell River, where the banks are damp and ferny. A picnic ground is set just off the east side of the Mirboo North-Thorpdale main road and it could be used for lunch either before or after the walk. The spot was once a saw mill. Apart from lyrebirds there are many other birds to be seen, especially near the Little Morwell River. Most of the walk circuit is in forest.

From the picnic ground walk 150 m north-east and fork right downhill on the main ferny walking track

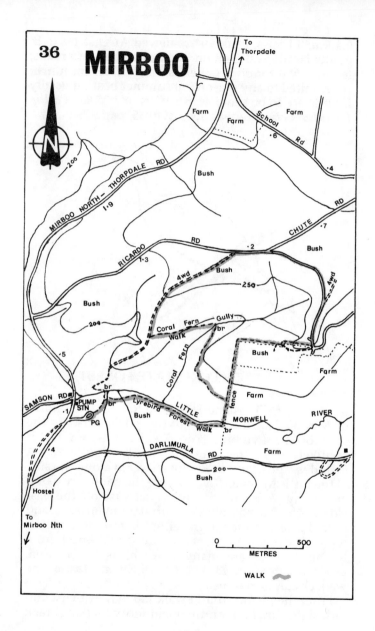

near the stream. Within 1 km cross the river at a bridge and farm fence and climb north steeply for 500 m distance, passing Coral Fern Gully Walk off left near the start of the climb. Just over the crest of the hilltop the track turns east at right angles, then leads for 450 m on the ridgetop to a minor road. The track divides to give two alternatives just before reaching the roadway. From this point turn left along the road which rises northwards, then sidles left across slopes to the junction of Chute Road and Ricardo Road 650 m away. This junction marks the highest point on the walk. Go west on Ricardo Road 200 m then diverge left down a jeep track. Within 600 m the other end of Coral Fern Gully Walk is reached after descending a spur. At this stage you could go directly back to the picnic area by continuing down the jeep track south-west for 500 m, but it is better to see the Coral Fern Gully with its displays of Coral Fern. Take this 800 m long track which basically follows the contour. Mauve coloured Tetratheca and heath flowers are common besides the Coral Fern. Once back at the farm fenceline at the east end of the track, retrace the route back to the picnic area by way of the Little Morwell River pad.

6 km; 2 hours; last reviewed February 1987; 'C' grade; family walk; all on tracks; carry water for lunch (Little Morwell River water could be polluted by farms); walk suited to any season; *Map:* 36, page 184 refers.

52   TIDAL OVERLOOK-SQUEAKY BEACH

Just north of Tidal River Camp at Wilsons Promontory is a ridge extending from Pillar Point inland to the Bishop Peak area. The ridge permits good views both north and south along the west coast of 'The Prom' and of several rugged offshore islands. A circuit from the car park serving Squeaky Beach is suggested as a most rewarding short walk and after the walk a swim at Squeaky Beach could be enjoyed. Initially you need to walk back up the sealed Squeaky Beach access road for 750 m, then right (south-east) along the main Tidal River Road for 650 m to reach the Lilly Pilly Gully car park. The road is flanked by low shrubs so that there are excellent views of the surrounding hills. Birds are common, and even though wombats are generally nocturnal they too are often seen in this location in broad daylight. The Tidal Overlook foot track leads off the main road 15 m south-east and opposite to the Lilly Pilly Gully car park entry. It sidles across slopes for a while and permits views of the Tidal River Camp, then it turns north-west and rises up round the slopes of a hill so that you overlook the Lilly Pilly Gully car park. About 1 km from the car park there is a short track, off left, for 150 m down to Tidal Overlook. There is a lookout on a large boulder and with access to it by a short steel ladder. The view from the granite boulder includes Norman Bay and its broad sandy beaches.

Return the 150 m to the track junction and continue south-west (left), initially sidling down across northerly aspect slopes, then onto a ridge crest. Once on the ridge crest views become superb to white sand Squeaky Beach as well as to yellow sand Norman Bay beach. One small knob gives a full panorama. Some 1.3 km from the Tidal Overlook track junction you should reach another junction where a track joins in from the left from the Tidal River Camp. Continue along the ridge 60 m further to another track fork. You should then take a really lovely side trip, 750 m each way, south-west to a knob on the end of Pillar Point. Some of the side trip is amongst dense tea-tree, but there is a large granite boulder on the knob at the end of the track and it affords a 360 ° view right along the west coast of 'The Prom' in both directions. Norman Island, the Glennie group of islands and the Anser group of islands are all in full view.

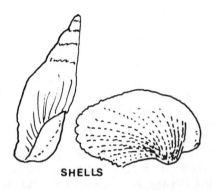

SHELLS

After the Pillar Point side trip, turn left down the Squeaky Beach track. The track is also part of a nature trail and has several pegs marking points of interest. Peg No. 6 is met almost immediately. It indicates an area of Coast Tea-tree, wind and salt-pruned and gnarled by the strong westerly prevailing winds. Peg 7 is nearby too. It is at an interesting granite rock known as Plum Pudding Rock. Its rock crystals are varied like most boulders on the Wilsons Promontory peninsula. There are quartz crystals which are clear or grey, mica which are black and feldspar which are white or pink. About 400 m from the ridge crest junction, the Squeaky Beach track doubles back north to sidle 700 m around to the south end of Squeaky Beach not far above the rocky shoreline. Along this 700 m long stretch, Peg 8 is in an area of low, severely wind and salt-pruned, herbage. Peg 9 indicates Coffin Rock next to a large sheet of granite. When waves break over Coffin Rock they appear like a shroud. Peg 10 is at a boggy spot and has many plants near it favouring boggy soils.

Peg 11 nearby indicates the rock pools on the shore,

then Squeaky Beach sand is reached. The sand is gleaming white and is almost pure quartz grains, so that if you shuffle your feet the grains squeak together with friction. It is an unusual beach, unlike Norman Bay nearby at Tidal River which contains shells also so appears more yellowish. Squeaky Beach is 600 m long and you should walk to its north end. Time could then be spent at leisure before heading inland for 250 m to the car park and end of the walk circuit. Toilets are locatred just near the start of the track to the car park. The area has dense tea-tree and is backed by white sand dunes being managed to prevent erosion.

7.5 km; 2½ hours; last reviewed April 1988; 'A' grade, family walk; all on tracks and beach; features coastal views and Squeaky Beach; water for lunch needs to be carried; walk suited to any season. *Maps: Vicmap 1:25,000 Wilsons Promontory South West* **refers as does Map 37, page 189.**

53   LILLY PILLY GULLY

At Wilsons Promontory, and near Tidal River Camp, is the Lilly Pilly Gully walking circuit. Adjacent Mount Bishop can be included to advantage when walking the circuit. The peak rises to 319 m and permits a spectacular view of Tidal River and the west coast of the promontory. The main part of the walk is in fact a nature trail, with ten pegs along its lower reaches to draw attention to points of interest between the main road and a pleasant picnic ground beside Lilly Pilly Gully itself.

From the car park at the main road, walk east downhill slightly to commence this walk. For about 2 km it contours near the adjacent flats of the Tidal

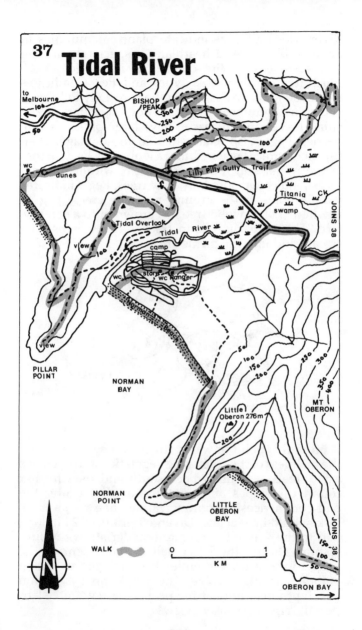

37 Tidal River

to Melbourne

BISHOP PEAK
300
250
200
150
100
50

Lilly Pilly Gully Trail

Titania Ck

swamp

JOINS 38

wc
dunes

Tidal Overlook

view
100
50

Tidal River

camp

wc store wc Ranger

Norman Beach

view

PILLAR POINT

NORMAN BAY

50
100
150
200

250
300
350
400

MT OBERON

Little Oberon 276m
200

NORMAN POINT

LITTLE OBERON BAY

beach

JOINS 38
150
100
50

WALK

0   1
K M

N

OBERON BAY

River. The trail pegs indicate plant communities in general, birdlife and heathland respectively; at Peg No. 4 some 1951 fire damage is indicated. Peg 5 illustrates eucalypt tree types and Peg 6 indicates the presence of koalas. Along the way, Lilly Pilly trees occur in a number of spots. They have dark green shiny leaves and in season have large pink or white berries. Peg 7 also relates to 1951 fire damage. Then the picnic area is reached, and a loop track leads across swampy parts in rain forest. Peg 8, within the rain forest, indicates more Lilly Pilly trees. Peg 9 indicates yabbie holes in the ground near the creek. Peg 10 is where a blackwood tree has grown onto a soft tree fern. Then the short loop track returns across the stream and into the picnic area.

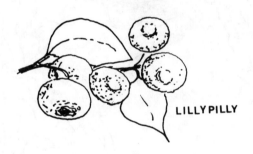

LILLY PILLY

From this point onwards the track rises away from the lushness of the creek-side vegetation and becomes a bit steep. It doubles back south and rises further round the slopes of Mount Bishop. Soon after the pad commences to contour, rather than rise, a track fork should be reached. Diverge right up a 2 km long pad to the summit of granite boulder-strewn Mount Bishop. During the latter half of the ascent to the peak top, the track doubles back to gain elevation before reaching a ridge. The whole area is within eucalypt forest until at the peak, where granite slabs permit most impressive views.

Back at the main circuit track, head west downhill. A small lookout should soon be passed. Its view is of Norman Bay and the Tidal River camp. Soon the car park and walk end should be reached after descending through more forest and past more granite boulders at the base of Mount Bishop.

9 km; 3½ hours; last reviewed April 1988; 'B' grade family walk; all on tracks; features Lilly Pilly trees and Mount Bishop view; creek water for lunch at Lilly Pilly Gully picnic area; walk suited to any season; *Maps: Vicmap 1:25,000 Wilsons Promontory South West* **refers as does Map 37, page 189.**

54   TIDAL RIVER-OBERON BAY

Wilsons Promontory is, without doubt, a superb place for beaches. This walk suggestion enables walkers to experience three glorious beaches, Norman Bay, Little Oberon Bay and Oberon Bay. An excellent well graded and clearly defined foot track connects the three beaches. Swimming could be an added attraction, although Little Oberon Bay can be a little too rough at times for safe swimming.

Start walking from the Tidal River camping area beach-front. Tidal River is the main tourist centre serving Wilsons Promontory. Walk south 1.5 km along the full length of Norman Bay Beach then follow a trail which commences at the south end of the beach. It gradually ascends up and around the rocky coastline, past a right, side-track turnoff to Norman Point, then down into Little Oberon Bay, a small but beautiful cove 4.5 km from Tidal River Camp beach-front. The track then continues inland from near the southern end of the 300 m long beach for about 100 m, then swings south again and follows the rocky coast 1.4 km around the base of dominating Mount Oberon to Oberon Bay. This is perhaps the most beautiful beach on the Promontory and is 2 km long. At the northern end of the beach Growlers Creek needs to be forded, and at the southern end is rugged Mount Norgate. The beach is backed by very large sand dunes which are completely bare over an extensive area. Lunch is suggested at Oberon Bay before returning to Tidal River via the same tracks.

12 km; 4 hours; walk last reviewed April 1988; 'A' grade, family walk; all on tracks and beaches; features beaches; carry water for lunch; walk suited to any time of year but cold in winter; *Maps: Vicmap 1:25,000 Wilsons Promontory South West* refers as do Maps 37 and 38, pages 189 and 193.

55   SEALERS COVE

On the east coast of Wilsons Promontory is secluded Sealers Cove. It has a crescent-shaped, white sandy beach 1.8 km long. Each end of the beach is dominated by rugged, forest-clad, high peaks featuring granite boulders. An excellent 9 km track leads to Sealers Cove from Mount Oberon car park at Telegraph Saddle. This takes about two and one half hours walking time, so the cove can be visited on a day walk. However it is far more enjoyable to spend time at the cove and camp out overnight. 'The Prom' has National Park regulations governing size of parties, camping availability and duration of stay at camps, so first register with the Ranger of the park and obtain a walker's camp permit for Sealers Cove.

From Mount Oberon car park, about 3 km from the Tidal River Camp, the gravelled foot track leads off east as a broad well-defined route. Initially there

South Point, Wilsons Promontory, National Park

Waterloo Bay, Wilsons Promontory, National Park

Sealers Cove, Wilsons Promontory, National Park

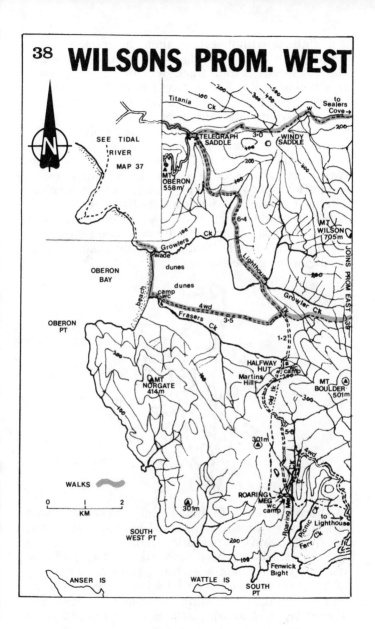

WILSONS PROM. WEST

SEE TIDAL
RIVER
MAP 37

Titania Ck

to
Sealers
Cove →

TELEGRAPH
SADDLE

WINDY
SADDLE

3·0

MT
OBERON
558m

200

6·4

Ck

MT
WILSON
705m

JOINS PROM EAST

Growlers
wade

dunes

OBERON
BAY

dunes

camp
WC

beach

Lighthouse

Growler Ck

200

4wd
3·5

Frasers Ck

OBERON
PT

1·2

200

HALFWAY
HUT
Martins
Hill

WC
camp

MT
NORGATE
414m

MT
BOULDER
501m

100

300

5·6

301m

4wd

WALKS

0   1   2
KM

ROARING
MEG
WC
camp

to
Lighthouse

Roaring Mg

Picnic Ck

Ferr Ck

301m

SOUTH
WEST PT

200

Fenwick
Bight

100

ANSER IS

WATTLE IS

SOUTH
PT

is a slight downhill section, then the track ascends gradually to Windy Saddle, 3 km from the car park. Midway there is a short track switchback. The general area is one of dry low eucalypt forest on northerly aspect slopes. Banksias, Hakea, Grasstrees and heathy plants predominate until near Windy Saddle, then some lush gullies occur. Windy Saddle lives up to its name, but affords good views to both east and west coasts of Wilsons Promontory from its open grassy area. The saddle is between Mount Ramsay and lofty Mount Wilson. The good track then narrows a bit as it continues east down south-easterly aspect slopes, around several very ferny gullies where there is a lot of dense, damp, shrubby vegetation including Sassafras and Beech. Water is usually available in a couple of the gullies.

FERN

About 4 km east of Windy Saddle, the track flattens out to cross swampy areas containing ferns, tea-tree, eucalypts and paperbarks. Long stretches of boardwalks have been erected to facilitate the crossing of the swampy sections. There are a number of 'siamese twin' ferns to be seen. They have their trunks joining and dividing. Eventually Sealers Creek should be reached after passing a lot of sword grass (cutting grass) and rushes. A good foot bridge provides access across Sealers Creek, past a toilet and on just 50 m to the gleaming white sand beach of Sealers Cove. A number of small trees provide shade along the beach and 500 m south-east along it is an excellent campsite. It is on the south-east side of the mouth of Sealers Creek within some forest and at the very end of the beach. Camp water can be obtained from a small side stream flowing through the campsite into salty Sealers Creek. Sealers Creek can require wading to above knee depth if there is a high tide.

It is interesting to know that Sealers Cove once had a jetty and network of timber-getting tramways spreading inland from the jetty. Today virtually nothing remains as evidence. While in camp you should consider walking a short side trip up the Refuge Cove track from near camp. The Refuge Cove pad climbs steeply to some large granite slabs which permit excellent views especially of Sealers Cove and beach. An evening stroll along the beach from camp can be most pleasant, especially on a clear night with a full moon rising in the east. On the second day, reverse the journey of day one and walk back to Mount Oberon car park.

19 km; 7 hours; 2-day walk, each day of 9.5 km and 3½ hours; last reviewed September 1987; 'A' grade, easy overnight walk all on tracks and beach; features Sealers Cove; water for lunches and camp from creeks; walk suited to any season; *Maps: Vicmap 1:25,000 Wilsons Promontory South West and 1:25,000 Wilsons Promontory South East* refer as do Maps 38 and 39, pages 193 and 196.

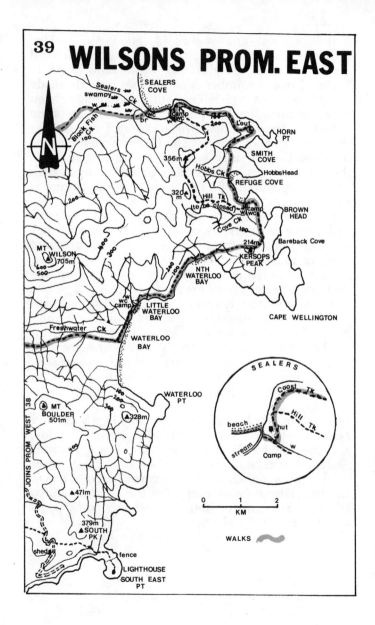

39 WILSONS PROM. EAST

N

Sealers
swampy
SEALERS
COVE
Black Fish Ck
100
w
Sealers Ck
Camp
br
wc
wwc
L'out
HORN
PT
SMITH
COVE
356m
Hobbs Ck
HobbsHead
REFUGE COVE
320m
Hill Tk
(to be closed)
Camp
w wc a
BROWN
HEAD
Cove Ck
100
214m
Bareback Cove
MT
WILSON
705m
600
500
300
200
KERSOPS
PEAK
NTH
WATERLOO
BAY
CAPE WELLINGTON
wc
camp
LITTLE
WATERLOO
BAY
Freshwater Ck
WATERLOO
BAY
WATERLOO
PT
MT
BOULDER
501m
328m
200
100
300
JOINS PROM WEST 38
471m
379m
SOUTH
PK
sheds
fence
LIGHTHOUSE
SOUTH EAST
PT

SEALERS
Coast Tk
beach
Hill Tk
hut
stream
Camp
w

0   1   2
KM

WALKS

196

Wilsons Promontory National Park would rank as one of Victoria's most scenic parks and is certainly visited by many campers and day trippers. Because there are so many visitors to the Tidal River area, limitations on people's movements have been imposed by the park authorities to prevent damage to the flora and fauna. It is regrettable, perhaps, that these limitations extend over the whole of this large park and, therefore, disadvantage long distance walkers who, by comparison to other visitors, number very few. For decades long distance tracks have not been extended and walkers are no longer permitted to leave these tracks or to walk in large groups. Campsites have similarly been limited and have consequently become 'overcamped' so that many experienced bushwalkers now adopt an attitude of no longer being interested in visiting the park because of a lack of wilderness atmosphere. However, if you have not seen the magnificent 'Prom' it is well worth the hassles.

One fairly remote bay to visit is Waterloo Bay. The track to it is very straightforward and despite the crossing of extensive swamps, long boardwalks prevent wet feet and permit fast walking. Camping is permitted at Little Waterloo Bay behind a high sand dune. The bay is north of Waterloo Bay and it is suggested that the spot be used. Register with the Ranger at Tidal River and remember to return the walk permit issued to the Ranger on return. Travel up to the Mount Oberon Car Park on Telegraph Saddle to start and finish the route.

From the car park, head south down the park service road known as the Lighthouse Track. It leads for 6.5 km down through scrubby slopes into eucalypt forest, then out across broad swamp and sand dune flats supporting a lot of leptospermum (tea-tree), banksia and melaleuca. Just 100 m south of a track turnoff right to Oberon Bay is a foot track turnoff left to Waterloo Bay and this should be followed next. The track ascends gradually along the crest of a densely covered sand dune then sidles east up around a fairly open spur. At the end of the climb some granite boulders are situated just to the right of the pad and it is well worthwhile climbing onto the boulders for a good view east to Waterloo Bay and your destination. From the boulders the track leads almost directly to the beach across fairly open slopes and flats, with several low points featuring dense melaleuca and leptospermum stands and swamps. Some 5.1 km from the Lighthouse Track, Waterloo Bay's magnificent beach should be reached. Turn left for 200 m to ford a stream at the north end of the long beach and have a late lunch beside the stream. A swim might also be welcome.

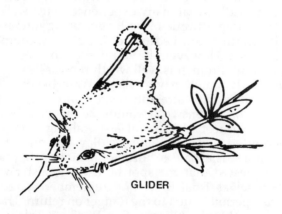

GLIDER

It is only another 1 km into camp so the afternoon can be spent leisurely either at Waterloo Bay or at camp. The track into camp leads from the north end of Waterloo Bay beach around the coastline, often well above the rocks, then directly into the southern end of the camp clearing which lies behind a sand dune in a sheltered wooded area behind Little Waterloo Bay beach and at the mouth of a creek.

Note: Firewood tends to be scarce.
On the second day reverse day one.

25.6 km; 8 hours; 2-day walk, each day of 12.8 km, 4 hours; last reviewed September 1987; 'A' grade easy overnight walk; all on tracks and beach; features Waterloo Bay beaches; water for camp at Little Waterloo Bay from creek; walk suited to any season; *Maps: Vicmap 1:25,000 Wilsons Promontory South West and 1:25,000 Wilsons Promontory South East* refer as do Maps 38 and 39, pages 193 and 196.

57   TIDAL RIVER-SEALERS COVE-WATERLOO BAY-OBERON BAY

This three day walk at Wilsons Promontory includes all the most beautiful bays of the southern part of the National Park and allows time for leisure and perhaps a swim at each bay. The circuit is so beautiful that it would be a pity to undertake it in less time despite a two-day walk with a camp at Refuge Cove being a quite feasible alternative. First, see the Ranger at Tidal River Camp, the main tourist centre, to obtain walk and camping permits. The campsites to be used are at Sealers Cove and Little Waterloo Bay. Park regulations prevent more than one night's stay at each of these campsites and party numbers are limited to twelve. The lighting of solid fuel fires is prohibited in the Park from November to April, so if wishing to cook, a small stove should be carried. Unless a car shuttle between Tidal River camp and Mount Oberon car park is possible, it is necessary to walk the 3.5 km distance, initially, to facilitate the walk circuit. At first you should walk out of the main camp entrance, then after about 1 km walking east, turn right up the road to Mount Oberon car park 2.5 km up the hill along the paved road. There are good views during the ascent which helps break the 'road bash' involved. The road is winding, so beware of traffic.

From the car park, which is on Telegraph Saddle, a gravelled foot track leads off east as a broad, well defined route. It initially heads downhill a little, then ascends gradually to Windy Saddle 3 km from the car park. Midway there is a short track switchback. Dry, low, eucalypt forest predominates in the locality which is one of northerly aspect slopes. It is not until almost at Windy Saddle that the slopes covered with heath—type plants, banksias, hakeas and grasstrees—give way to gullies with lush vegetation. Windy Saddle is a windy place very often, but affords good views to the east and west coasts of 'The Prom'. It has a grassy open area and is situated between Mount Ramsay to the north and lofty Mount Wilson to the south. The track then narrows a bit and continues east down south-easterly aspect slopes, around several very ferny gullies in damp forest of sassafras, myrtle beech and smaller type trees. Water is usually available at a couple of the gullies. Lunch could be eaten either on Windy Saddle or at one of the gully water supplies, the first of which is only a very short distance from Windy Saddle.

Upon continuing some 4 km from Windy Saddle the track reaches flats including areas of tree ferns and, in some swampy parts, tea-tree and sword grass (cutting grass). Boardwalks cross these swampy sections. About 6 km from Windy Saddle, the track crosses Sealers Creek on a bridge, passes a toilet facility and meets the magnificent, secluded, crescent-shaped, white sand beach of Sealers Cove. The beach is 1.8 km long and each end is dominated by rugged peaks. Tea-tree along the beach gives good shade to some of the sand. Walk 500 m south-east along the beach to a camp site on the south-east side of the mouth of Sealers Creek. The camp is among tall eucalypts right at the end of the beach across the creek. Camp water supply is from a small stream which flows west through camp into Sealers Creek.

The water in Sealers Creek is salty. Also the water in Sealers Creek can be deep enough at high tide to require wading to just above knee depth. It is interesting to know that Sealers Cove once had a jetty and a network of timber-getting tramways spreading inland from the jetty. Today virtually nothing remains as evidence. The first days walk distance is relatively short so an evening stroll along the beach from camp could be of added interest, especially if it is moonlight.

On the second day, take the Refuge Cove foot track northwards from camp passing behind a Ranger Station. Currently two tracks exist from just north of the Ranger Station building. The Hill Track follows ridges and there are plans to close this route. A newer Coastal Track (left fork) is the suggested route. It ascends gradually to Horn Point Lookout at about 100 m above sea level then turns from an easterly direction to a southerly direction. Forested country is then traversed down to the mouth of Hobbs Creek on North Refuge Cove beach. Another short track then links North Refuge Cove beach with the southerly beach in the cove. It leads along slopes above the rocky foreshore to camp areas. A bridge over Cove Creek facilitates creek crossing. It is some 5.6 km via either the Hill Track or the Coast Track from Sealers Cove to Refuge Cove.

Lunch is suggested at Refuge Cove on the beach, and a long break could be taken before moving on to Little Waterloo Bay for the night. Refuge Cove is almost surrounded by rocky peaks. It is frequently visited by ocean-going yachts. A camp is behind the beach on the east side of Cove Creek and fresh water is available from Cove Creek upstream of the camp. The departure track to be followed leaves the eastern end of the cove beach and rises up across granite slabs which enable views of the cove. It soon turns south-east on a ridge and crosses a couple of minor saddles before rising south onto a main easterly spur of Kersops Peak.

Some 2.2 km from Refuge Cove, the track attains 214 m elevation at Kersops Peak. Views southwards include Wilsons Promontory lighthouse, conical Rodondo Island in Tasmanian waters some 12 km offshore, and a panorama that takes in fifteen islands in total. Just 1.7 km from the peak is the next objective and it can be seen fully from a few metres west of the crest of Kersops Peak as you follow the track.

The focus is the two delightful beaches in North Waterloo Bay with a rocky headland between them. To reach these beaches the pad descends across a bit of low, heathy ground cover, then through low forest. A streamlet is crossed as the east end of the nearest beach is reached. Further on, a short track connects the two sections of beach walking, then at the west end of the latter beach the track resumes in light forest above the rocky shore. Sheoaks and Banksias become prolific. As you progress there are good coastal vistas especially at two points where a granite boulder and a huge granite slab respectively enable access to view points.

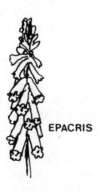

EPACRIS

The track rises up round a gully then descends sharply to meet the beach at the north end of Little Waterloo Bay. Freshwater Creek's mouth is at the beach and needs to be forded. Campsite is behind a dune and adjacent to the creek. Many trees make the camp very sheltered and lilly pilly trees grow in profusion, especially up the slopes near the toilet block. The second days distance, like the first, is short but includes climbing. Some Park information overstates the distance from Refuge Cove to Little Waterloo Bay by 2 km. Firewood can be scarce at the camp.

On the third day, walk south out of camp from behind the dunes. The way soon rises and follows near the rocky coastline of granite boulders, then within 900 m reaches the north end of Waterloo Bay Beach. A lagoon exists behind the north end of the beach and it is necessary to ford its outlet. Walk south along the beach for 300 m, or for the same distance along a track on a low dune immediately facing the beach, to reach the main walking track, inland, westwards.

Follow this good track towards the Lighthouse Track area. There are long boardwalks at times across swampy flats, then the pad leads gently up a broad valley between Mount Wilson on the right and Mount Boulder on the left. Vegetation varies from very low salt and wind-pruned herbage to 3 m high eucalypts, tea-tree and paperbarks. Some 1.8 km from Waterloo Bay beachfront, the track lies beside some granite boulders worthy of climbing for a good view back to Waterloo Bay.

About 300 m later the crest of a low divide is crossed. High on the slopes of a northerly spur of Mount Boulder are huge granite tors. One tor appears just like the image of former Australian Prime Minister, Malcolm Fraser, when viewed from the divide area. The track continues across another fairly swampy section and rises to its high point within 1 km of the divide, then it sidles south-west onto a pronounced sand dune bearing many huge coast banksias. It then descends the dune crest west to the Lighthouse Track which is a jeep track, some 5.1 km from Waterloo Bay.

Turn right (north) and within 100 m turn left onto

another track which leads west to Oberon Bay and the Frasers Creek camp area and beach.

The vehicular track leads through coastal scrub to the mouth of Fraser Creek and is 3.5 km long. Once on Oberon Bay beach, lunch is suggested. Water from Fraser Creek at the camp site is suitable for drinking if needed. Oberon Bay beach is yet another superb beach dominated by 558 m Mount Oberon at its north end and 414 m high Mount Norgate at its south end. The beach is 2.2 km long, but you need to walk 1.4 km along it only to reach its north end after lunch. Huge sand dunes exist behind the beach.

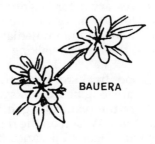

BAUERA

Salty and shallow Growlers Creek mouth needs to be forded at the beach end, then an excellent foot track can be followed around the coast, but above granite boulders and cliffs. The track is among a lot of low herbage plus sheoaks and banksias as it skirts around and below Mount Oberon to Little Oberon Bay beach in 1.4 km. This small beach 300 m long, is beautiful, but *dangerous for swimming*. Continue along the coast track from the north end of Little Oberon Bay beach for 3 km, crossing the spine of Norman Point and on to the south end of Norman Bay. Views of the coast and offshore islands are especially good near the Norman Point vicinity. To finish the three day circuit you then need to walk 1.6 km along Norman Bay beach to the Tidal River Camp.

44 km; 13-14 hours, 3 days walk, each day of 13 km, 3½-4 hours, 13.3 km, 4 hours, and 17.7 km, 5½-6 hours

respectively; walk last reviewed September 1987 and April 1988; 'A' grade; medium walk; all on tracks, roads and beaches; features some of Victoria's best beaches; water for camps and lunch spots from streams; walk suited to any season *Maps: Vicmap 1:25,000 Wilsons Promontory South West and 1:25,000 Wilsons Promontory South East* refer as do Maps 37, 38 and 39, pages 189, 193 and 196.

58   TRAPYARD HILL

The Trapyard Hill area is one alpine locality which provides easy walking and a high point with commanding views. The summit is fairly close to an access road. Also of interest is the adjacent alpine Wellington Plains area. Access by road is from Heyfield through Licola, then up spectacular Tamboritha Spur Road to Arbuckle Junction 47 km from Licola and along Moroka Road a further 11.5 km to McFarlanes Saddle. *The whole area is snowbound is winter.* The saddle carpark is the main departure point for walkers heading for Tali Karng. From McFarlanes Saddle car park, walk 500 m south-south west on a foot track to a disused jeep track swath (aligned east-west) through some snow gums. Turn left on the grassy track and head east for 2 km to a point just north of the summit of prominent Trapyard Hill. On the way, fork right at a minor jeep track junction. The main jeep track skirts the peak then descends steeply to the Moroka River area. The whole area is covered with delightful alpine vegetation and has numerous view points. Leave the jeep track and scramble south up the steep grassy slopes to the rocky summit of Trapyard Hill for quite spectacular views, especially northwards towards

Moroka Gorge and Snowy Bluff. The ascent is quite short and the summit is some 1585 m above sea level.

HELIPTERUM

5 km; 2 hours; walk last reviewed February 1988; 'A' grade, easy Alpine walk; 95% on tracks, 5% alpine grassland; features views; carry water; suited October to April only; (district subject to blizzards March to November); *Maps: National Mapping 1:100,000 Howitt* **and Map 40, page 207.**

59   MOUNT WELLINGTON

The Wellington Plains area is alpine and part of Victoria's high country cattle grazing lease areas. The plain provides easy walking and such adjacent high peaks as Trapyard Hill and Mount Wellington can be easily reached. An historic cattlemans hut (Millers) is also an attraction. It is set amid very beautiful snow gums which have pink and orange-red trunk markings, especially in autumn.

Access to this walk is the same as if going to Tali Karng. The area is completely snowbound in winter and blizzards occur March to November. From Heyfield in Gippsland head north into the mountains via Licola, up the Tamboritha Spur Road for 47 km

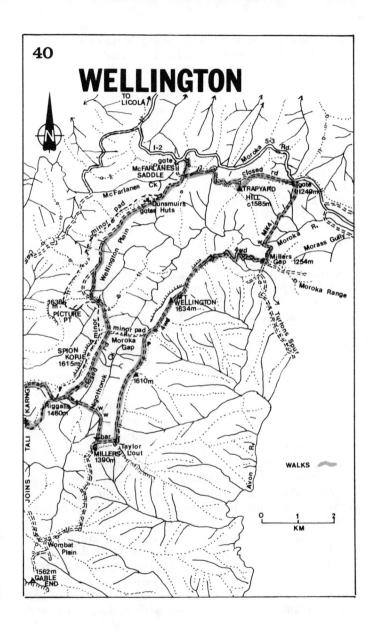

40

WELLINGTON

TO LICOLA

N

McFARLANES SADDLE
gate
1-2
McFarlanes Ck
Dunsmuirs Huts
gates
Wellington Plain
minor pad

Moroka 5.3 Rd.
closed rd
TRAPYARD HILL c1585m
gate 1240m
MK4
Moroka R.
Morass Gully
4wd
Millers Gap 1254m
Moroka Range

1638m PICTURE PT
minor
closed rd
minor pad
Moroka Gap
SPION KOPJE 1615m
Nigothoruk
WELLINGTON 1634m
1610m
Turtons Spur

TALI KARNG
JOINS
Riggalls 1460m
w
w
bar
MILLERS 1390m
Taylor L'out
Avon R.

WALKS

0   1   2
KM

Wombat Plain

1562m GABLE END

207

to Arbuckle Junction, then along Moroka Road 11.5 km to McFarlanes Saddle Car Park. To avoid navigation problems at Trapyard Hill it is best to undertake this walk circuit anti-clockwise.

From the car park go 500 m south-south-west through snowgums via a pad to reach a disused jeep track swath aligned east-west. Cross the swath and continue along the Wellington Plains Track. Soon alpine grassland plains are reached. About 1.5 km from the walk start avoid the minor pad off right towards the Spion Kopje Range. Another 500 m sees you at gates and the two fairly derelict Dunsmuirs Huts. The main plain area is then crossed and no doubt some cattle will be seen. The track leads south-west then south-east across the Moroka River-Carey River saddle then passes over a low ridge and continues south-west along the eastern slopes of the Spion Kopje Range still in alpine grassland. Some 9.5 km from the walk start leave the Tali Karng access route and turn east (left) 1.5 km to Millers Hut for camping. Nigothoruk Creek and tiny tributaries are crossed as close as 400 m to Millers Hut and water for camp could be collected as you pass. Just north of the hut, a jeep track joins in from the east amongst snow gums. It is the Mount Wellington Track. The historic hut has good camp spots around it. A 2 km return walk to 1514 m Taylor Lookout up the Mount Wellington Track is highly recommended to finish off the day. The lookout area is just south of the jeep track at rocky outcrops near the hilltop. There is 120 m ascent from Millers to the lookout area.

Next day return up the Mount Wellington Track and follow it north-north-east to the 1643 m Mount Wellington summit 5 km distant. Snow gums and small alpine grass clearings are passed during this gradual ascent. The summit views include Bass Strait 80 km away. A 4 km long jeep track descent north-east then east, losing 380 m elevation to Millers Gap, follows. The track leaves the alpine tops and descends via hairpins into forests. At Millers Gap turn left (north) on MK4 road and within 800 m reach the Moroka River for lunch.

After the break continue along the quiet road to reach the main Moroka Road. At this junction an old jeep track leads west up into scrub, it being the former cattlemens route before Moroka Road was built. Despite some obstructions of fallen limbs and regrowth, ascend this old track so that after 1.7 km you reach the summit of Trapyard Hill. The track bypasses the actual top via the northern slopes and in that vicinity fades among snowgrass and rocks. Trapyard Hill some 1585 m high is covered with delightful alpine vegetation and rocks. There are spectacular views north towards Snowy Bluff and Moroka Gorge.

GENTIAN

Descend the north-west slopes 200 m onto the old grassy cattle track, then head westwards for 1.8 km to rejoin the previous days outward walk route 500 m south of the McFarlanes Saddle car park. That last 500 m involves turning right into snow gums from the jeep track swath.

28.5 km; 9½ hours; spread over two days of 13 km, 4 hours and 15.5 km, 5½ hours; walk last reviewed February 1988; 'A' grade, medium overnight Alpine walk 95% on tracks 5% alpine grassland; features views; carry water from Nigothoruk Creek and

Moroka River; walk suited to October to April only; *Maps: National Mapping 1:100,000 Howitt and Vicmap 1:25,000 Tali Karng* refer as does Map 40, page 207.

60   TALI KARNG

Tali Karng, a sparkling lake, cool and refreshing, set amid tall timber and tucked away in a rather remote rugged part of the mountains has long been a favourite destination for walkers. It is set at the western rim of a geological formation similar to a glacial cirque and the lake itself apparently has been caused by an ancient landslide blocking the Wellington River valley. Spion Kopje, Gable End and The Sentinels, each about 1600 m high, tower above the waters which lie at 855 m, while, below the lake, the valley descends very rapidly to about 600 m within 1.5 km. A further unusual feature is that the lake waters drain out underground at its western edge into the Wellington River some 500 m away, and although there is a natural surface outlet it does not flow. The lake level fluctuates tremendously and consequently varies the size of the lakeshore camping area, but never rises to a point where no camp areas are left dry.

The lake is heavily used as a bushwalking destination. There are several routes to the lake, but only walkers can go there now as the former jeep track access has been closed. The easiest and most popular approach is from McFarlanes Saddle and these notes describe that routing. The saddle is 58.5 km from Licola in Gippsland via the Tamboritha Road and Moroka road. *The whole district is quite snowbound in winter.* Warm and waterproof clothing is essential

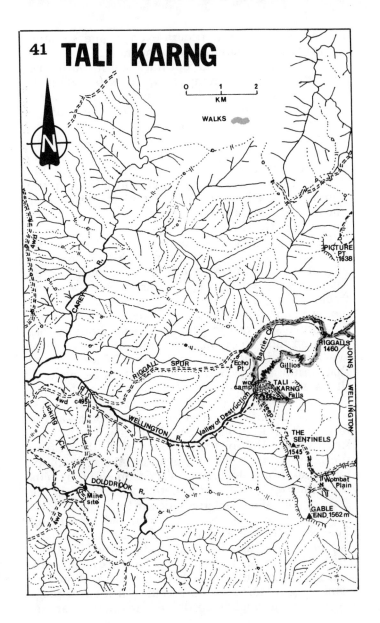

WALKS

O   1   2
KM

N

CAREY R.

PICTURE
PT
1638

RIGGALL SPUR

Barter Ck.

Echo
Pt

Gillios
Tk

RIGGALLS
1460

JOINS

WELLINGTON

wod
camp

TALI
KARNG
Falls

455

steep

Valley of Destruction

WELLINGTON R.

THE
SENTINELS
1545

4wd c495

4wd

licking Ck

DOLODROOK R.

Mine
site

Wombat
Plain

GABLE
END 1562 m

for the walk as snow occurs even in mid summer. Blizzards occur March to November.

Initially follow a good foot track south-south-west from the car park among snow gums for 500 m to reach a swath through the trees where a disused jeep track exists. Across this cleared strip the route to follow is on an old jeep track known as the Wellington Plains Track. Soon snow gums are left and open alpine grass plains are crossed. About 1.5 km from the walk start, keep to the old jeep track short route to Tali Karng rather than to diverge right onto a longer route minor foot track to the lake. Another 500 m finds you at gates and at the two fairly derelict Dunsmuirs' huts beside the track.

The track ahead leads south-west for 4 km on the Wellington Plains, then turns south-east to cross the end of the plain at a saddle on the Moroka-Carey River divide. A low ridge is then crossed and the track swings south-west again to continue on more alpine plains on the eastern slopes of Spion Kopje. On either side of the low ridge you should avoid tracks off right to Spion Kopje and off left to Mount Wellington via Moroka Gap. Another 2.5 km on from that turnoff is a second track off left, to be avoided. (It leads to Millers Hut and Gable End.) The junction is some 9.5 km from the walk start. Proceed almost westerly for another 500 m for a lunch break at the former site of Riggalls Hut at about 1460 m elevation. At this point the tops need to be left to descend to the lake at about 855 m elevation. Also, the minor foot track from McFarlanes via Spion Kopje rejoins from the right. Just a few metres west again is the start of the Gillio foot track down to the lake. (The track is named in memory of an old stockman.) Consequently there is a choice of descent via the old jeep track (Riggalls Spur Track) or the Gillio foot track. Most prefer to use the Gillio track as it is the more beautiful of the two. Both routes are about the same length (some 4.5 km). Gillio's has twelve zig-zags over the final steep descent to the lake shore.

It leads through snow gums at first on the tops, then descends through fine alpine ash stands. It is therefore recommended that walkers use this route.

Once at the lake shore, you need to follow the water's edge to the west end of the lake for camping. The spot is heavily camped and walkers should ensure that rubbish is taken out with them. If time permits, there are pleasant falls to be seen at the east end of the lake as a side trip from camp. A pad circuits the lake.

On the second day you should climb via the Riggalls Spur route to Riggalls (605 m), then reverse the route of day one, but remember that there is a big initial climb so that you should not leave the lake too late.

Some may prefer to return along the ridgetops walking track over Spion Kopje, west of the main jeep track. In so doing the distance is increased by about 2 km and an extra two hours should be allowed as you need to climb over the summit of Spion Kopje and other high points. The pad is quite indistinct at times.

PROSTANTHERA

29 km; 10 hours walking spread over two days of 14.5 km each, taking 4½ hours and 5½ hours respectively; walk last reviewed February 1988; 'A' grade, medium, overnight, Alpine walk; all on tracks; features Tali Karng; suited to summer months only; carry water for lunch, camp water from lake; *Maps: National Mapping 1:100,000 Howitt and Vicmap 1:25,000 Tali Karng refer as do Maps 40 and 41, pages 207 and 211.*

Wonnangatta Valley has for many years been one of those beautiful far away valleys that bushwalkers consider the ultimate in bushwalking venues. Many think that the valley is a must because, as well as walking, the swimming in the Wonnangatta River and the camping situation are ideal. In season, there are blackberries, raspberries, fruit trees, fish, rabbits, mushrooms and even chestnuts.

Best access to the valley is from a point on the Snowy Range 65 km from Licola via the Tamboritha and Howitt Roads to Guys Hut Car Park on the right-hand side of the road. A good marker is a cattle grid across the road at 64.7 km. A closed jeep track leads to historic Guys Hut on an alpine meadow called Bryces Plain. Bryce is a famous name in Victoria's high country, being the family name of the early cattle graziers of the Wonnangatta Valley. William Bryce, a Scottish university graduate who ran a packhorse business between Myrtleford and Grant, a once gold boom town, bought out the original settler Oliver Smith after Smith had been grazing cattle only a few years. He extended the homestead and became well known as he expanded both the property and his family to ten children. The family lived an active social life, frequently travelling to nearby Grant. They became respected for their horsemanship in their work of mustering cattle in such rugged country. However, by 1914 the family had grown up and dispersed and the property was sold to a Myrtleford man who installed a manager. This manager was later murdered and a mystery ensued when the prime suspect was himself found murdered. Later the homestead was destroyed by fire and all that remains today is the Bryce family cemetery, some old stockyards and post and rail fences, a small hut and some exotic trees. Cattle no longer graze the rich alluvial river flats but the Bryce name can be seen on the cemetery headstones. Additionally, Bryces Gorge is quite an attraction, it being in the headwaters of Conglomerate Creek upstream of the homestead site. The gorge is very rugged with cliffs up to

OLEARIA

300 m high. Pieman Creek and Conglomerate Creek both plunge headlong over the cliffs in fine waterfalls, whilst Pieman Pool, at the very head of the Pieman Creek Falls, is a very pleasant but cool spot for a swim on a hot day.

Start walking 100 m north-west down the jeep track out onto the snowgrass plains and diverge right onto the Bryces Gorge foot track. Follow it north east 800 m to cross Pieman Creek then head east 800 m on the north bank to Pieman Pool and falls at the lip of Bryces Gorge. The best vantage point for appreciation of the falls is 200 m north via a gorge rim foot track. Next continue along the pad fairly near the rim for 1 km to a cliff top vantage point from which Conglomerate Creek Falls can be best seen. The spot is about 200 m short of the head of these superb falls which would be one of the best in Victoria. They drop then rush down a chute into Bryces Gorge.

Walk the 200 m north-east to the head of the falls, then go 1.3 km west, on a foot track over snowgrass upstream along Conglomerate Creek to the spot where Bryces outstation hut once stood in a large clearing. There is a fairly prominent ford in the clearing, beside a conspicuous red-brown patch of bare earth. It is where the creek turns north sharply after flowing east. Lunch is suggested while near water. Locate a cattle pad which leads north-west from the ford, it soon becomes a marked foot pad. Follow it up the herb covered clearing, swinging north across a shallow gully into snowgums, and on to reach a broad ridgetop 1.5 km from the ford. You then start the 5.5 km descent on a marked foot track to the Dry River.

At first the marked track leads down through fairly open alpine vegetation and descends a rocky sector via two zig-zags to a north-sloping spur. It then sidles down the eastern slopes of this spur and swings east onto a pronounced subsidiary spur. Continue down to a saddle, then veer left to descend northwards contouring across well timbered slopes and out onto a north-west sloping spur which leads to the Dry River valley itself. However, rather than reach the river immediately, the track leads north-east among blackberries for about 500 m, then joins a well defined foot track from Howitt Hut. Once on the Dry River flats, walk north-east 1.3 km to a ford, by which time the foot track has become a disused jeep track. Follow the river downstream, not far from its north bank, for 300 m to another ford of a tributary stream, then on 2.7 km to a jeep track junction at the Dry River-Zeka Creek confluence. This latter 4.3 km of walking is all across lightly timbered parklike flats.

Next, head east, then north-east, for 800 m out onto the open main Wonnangatta River flats and join the main valley jeep track. Turn right (south-east) and walk the day's final 2.5 km down the valley to within 500 m of the old Wonnangatta Homestead site. The homestead area is easily discernable ahead due to the many exotic trees around it. Camp beside the river where the river and jeep track are nearest each other. Then, after camp is established, wander south-

216

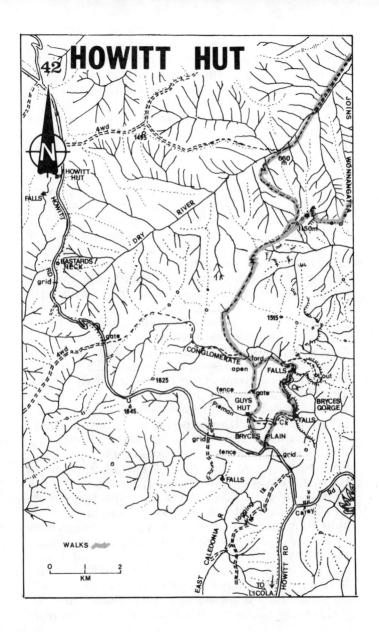

42 HOWITT HUT

N

4wd

1495

660 m

JOINS WONNANGATTA

HOWITT HUT

FALLS

HOWITT RD

DRY

RIVER

150m

BASTARDS NECK

grid

4wd

gate

1515

CONGLOMERATE

ford

open

FALLS

lookout

Ck

1625

fence

gate

GUYS HUT

BRYCES GORGE

1645

Pieman

Ck

FALLS

BRYCES PLAIN

grid

fence

grid

FALLS

Carey

WALKS

0   1   2
KM

EAST CALEDONIA R

logging tk

HOWITT RD

TO LICOLA

east 200 m to see the old family cemetery amid several large cypress and pine trees. From camp site views are very good down the valley, and from the adjacent slopes near the jeep track The Viking can be seen dominating the head of the valley.

Also walk to the homestead site to browse about, making sure that you include a detour east along the jeep track continuation for about 400 m in and among the magnificent and historic exotic trees.

Next morning a decision needs be made. If your party is not well experienced and able to cope with very difficult trackless terrain, simply retrace the previous day's route back to the tops. For those continuing, spectacular scenery is assured by heading up Conglomerate Creek from the homestead site.

At first follow a jeep track for 1.5 km south-west on the west bank then across a ford onto the east bank. This section is grassy with many fruit trees and briar roses. A quite minor pad then leads for 3.5 km on the east bank usually 20 m to 40 m up the very steep slopes from the stream. Make sure side valleys are not taken, especially about 1.5 km from the ford. At a second side gully 2.5 km from the ford the pad temporarily crosses to the west bank. Thereafter a broad lightly timbered river flat is reached. Another 1 km on, where the broad valley is turning to a south-north alignment, have an early lunch as there is no water for the next section.

After lunch start a steep trackless climb up to Guys Spur track. To do this, climb 1 km west up one of the relatively open, but very steep, spurs; turn south up the fairly flat ridge of the Conglomerate Creek-Dry River Divide to a distinct knob and bend in the spur. Climb steeper and steeper west up through cliffs to a high prominent knob. It is best to skirt around the right of the cliffy sector, but the ascent is still awkward. (Inexperienced walkers could become nervous at the cliffs.) Good views on the top will no doubt help dissipate any tired feeling from the sudden 640 m rise in elevation over the 3 km from

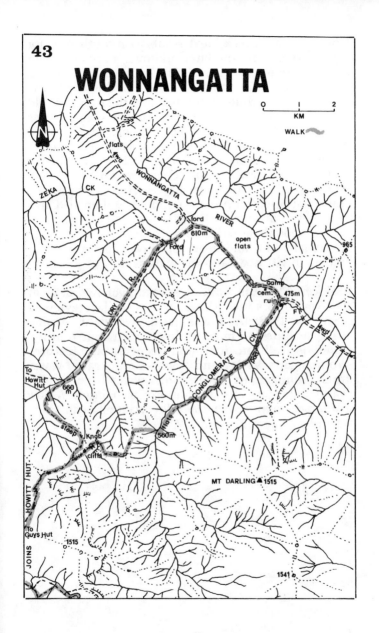

43

WONNANGATTA

0   1   2
KM

WALK

flats

4wd

WONNANGATTA

ZEKA   CK

ford

610m

RIVER

Ford

open flats

DRY R.

camp

cem. ruin

475m

Ft.

4wd

965

To Howitt Hut

660 m

CONGLOMERATE   CK

660

steep

Knob

560m

cliffs

HOWITT HUT

To Guys Hut

MT DARLING ▲ 1515

1515

JOINS

1541

Conglomerate Creek. Next, scrub-bash south-west for 800 m down from the knob and over a second lower knob to meet the Guys Spur Track in a saddle as it sidles up from the Dry River. At this point the previous day's route is rejoined and the route should then be reversed for 4.5 km as far as the site of Bryces Hut on the upper Conglomerate Creek. *However, when ascending, the track can be hard to follow despite markers on trees. The correct route is south-south-west to the top of the ridge then south down to Conglomerate Creek.*

A jeep track leads from Bryces Hut site ford area south-south-east up over a shoulder, then to Guys Hut, 2 km away, mostly through timber. Midway, a gate should be passed. See historic Guys Hut, (a cattlemans hut) and head south-east 700 m back up to the Howitt Road and the walk's end.

36.4 km; 14 hours walking spread over two days of 20.4 km 7 hours and 16 km 7 hours; walk last reviewed February 1988; 'A' grade, hard, overnight, Alpine walk; includes 4 km of trackless open spur routing, otherwise all on foot and jeep tracks; features Wonnangatta Valley and Bryces Gorge; camp water from Wonnangatta River, lunch water from creeks; walk suited to any season except winter; *Maps: National Mapping 1:100.000 Howitt* refers as do Maps 42 and 43, pages 217 and 219.

WESTERN REGION

62 HARCOURT PLANTATION-MOUNT ALEXANDER-KOALA PARK

Mount Alexander is a classic example of how our society tends to abuse nature in the quest for material things but it also shows how, with the aid of care shown in these slightly more enlightened days, nature quickly recovers if only given the chance. The 741 m high peak seems to be relatively unknown to most Victorians, yet few mountains have had such a notable history. Named after Alexander the Great

KOALA

by explorer Major Mitchell after he climbed it in 1836, it became the focus for thousands of diggers converging on the large Mount Alexander goldfield from 1851 onwards. They came mostly from Melbourne via Mount Alexander Road, Essendon and across the Keilor Plains. While the surrounding, undulating country yielded gold, especially at nearby Chewton and Castlemaine, the mountain itself became famous for Harcourt Granite (granodiorite) which has found its way into numerous well known buildings such as the old Parliament House Canberra and Flinders Street Station Melbourne. The friendly aboriginal peoples who inhabited the area initially, suffered terribly, particularly from disease brought by the gold diggers, and died out. The mountain was stripped bare of its timber by miners and former large colonies of koalas were exterminated for their fur by 1920. In 1880 a disastrous bush fire added to the desolation then, more recently, plagues of rabbits, erosion and drought occurred. Only since the 1950s have conditions changed somewhat for the better, although three modern towers now starkly dominate the summit to provide television and communication links, and granite continues to be quarried in numerous and widely scattered spots rather than in a better managed concentrated area.

Following establishment of a State Forest in the area, the lower western slopes of the mountain were planted with pines, oaks and cedars to help prevent erosion and to provide wood for packing cases for the adjacent Harcourt fruit growing area. The remainder of the slopes has been left to regenerate naturally and there has been rapid regrowth, especially of manna gums. Kangaroos and wallabies are now quite common and a koala sanctuary has been established and expanded to a new site, creating an excellent place to see the quaint little mammals. Obviously more could be done to assist nature, but today the mountain is once again beautiful and a delight to walkers. Try the following circuit walk from the State Forest boundary and attempt to comprehend the significance of history from the peak.

Access to the starting point is from the Calder Highway at Harcourt, east along Market Street for 1.3 km to intersect Government Road, then on further east 1 km to enter the forest. Immediately following entry to the reserve, walking should begin.

Head left on a minor road through pine forest to

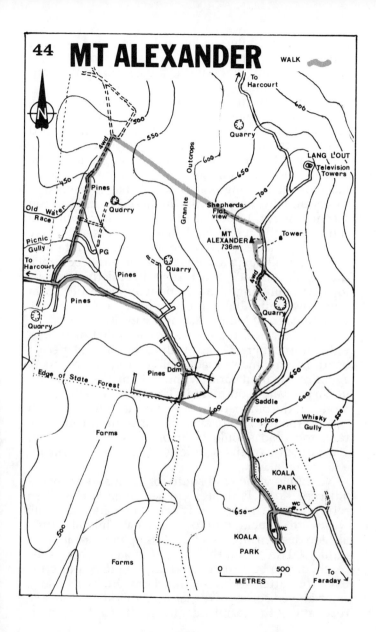

44 MT ALEXANDER

WALK

To Harcourt

N

4wd

500

550

Quarry

606

Granite Outcrops

600

650

700

LANG L'OUT

Television Towers

450

Pines

Quarry

Old Water Race

Shepherds Flat view

MT ALEXANDER 736m

Tower

Picnic Gully

PG

To Harcourt

Pines

Quarry

4wd

Quarry

Pines

Pines

Quarry

Dam

650

Pines

Edge of State Forest

600

600

Saddle

Fireplace

Whisky Gully

550

Farms

KOALA PARK

650

WC

500

KOALA PARK

WC

Farms

0   500
METRES

To Faraday

cross Picnic Gully among oaks and cedars after 500 m. A small picnic area exists just to the right under the exotic trees and is a particularly pleasant spot in autumn.

Continue north amid pine forest and gradually ascend to a prominent saddle 1.3 km away. Fork right on the saddle, then after 100 m leave the minor road and start to climb the crest of a spur steeply. There is no track, but a virtual absence of any scrub in the area. Trees and numerous rocky granite outcrops make an interesting walk and all that is needed is to continually keep to the highest ground as you ascend. About 1.3 km up the spur, after swinging south on the crest and having crossed grassy Shepherds Flat, a rocky viewpoint should be attained. It reveals quite expansive views west and a foot track then leads east 400 m across rocky, relatively open, tops to a main range top road right opposite a Telecom relay tower, just 100 m north of the 3 m high granite summit cairn of Mount Alexander itself.

Visit the cairn, then wander south 400 m to fork right onto a minor road leading south-west near a bend in the main road. Follow the minor road, avoiding two left forks within 200 m then head on down the range southwards. The route becomes quite faint, but the old road alignment is a useful navigation guide. About 1.7 km south of the summit cairn, the rangetop road should be rejoined in a saddle, and 100 m south of the saddle is a fireplace useful for a lunch break.

Next follow the road south for 1 km and enter the adjacent Koala Park areas to see some koalas, then return to the fireplace. Leave the road and walk westwards. Rocky outcrops dominate initially, then a steep descent through trackless open forest follows until, 800 m from the road, farmland should be reached. It is best to descend keeping to a spur crest over the latter sector so that farmland is met at a right-angled corner of the farm. At this spot a forestry road abuts the farmland and itself bends at right

Snowy Bluff from Trapyard Hill

Wonnangatta Valley

Tali Karng. Remote lake in the Upper Wellington River Valley

angles. Follow the road north, down amid pine plantation 400 m to a gully, then north-west, then west, down the small valley for 1.5 km to complete the walk circuit. Part of the latter sector is on bitumen road within the plantation.

GALAHS

10.5 km; 3½ hours; plus Koala Park walking; walk last reviewed January 1987; 'C' grade; medium walk; partly off tracks but on open slopes; features Koalas; walk suited to any season, but could prove hot in summer; normally no water for lunch at any point; Maps: Vicmap 1:25,000 Barker and 1:25,000 Chewton refer as does Map 44, page 223.

63   MALDON-MOUNT TARRANGOWER

Maldon is an outstanding example of a nineteenth century gold mining town largely untouched since the turn of the century, and it is notable for its historic atmosphere; its public buildings, verandahed shopping streets, houses and mining structures depict an era. As a result the Maldon Planning Scheme has been enacted. It is unique in Victoria in that it is the first statutory attempt to achieve historic conservation of a whole town as opposed to individual buildings. The central commercial area is of prime historic interest with the main access routes into and through the town being worthy of special protection. The town's character is found not in the importance of individual buildings, but in the many small miners' houses and old European trees associated with the main buildings. The discovery of rich alluvial gold at Maldon in 1853 was responsible for early development, and with the advent of later quartz mining the town grew from a collection of tents and huts to a thriving community, at one time the eighth largest town in Victoria. Gold contributed directly to Maldon's development for over seventy years but, due to the lack of sufficiently rich nearby farmland to support a large town, it declined with the decline of gold and today has a population of about 1000 people.

The town is overshadowed by 571 m high Mount Tarrangower and the goldfield used to be known as the Tarrangower Diggings. A walk circuit including both this mountain and the historic town provides a most interesting day. The mountain slopes feature many wildflowers in spring and a high lookout tower on the summit permits a very good view. Maldon is close to both Bendigo and Castlemaine. It is suggested that walkers go to a gold memorial cairn to be found 1 km towards the south end of the town at a bend, and on the east side of the Castlemaine to Maldon Road. If time permits, a little gold panning could be tried as an added attraction for the day.

Walk 400 m towards the town then turn left (southwest) into Parkins Reef Road. Continue for 200 m then turn right into Gray Street and climb up a minor 800 m long pine tree-lined avenue to Anzac Hill for a view of the town. Next, head west up a minor road

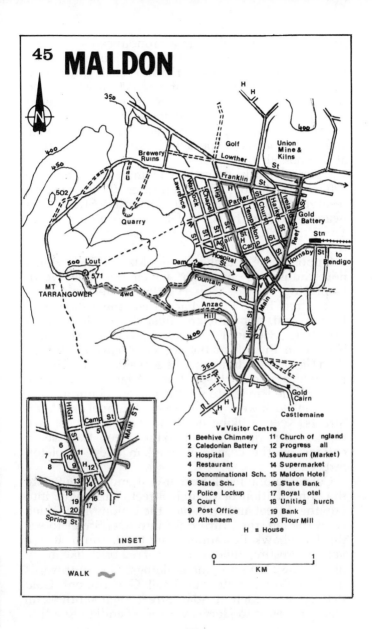

45 MALDON

N

35o

400

450

502

400

Brewery Ruins

Golf

Union Mine & Kilns

Lowther

St

Franklin St

Lawrence

Warrock

Chapel

High

Parker

St

Church

Harker

Ireland

Reef

St

4

Gold Battery

Stn

Quarry

St

St

St

St

St

Adair

H

Camp

St

St

St

500 L'out

571

Dam

Hospital St

St

St

Hornsby St

1

to Bendigo

MT TARRANGOWER

4wd

Fountain St

V

Anzac Hill

High St

Main St

400

350

H

Gold Cairn

to Castlemaine

INSET

HIGH ST

Camp St

5

MAIN ST

6

11

7   10

8   9   H 12

13

14

15

18   16

19   17

20

Spring St

V = Visitor Centre

1 Beehive Chimney	11 Church of ngland
2 Caledonian Battery	12 Progress all
3 Hospital	13 Museum (Market)
4 Restaurant	14 Supermarket
5 Denominational Sch.	15 Maldon Hotel
6 State Sch.	16 State Bank
7 Police Lockup	17 Royal otel
8 Court	18 Uniting hurch
9 Post Office	19 Bank
10 Athenaem	20 Flour Mill

H = House

0   1
KM

WALK ～

from the lookout following a pronounced spur crest and, after 600 m, note another road joining in from the right. This is the (later) route back down into the town, but first keep climbing 800 m west up to the Mount Tarrangower summit and three-tiered lookout for a really good 360° view. During the climb, which is through open dry forest, many wildflowers should be passed, especially in spring-time. Lunch at the lookout is suggested.

Descend back down the minor road for the 800 m, fork left to go down a further 500 m to a small reservoir at the western end of Fountain Street, then head east down the 600 m length of Fountain Street. The Uniting Church should be passed. It is on the right.

Opposite the church is an old Market Place which now houses a museum which is well worth inspecting. Turn left up High Street for one block to the red brick Post Office, then the Athenaeum Library and, opposite, an unusual brick house and the stone 1860 Anglican Church. Next see the State School on the left at the corner of Hospital Street, then *Glendonald* a house on the east side of High Street midway between Hospital and Adair Streets. Take a short side trip left to see the Hospital built in 1859. It is one block west at the corner of Chapel and Adair Streets. Keep walking north on High Street for two blocks, turn right into Franklin Street, then see a cottage on the corner of Franklin and Templeton Streets.

Continue one block further east and turn left into the continuation of Church Street. Turn right into Lowther Street and walk past the Union Mine which is on the left, then turn right into Reef Street to see the Eaglehawk Restaurant, one block south. It is a very interesting building made of red brick like many of the town's important buildings. Go southwards in Reef Street, note the small Government Gold Battery on the left at Adair Street, then south again and turn left into Hornsby Street (Bendigo Road) to complete a short side trip to the Railway Station. Next visit the conspicuous Beehive Chimney, 25 m high; head south again, then continue through Main Street noting Dickensons' Supermarket building on the right and Maldon Hotel and Stables, then the State Bank and the Royal Hotel on the left.

Back on High Street, still heading south, see Oswalds' bluestone cottage on the right and the ruins of the Caledonian Crushing Battery on the left, then fork left onto Castlemaine Road and walk the final 400 m back to the gold memorial cairn.

9.5 km; 3 hours; walk last reviewed January 1987; 'B' grade; easy walk; all on tracks and roads; features National Trust Classified buildings; water not available for lunch on Mount Tarrangower; walk suited to any time of the year; *Map:* 45, page 227.

CALADENIA

64   MELVILLE CAVES

Melville Caves is a forested, hilly area north-west of Inglewood and Bendigo. It is a relatively dry and quite rocky place and derives its name from Captain Melville, the bushranger who once hid among the rocks in the many crevices and overhangs.

The district is well known for bird life, especially

229

cockatoos and galahs, and also for its wide range of flora. The Kooyoora Park establishment recognizes these attractions.

There are good picnic facilities and an extensive network of foot tracks to the numerous points of interest. This walk suggestion involves easy walking along the longest of the constructed foot tracks in the picnic ground vicinity.

Start walking from the picnic area which is just south of the rocky hill known itself as Melville Caves. Walk south-east up the tarred road for 500 m to the second foot track branching off to the right. It is on the crest of an east-west ridge. Walk east on the foot track, forking left twice, so that you reach a viewpoint within about 400 m. From the viewpoint follow the foot track south-east down the rocky and open spur and note the interesting rock formations and views to the north and east especially. The track eventually crosses a very large rock slab well down the spur at a point where the land starts to flatten out, then it turns west and back north-west very shortly. The track then virtually follows the contour, generally westwards then northwards, back to the walk starting point at the picnic ground. Pieces of white quartz rock act as a guide for most of the route.

The beauty of the walk lies in the variety of flora and fauna combined with views and rock formations, so it is important that you do not rush and that you walk quietly if you are to see the wildlife. Wattle is a particular attraction during early spring.

5 km; 2 hours; walk last reviewed January 1987; 'B' grade, family walk; all on tracks; features open forest, rocks and birdlife; carry water for lunch; suited to any time of year, but hot in summer; *Maps: National Mapping 1:100,000 Dunolly* **refers as does Map 46, page 231.**

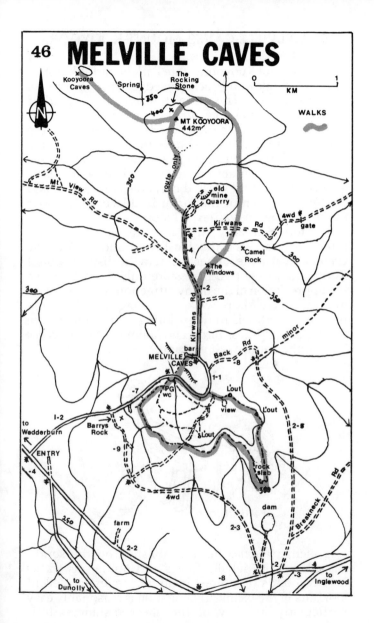

46 MELVILLE CAVES

Kooyoora Caves

Spring

The Rocking Stone

350

400

MT KOOYOORA 442m

route only

WALKS

N

Mt View Rd

350

old mine Quarry

Kirwans Rd

1·7

4wd gate

Camel Rock

300

Kirwans Rd

The Windows

·4

·2

350

300

minor

bar

Back Rd

MELVILLE CAVES

·8

·4

1·1

PG wc

·7

L'out

view

L'out

1·2

to Wedderburn

Barrys Rock

·9

L'out

2·5

ENTRY

·4

rock slab

300

4wd

dam

Breakneck Rd

250

farm

2·2

2·3

·2

to Dunolly

·8

·3

to Inglewood

0 KM 1

231

The creation of Kooyoora State Park in park-like forest west of Inglewood acknowledges the worth of Melville Caves. This is a forest with a marked difference to those of other Victorian areas. It is relatively dry and barren, yet the low hills have a real fascination. There are huge granite tors, balancing rocks, shelters, overhangs, caves and colourful rock markings, and an abundance of birdlife, particularly galahs and sulphur crested cockatoos. In August and September much of the forest is ablaze with colour especially due to wattles in bloom.

The forest is fairly large but the section of most interest to walkers is that locality around the Melville Caves and also the highest point in the district, Mount Kooyoora. These two places are only 3 km apart, so full appreciation of the many attractions can be gained in a relatively short walk. It is suggested that you wander about, leisurely exploring and enjoying the geological oddities, birds and animals. Main access is from the south-west entrance.

EMU CHICKS

A picnic site has been established on the south-east slopes of Melville Caves and numerous tracks lead to points of interest including several excellent lookouts in the vicinity. Navigation is reasonably easy particularly in view of the short distances. It is probably best to be at the walk area very early in the morning and while the animals are feeding follow some of the many short tracks in the vicinity of the picnic area. Wander among the rocks at Melville Caves themselves. Ponder over how much 'Captain Melville', the bushranger, must have enjoyed his stay among the caves amid such striking scenery. Afterwards walk north to the crest of the ridge of Mount Kooyoora via the Crystal Mine area, then have lunch.

The afternoon could be spent ambling and climbing round Kooyoora's peak and along the west-north-west ridge which has many interesting tors and overhangs. At Kooyoora Caves, there are numerous rock crevices wide enough to walk through. These

RED BROWED FINCH

are quite deep and worthy of investigation. After a good look round, return south via the eastern slopes of Mount Kooyoora and explore the gullies and bird habitats as you swing south. There are several ledges and window formations and numerous large granite tors along this return route southwards to the picnic area.

9 km; 4 hours to 5 hours; walk last reviewed January 1987; 'B' grade, medium walk, mostly across trackless open country; water scarce for most of the route; walk suited to autumn, winter, or spring; *Maps: National Mapping 1:100,000 Dunolly* refers as does Map 46, page 231.

A desert area south of Mildura strangely provides lovely walking country, especially during the cooler winter months when skies are often cloudless, similar to Central Australia. Summer can prove a bit hot and dry. The Murray River periodically floods desert channels and lakes and red gum trees proliferate near the water margins. Kangaroos, emus and water birds plus many birds of the parrot family all add interest. Part of the flood plain is zoned the Hattah-Kulkyne National Park.

EMU

A day walk around the main walking track circuit in the National Park should prove most rewarding. This track should be joined at the camping ground on the western end of Lake Hattah.

At the north-eastern end of the camp ground there is a small weir for controlling lake water levels. Cross this weir, then commence to walk along a sandy, low ridge track which lies just north of Lake Bulla's north shore and continue past the north side of Lake Brockie. The trail should be followed for 3.3 km to a junction, and along the way kangaroos and many varieties of parrots may be seen. The lakes are in view most of the way.

At the junction, double back north-east and follow a trail past the north end of Lake Tullah, a lake which is often dry, then, in about 1.5 km a further track junction should be reached not far from a high Kangaroo-proof fence. The spot has some broad open views eastwards and would be suitable for lunch, although there is no drinking water.

Next, walk along a track southwards into open sandy tracts and to areas of Buloke trees. Gradually swing south-west, then west, so that within about 3 km you are south of Lake Brockie where tracks join in from both north and south. Dry looking black box trees grow extensively in this area. As you head further west across blackened flood plain you should pass Lake Arawak, then return into sand dune country. About 2.3 km from this last junction a minor tourist road aligned east-west should be met. Walk 200 m west on the road to a road junction which is near the south shore of Lake Hattah. This road is a motorists' nature trail. Cross it and head down to the lake, then follow the shore right round to the park camp ground which is plainly visible.

On the way west, the red gum trees are most attractive as they spread out across the water. One large tree near the water's edge has bark removed, indicating it was used to make an aboriginal canoe. A little further west is an old pump station which supplied water for former steam trains passing through Hattah station.

12.5 km; 4 hours; last reviewed April 1987; 'B' grade, easy walk; mostly on tracks with a little easy lakeshore walking; features desert lakes; no water for lunch; summer walking too hot, but suited to any other season especially winter; *Maps: National Mapping 1:100,000 Mildura-Nowingi* refers as does Map 47, page 236.

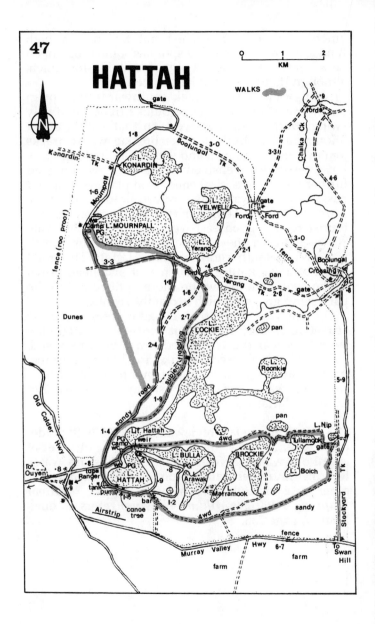

HATTAH

South of Mildura is a desert where the Murray River periodically floods a number of lakes. Red gum trees grow around these lakes and along watercourses feeding them and these features, plus an abundance of emus, kangaroos and waterbirds, all contribute to an excellent desert walking area. A section of the desert is designated as the Hattah Kulkyne National Park. Being a desert area with some extreme summer heat, it is occasionally necessary for walkers to be controlled by the Park Ranger. The ideal time for a walk in the district is winter, in fact it has become almost a tradition with many bushwalking clubs from Melbourne to head for Hattah for the June Queen's Birthday holiday weekend when, year after year, the skies seem to be cloudless and walkers escape Melbourne's dull winter.

There are times when water can be a problem for drinking but, on the other hand, the river occasionally floods in and swamps many low areas, drastically altering the shape of the lakes. For this reason it is difficult to draw a map of the lakes as their limits change so much. After a long dry period the lakes become quite brackish, so be prepared to carry drinking water.

A Park camping ground exists at the western end of Lake Hattah itself, which is 8 km east of Hattah railway station.

From the camp ground walk to the road intersection of Mournpall Track 300 m west then turn right along the sandy route to Lake Mournpall. After 1.4 km of walking in sand dune country, veer right onto a minor jeep track so as to head basically northwards for 4.6 km along the western shore of Lake Lockie. At times the jeep track gets flooded by the lake, in which case follow the western shore. There are large stands of Buloke trees in the area. The jeep track eventually joins another minor road near a watercourse which often links Lake Lockie with nearby Lake Yerang. The channel area is reached by turning right along the road a short distance. Remain on the west side of the channel—which can be dry—and walk north-west amid red gum trees so that within 700 m you arrive at a car park and the south-east corner of Lake Mournpall. This locality usually teems with bird life. Lunch is suggested at the spot.

WALLABY

Next walk the southern shore of Lake Mournpall westwards for 2 km to a picnic and camp area at the lake's western end. The whole of the lake shore sector of the walk features really big and beautiful red gums. Mournpall Track leads past the picnic area in a north-south direction and should be followed next. For 1 km go south into dune country, then, using a compass, leave the road and walk across the desert south-south-east for 3 km so as to rejoin Mournpall Track and cut short the road route. No doubt the desert walk will reveal a lot of kangaroos and emus. It will also permit you to fully appreciate the colourful dune landscapes.

Provided navigation is good, you should then have 2.2 km to walk the road southwards before reaching a road intersection just west of the Lake Hattah camp. If you have no compass—shame! You will miss an interesting shortcut and should instead remain on Mournpall Track for 7.9 km. Without the compass you would be unwise to leave the road, especially in the warmer months. The walk finishes with the retrace of the 300 m into the camp.

15.5 km; 4½ hours; walk last reviewed April 1987; 'C' grade; easy walk; mostly on minor roads, but with

3 km of cross country desert walking; features desert scenery and wildlife; CARRY WATER; walk unsuited to summer and best in winter; *Maps: National Mapping 1:100,000 Mildura-Nowingi* refers as does Map 47, page 236.

68   HOLLOW MOUNTAIN

The remarkable Mount Stapylton area, equally as good as Wonderland, is 30 km north-west of Halls Gap but remains virtually unnoticed by tourists. The road between the two points is very sandy and can be impassable after much rain, but is gradually being upgraded. One of the best spots near Mount Stapylton is Hollow Mountain. It is a fantastically wind-eroded spur of Mount Stapylton. Access is from the Halls Gap-Mount Zero Road 1.5 km short of the Mount Zero picnic area. Rocky conditions make this walk not suitable for the less agile and children aged less than about ten years. Start to walk at the Hollow Mountain Picnic Area which is within an old quarry. The Hollow Mountain Picnic Area is a favourite with rock climbers who frequent adjacent cliff faces.

Leave the southwest side of the quarry on a foot track south for 200 m, diverge right across a usually dry creek gully to link with a pad near the west bank, then walk 500 m slightly uphill south-east on a good foot track onto a low ridge, passing sandstone stacks and cliffs on the way. You then should meet a cliffline and need to walk 30 m to the left. At this spot, painted arrows on rocks indicate the route up through a cleft in the cliff and under overhanging cliff. It is necessary to climb steeply for some 200 m, bringing you to a high very broad sloping 'ledge' overlooking the valley. In places it is a bit of a scramble to reach the broad ledge. Next, climb slightly westwards to see a large rock window and overhang, climb through it and up onto its roof for a first class view. Also, a few metres south-west to cliff rims, there are good views of Flat Rock.

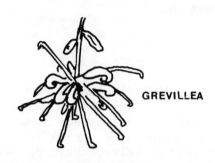

GREVILLEA

Return to the broad sloping ledge, then walk south-east to the base of the cliffs. Go to the cliffs on the north side of a wide split in the ridge. You will see that this spot, known as Hollow Mountain, is a series of wind-blown chambers. You should next climb the 'mountain' through its inside to emerge near the top. The inside passages are well lit by daylight and the climb is fairly easy and short. Painted arrows show the start of the climb which involves squeezing under a horizontal slit about seventy centimetres high, but many metres wide. You should reach a narrow ledge on the outside of the mountain from which a spectacular view of an amphitheatre to the south is obtained.

Please ensure that children do not deface the magnificent sandstone cave interiors by writing names, etc. Likewise do not light fires in the caves and so mar the white sand.

To reach the ridge top over Hollow Mountain, for bushwalkers there are only two alternative routes available. (Other alternatives are strictly for experienced rock-climbers.) The easiest way, providing you have good strong nerves, is to scale the slope directly from just west of the exit from the inside of the mountain. For those who worry about the drop at the edge of the ledge, take the awkward but safer route. It is just to the east of the exit from the mountain. It is a crack between two slabs of the cliff. The crack can be climbed by 'chimneying' into a small rock chamber above, then climbing through a hole in the low roof of the chamber. Once on the top of the mountain it is a fairly easy rock-hop and scramble along the ridge south-east. However, soon after reaching the ridge, an appalling looking chasm will be met. The chasm is very easy to jump across, but good nerves are needed. The opposite side of the gap is about 1.5 m lower. The gap is quite narrow but very deep. Many may prefer to make the chasm their turn around point for the walk. Others could explore the area a bit before returning by retracing the route.

Rock pools of water are often on the tops, but should not be used for lunch water if lunch is taken to the tops. Animals drink and contaminate the pools.

2.5 km; 2 hours; walk last reviewed April 1988; 'A' grade; medium walk; features rugged cliffs; *Maps: Vicmap 1:25,000 Mount Stapylton* refers as does Map 48, page 242.
* Warning: this walk is only suited to the more agile person.

69   FLAT ROCK-MOUNT STAPYLTON

At the extreme north end of the Grampians is the Mount Zero Picnic Ground just adjacent to Flat Rock. This locality, including nearby Mount Stapylton, would be about the most rugged in the Grampians with extremely good walking.

The remarkable Mount Stapylton area, equally as

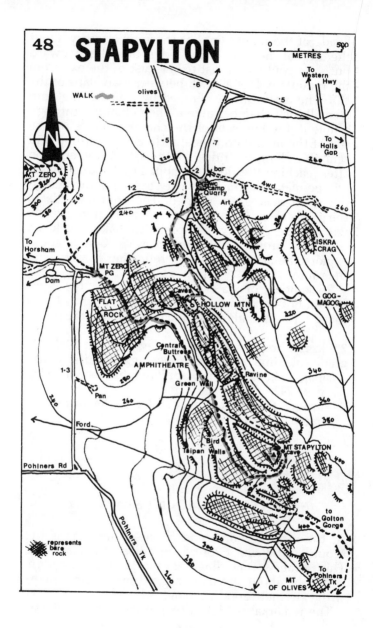

good as Wonderland, is 30 km north-west of Halls Gap yet remains virtually unnoticed by tourists. The road between the two points is very sandy and can be impassable after much rain, but is gradually being upgraded.

There is a good walking track from the picnic ground to Mount Stapylton, permitting access to some of the most scenic spots. The route is reasonably easy with the exception of the final 100 m or so right at Mount Stapylton summit. Some may prefer not to scale this last section in view of the exposure on the rock. The view just below the part exposed is almost as good as the top if the south approach is used.

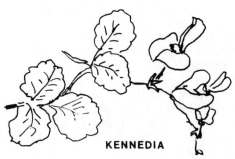

KENNEDIA

From the Mount Zero Picnic Ground, walk south-east up Flat Rock, a broad sandstone slope with about a 15° angle. Painted arrows on the rock indicate the route to follow. It tends a little to the left as it rises. At the top of Flat Rock, the pad is just south of a cliffline. It then descends slightly and crosses the floor of a huge amphitheatre on the southern side of Mount Stapylton. Massive colourful cliffs ring much of the amphitheatre and are a rock climbing venue.

Continue on the pad up from the amphitheatre south-east via a broad ramp and past a large bird-shaped rock just beside the track. The pad attains more level heights just south of Mount Stapylton summit and reaches a track junction 2 km from the walk start. Avoid the track down southwards (right to Pohlners Track) and continue round and over a small ridge into a hollow and ravine area just east of Stapylton summit. As the ravine rises and narrows, the pad divides right at a tiny gully and abutting rock.

From this point there are two routes to the peak summit. Here a decision must be made for both routes have their advantages and disadvantages. The left fork enables walkers to get very good views without reaching the top *if* they feel the rock is too exposed, while the right fork is the less exposed and far more walkers would be likely to get to the top, but there is no good view via the right fork *unless* the top is reached.

The left fork rises up bare, sloping rock immediately. It passes a big and lovely wind-scoured cave in the cliffs, right alongside the climbing route. Some 100 m up the slope is a rocky viewpoint where the route seemingly ends. The lookout is only about 40 m short of the actual summit. Many may prefer to go no further, but the adventurous can scramble up bare rock to reach the peak from this southern side. The latter 30 m is fairly easy. The summit is the highest point in the district and one gets a real appreciation of the rugged terrain. A short wander west, down the summit crest, is most rewarding before returning.

The right fork access to the summit involves walking only a few metres up the ravine to a narrow rock spine protruding east in the middle of the ravine. Scramble onto this spine and walk west up it. It joins onto the face of Mount Stapylton and from there climbers simply head up south to the top. Only one spot, about 3 m long, is awkward to negotiate and that occurs right where the spine joins the face. The difficulty at this spot is noted more on the return as the experience is really just a telling on one's nerves rather than the incurring of any physical difficulty. It is stressed that, if using this approach to the top, the access point to the face from the spine should be remembered for the return descent. It is hard to pin-point at any time.

After climbing Mount Stapylton, simply retrace the route back to the walk start.

5.5 km; 2¼ hours; walk last reviewed April 1988; 'A' grade; easy walk; features rugged cliffs; *Maps: Vicmap 1:25,000 Mt Stapylton and 1:25,000 Lah-arum* refer as does Map 48, page 242.
* Warning: The final ascent of the peak is suited only to the more agile.

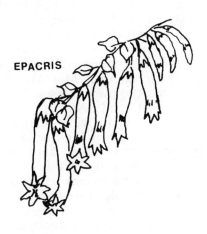

EPACRIS

70   BEEHIVE FALLS-BRIGGS BLUFF

A walk to Briggs Bluff provides an unforgettable experience, one likely to be remembered for life. It is through some of the best walking country in Victoria. There is a foot track all the way, but it is rough in places and sturdy footwear is essential. The walk is not suitable for children under about ten years of age. The track commences about 800 m west of the intersection of the Halls Gap to Mount Zero Road and Roses Gap Road. A small car park exists at the start on the side of Roses Gap Road.

Initially, a broad, fairly level track leads south 700 m to a spot once used for camping. The track then narrows considerably and leads 400 m south-west up the west bank of Mud Hut Creek to a log and ford crossing of that creek. Next, walk up the east bank for 500 m to reach lovely, 25 m high Beehive Falls. The cliffs in this area get very colourful at times when the sun is low. Cross the creek below the falls and scramble up a steep track till the cliff's top is reached. A second, usually dry, small fall should be passed during this short ascent.

The pad swings south-west then south-east, to cross a gully and ascend into wild, rocky, sandstone terrain. Continue up past many rocky turrets, ravines and escarpments, then swing south-west onto a ridge. Clifflines abound in this locality. There is a very pretty stream gully just to the east of the pad. About 2 km from Beehive Falls, the track crosses a broad saddle after swinging east, and rises up towards most impressive cliffs with many wind-scoured caverns in them. An arch exists across the track and then the pad swings north-east to reach the main cliff tops. From here, 2.6 km from Beehive Falls, walk down the left fork pad. It soon swings north to lead along bare rock near a cliff top, then across a couple of minor streams and up the rocky slopes of Briggs Bluff. It is about a kilometre from the track junction to the bluff crest.

If you dislike heights, keep away from the bluff's northern face as there is a 400 m drop over the rim. However, the views are nothing short of spectacular. The spot would be good for a lunch break (without water). Return to the walk start by retracing the same pads.

10.5 km; 4½ hours; walk last reviewed April 1988; 'A' grade, easy walk; all on tracks; features Briggs Bluff and wild sandstone terrain; no water for lunch at Briggs Bluff, but sometimes creek water available in other areas of the walk route; walk suited to any

71   TROOPERS CREEK-MOUNT DIFFICULT

Geologically, the Mount Difficult Range is most interesting as it consists of a huge synclinal structure or basin with Lake Wartook in the middle and the surrounding ranges forming the rim of the basin. Mount Difficult itself is a high rugged point on the basin's western rim and the peak permits superb views of the geological formation. Also, to the north-west there are views of the folding and twisting of the lower adjacent sandstone ranges. Mount Difficult is sufficiently high above the surrounding country to enable an almost aerial view of the structures. Any view from it is a very informative experience for budding geologists.

The peak can be climbed by foot track from north, east or west sides. The route described here is the more strenuous one from Troopers Picnic Ground to the west of the mountain. Troopers was once the site of a Police Post on the old Melbourne to Adelaide Road (now called Roses Gap Road). The police at the post aimed to protect the men travelling to the Victorian goldfields. The climb from Troopers to Mount Difficult is steep and time consuming, but most rewarding. It is best to take lunch and water and make a day of the trip. There is rarely water available on the peak.

The pad leaves the picnic area adjacent to some toilets to the south-east. Follow the track up east-south-east and, within 300 m, arrive at a large sandstone boulder with a wind-scour in it known as Wind Cave. The pad encircles the boulder and there is a fork track off left to Tilwinda Falls. The

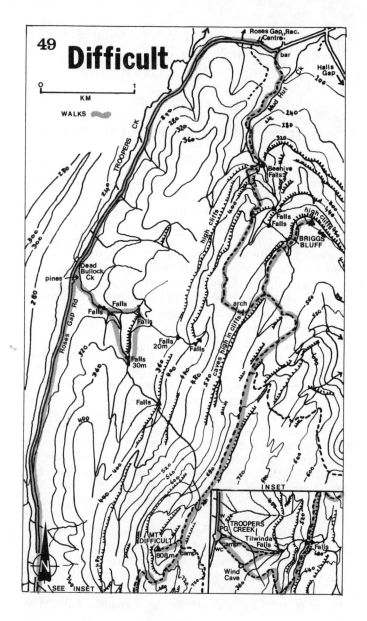

49 Difficult

WALKS

Roses Gap Rec. Centre

bar

Halls Gap

Mud Hut Ck

TROOPERS CK

Beehive Falls

high cliffs

Falls Falls

high cliffs

BRIGGS BLUFF

Dead Bullock Ck

pines

Roses Gap Rd

Falls

Falls

Falls

arch

Falls 20m

Falls

Falls 30m

caves high in cliffs

Falls

INSET

MT DIFFICULT

808 m

camp

TROOPERS CREEK

w PG

Tilwinda Falls

camp

WC

Falls

Wind Cave

SEE INSET

N

248

route to take is up the slope, which gets steeper and steeper. The pad zig-zags to gain elevation.

It then reaches the base of some high cliffs 1.2 km from Troopers and considerably higher. The cliffs are a favourite spot for rock climbers.

Turn left and head along the pad at the cliff base north-north-east for 1.4 km. The track contours under huge overhangs, across rock ledge areas, past some falls and a rugged associated gorge then begins to rise significantly to the cliff rim. Just as the cliff top is reached after a hairpin bend and bush is much less dense, there is a large rock on the right of the track from which good views can be gained. It is a

GREVILLEA

good place for a rest after the ascent. It is then 500 m up across the tops to the junction of a track from the east side of the mountain. On the approach to the junction several usually dry, rocky watercourses are crossed. There is a small camp area at the junction. Next, walk north on the pad towards Briggs Bluff, but within 150 m turn left onto rock. Head to the south-west and within 250 m the summit rock cairn of Mount Difficult should be attained. The 808 m high 360° view includes much of the entire Grampians system of ranges. There is an excellent view of Troopers Creek area over 400 m below, and one wonders how any track could negotiate the distance and the cliffs between the two points.

The return walk is a retrace of the climb except that at Wind Cave walkers may like to turn right and make the short detour to Tilwinda Falls. The extra distance is only 500 m and there is a direct pad from the falls to Troopers Creek Picnic Ground so there is no need to return back past Wind Cave. However, the falls are small and can be dry in late summer.

6.5 km; 4 hours; last reviewed April 1988; 'A' grade, medium walk; all on tracks; features Mount Difficult's rocky summit; normally no water on tops for lunch; walk suited to any time of the year; *Maps: Vicmap 1:25,000 Mount Difficult* refers as does Map 49, page 248.

72 BRIGGS BLUFF-MT DIFFICULT

This walk circuit includes both the Briggs Bluff walk (No 70) and the Mt Difficult walk (No 71) plus an overnight camp at the Troopers Creek Picnic Ground. The circuit is suitable for only the more agile walker. It includes some of the most beautiful terrain in the Grampians. The start and end is near Roses Gap.

Follow directions as indicated for walk seventy but drop packs at the turnoff and take a side trip 1 km each way to the summit of Briggs Bluff before continuing southwards to Mount Difficult. Avoid the left fork track 1 km south of the Briggs Bluff turnoff so as to walk south-south-west 2 km. Much of this section is close to the base of cliffs and through very rocky country with good westerly views. The turnoff to the summit of Mount Difficult should then be reached and again packs could be dropped for the short side trip to the lofty summit at 808 m above sea level. The side track is across extremely rocky terrain and is some 250 m long. The view from the summit is very interesting geologically in that a huge syncline containing Lake Wartook is included. The twisting lower adjacent ranges are also noteworthy. Troopers Creek drains the deep valley westwards and is the goal for the day. If time is short however, there is a small waterless camp area just 150 m south of the junction of the side track to Mount Difficult. It is 3.1 km from this camp spot down to the large comfortable camp area at Troopers Creek, but the rocky conditions cause progress to be slow. In proceeding to Troopers Creek, avoid the track off east from the camp spot and start the descent south-west.

PLATYLOBIUM TRIANGULATUM

Within 500 m the top of the main cliffs are reached and you need to walk down round a hairpin bend to get below the cliffs. It is then a 1.4 km-long walk, basically at the cliff base, before a further sharp descent can be made to Troopers Creek via some zig zags and past Wind Cave. The distance from the cliff base to the main camp near the creek is 1.2 km, of which the last 300 m is below the Wind Cave contour. It is probably best to omit the possible short detour into the camp from Wind Cave via Tilwinda Falls.

The second day's walk includes 7.4 km along quiet Roses Gap Road to complete the circuit. Whilst clearly a car shuttle would obviate the road walk, it is suggested that the walk be undertaken. It is basically a downhill route always near to Troopers Creek. In winter and in spring the wattles in flower are magnificent and for much of the distance there are good views eastwards up to the massive cliffs of Mount Difficult.

It is also suggested that a break be taken at Dead Bullock Creek, and that packs be left whilst a short exploratory side trip is taken south-eastwards to the many lovely waterfalls on Dead Bullock Creek and its tributaries. There are five falls within 1 km of the road. There are a further four falls upstream and one fall has a 30 m drop. No tracks exist to connect the road and falls, so good navigation is needed. The scrub can be thick, so leg and arm protection is needed. Dead Bullock Creek crosses Roses Gap Road some 3 km short of the walk end. Allow an hour for the 3 km walk and spend time at the falls for as long as possible. A good plan would be to follow the streams and walk a triangular route by way of cliff tops linking two of the better falls (as indicated on Map 49) totalling some 2.6 km of off-track walking.

23.3 km, 11 hours spread over two days of 13.3 km, 6 hours and 10.0 km, 5 hours; last reviewed April 1988; 'A' grade medium overnight walk on tracks and roadway except for 2.6 km of optional trackless scrub; features Briggs Bluff and Mount Difficult; walk suited to any season but better to avoid summer and early autumn heat; *Maps: Vicmap 1:25,000 Mount Difficult and Mount Stapylton sheets* refer as does Map 49, page 248.

73   THE FORTRESS

Perhaps the most impressive peak in the Grampians is The Fortress. It is high on the crest of the remote central part of the Victoria Range and its rugged features make it a rock climber's venue. Any walk to it should include exploration. Tracks used mainly by rock climbers lead around part of the peak and in many places one can scramble about to gain pinnacles and attain lofty ledges from which there are good views.

The Fortress area is some of the wildest country in the Grampians and indeed in Victoria. Adjacent are the extremely wild Deep Creek valley and the Honeysuckle Creek valley. Only fit persons should attempt this walk route which starts at a road barrier across the Deep Creek jeep track where it leaves Harrops Track south of Buandik and the Billywing Pine Plantations.

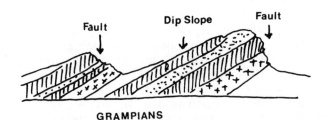

GRAMPIANS

Initially walk east on Deep Creek jeep track for 600 m on a flat sandy track. The foot track to be taken then forks off to the right (south) and immediately begins the long climb which persists until almost at campsite. The foot track ascends to the crest of a long spur and leads basically south-east, on the crest for much of the distance. Wildflowers seem particularly prolific in the area. About 3 km from the walk start and some 300 m higher in elevation, the track leads round the south side of a knob on the spur then soon after, starts to sidle the northern side of the spur. About 3.7 km from the start the track suddenly leaves the spur area and turns sharp left, steeply down from a small saddle and adjacent to a cliffline, to reach a creekbed within some 300 m. The wild nature of the gully makes location of the track difficult once the creekbed is reached.

Camp spots, however, exist just upstream under massive sandstone cliff overhangs and in caves. It is suggested that camp be established in this location. Probably rock climbers will also be present as the spot is very popular with climbers.

Immediately upstream of the camp cave area, the foot track continues. It rises eastwards up a long ravine close by the dramatic cliffs of The Fortress. After settling into camp, head off to explore The Fortress area via the track up the ravine. Some 200 m elevation is gained, then the track leads south-east along the northern side of The Fortress complex to its eastern end, 1.5 km from camp. At a number of points pads can be seen and explored as they head onto the peaks, ledges and platforms and among ravines. Take great care if the rock is at all wet or slippery and take notice of your location at all times. The locality is so rugged and so complicated that it is easy to loose bearings. Once back at camp it is a most pleasant experience to find some rocky point at sunset from which to see the change of colour of the huge west-facing rock faces as the sun sinks in the west.

The Fortress is so interesting that most people visiting the area will no doubt wish to spend more time on the morning of the second day exploring the area upstream of the camp cave area. They could then, after an early lunch, retrace the track back along and down the spur to the Deep Creek jeep track and walk's end.

An option is to undertake the very short Cave of Hands walk (No 74) in this book after completing the walk to The Fortress. This other walk starts just across Deep Creek and at the creek there is a campsite and good water.

11.5 km; 7 hours spread over two days of 7 km, 5½ hours and 4.5 km, 1½ hours; last reviewed April 1988; 'A' grade medium overnight walk on tracks basically; features extremely rocky peak; walk suited to any

**ASTROLOMA
CRANBERRY HEATH**

74   CAVE OF HANDS

In the western Victoria Range there is a lot of aboriginal rock art. Most sites are in hard-to-find places, but a few are accessible and protected by wire mesh screens. The Cave of Hands is one rock art site which is well worth visiting. It has some of the better-preserved art and like many other sites is in an overhang facing north. There are many red ochre

**ROCK
ART**

stencilled hands in the artwork. There are thought to imply ownership of land as far as the eye can see. The rock-stack containing the art is well worth climbing for a view. It can be climbed from the south-east side. Harrops Track, a minor road, gives vehicular access south from the Buandik area at the base of the western side of the Victoria Range. Travel this

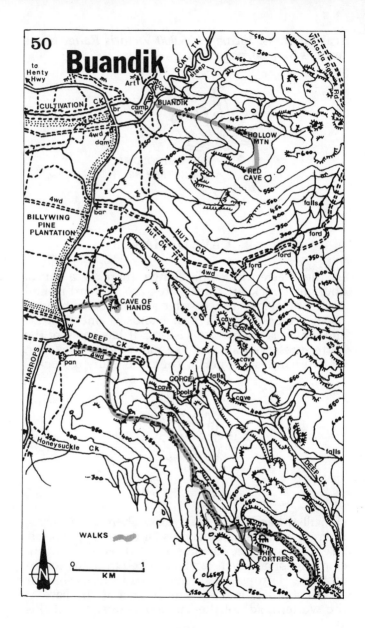

50
Buandik

to
Henty
Hwy

GOAT TK
steep

Victoria Range Rd.

CULTIVATION   CK
br
camp
wc

wc
PC
BUANDIK

Art

HOLLOW
MTN

RED
CAVE

4wd
dam

falls

ford

4wd
bar

BILLYWING
PINE
PLANTATION

HUT   CK

Hut Ck Tk

falls
ford

4wd   ford
ford

CAVE OF
HANDS

cave
cave

cave

HARRORS

DEEP   CK

w

bar   4wd
pan

cave

GORGE   falls
cave   pools
cave

Honeysuckle   Ck

falls

DEEP   CK

WALKS

THE
FORTRESS

N

0   1
KM

256

road for 2.7 km south-south-west of the road junction just west of Buandik Picnic Ground. The Billywing pine plantation should be on the right (west) during the drive. A sandy road then forks off left for 200 m to a car park serving the Cave of Hands. A gate prevents traffic proceeding to the cave.

Commence walking and head up east for a kilometre to a very prominent sandstone bluff. There is a minor intersecting jeep track as you climb east to the bluff. It should be passed. At the left (north) side of the bluff, the sandy road terminates and a foot track leads south 50 m to the rock art site in the cave. Right near the end of the road there is a very minor jeep track off north (left) and it should be avoided. After a look at the art, climb the rock-stack for a view. Head round the east side of the rock, then scale it from the south-east. There are good views of much of the western Victoria Range. The return walk suggestion is to retrace the same track. **Note** that National Parks plans include an intention to realign and upgrade the access track to the Cave of Hands in the future. The realignment is likely to be via the more northerly jeep track approach.

2 km; 1½ hours; walk last reviewed April 1988; 'A' grade, family walk; all on tracks; no water available in vicinity of walk; walk suited to any season; *Maps: Vicmap 1:25,000 Victoria Range* refers as does Map 50, page 256.

75   BUANDIK PICNIC GROUND-RED CAVE

The western slopes of the Victoria Range have a number of large and interesting wind-scoured sandstone caves. Two of the better examples are Hollow Mountain and Red Cave, both of which are not far from the Buandik picnic and camp area. When visiting the caves, walkers are reminded not to light fires in them and so spoil the lovely white sand and formations. Children should be instructed never to deface these caves with graffiti. There have been recent suggestions for construction of a foot track to the Red Cave area, but currently intending visitors still need to scrub-bash in quite light scrub.

THELYMITRA

From the entrance to Buandik Picnic Ground on the Goat Track head off 1.4 km east-south-east directly up a broad spur in light forest. As the crest of the spur is climbed, you will see a small cave and be forced by rugged terrain to skirt the northern side of the rocky knob in which Hollow Mountain is located. That knob is the easternmost in the locality. The cave is concealed and high up. To get to it you should scale a small gully on the north face. The cave would be 50 m wide and has a dress circle formation inside it.

The next objective is Red Cave, easily seen from Hollow Mountain. It lies south across a valley. To reach it, 1 km distant, scrub-bash to the east end of the cliffline in which Red Cave is located, then walk along the cliff tops to a porthole in the cave's roof. Its grandeur can then be viewed through the porthole before retracing the route back to Buandik.

5 km; 2½ hours; last reviewed April 1988; 'A' grade, easy walk; no tracks and light scrub so good

navigation is essential; no water for lunch; walk suited to any time of year. *Maps: Vicmap 1:25,000 Victoria Range* refers as does Map 50, page 256.

76 STONY PEAK-TOWER HILL-CALECTASIA FALLS

In western Victoria in the Grampians and west of Mount Rosea is some delightful wild country into which few walkers seem to venture. It is an area frequented more often by rock climbers. The district has many sharp rock faces and rock stacks such as those found on Stony Peak and at Tower Hill. The streams too are rather pleasant in the area. Mount Rosea Creek has delightful Calectasia Falls on it. A most enjoyable walk could be taken from the junction of Stony Creek Road and Mount Rosea Track some 2.3 km west of Mount Rosea Picnic Ground.

The suggestion is to walk from the junction south to Stony Peak, then on to Tower Hill and the falls. One could drive along part of Mount Rosea Track, but it is better to walk this minor road which is rough and is sometimes closed due to bad weather anyway. The best lunch site is at the waterfalls. These falls are fairly big and there is a very pleasant cascade area just above the main drop. The region is remote, so ensure that any young children do not get separated along the track.

First walk 900 m south along Mount Rosea Track to a pad off right up to Stony Peak. Climb that pad westwards through a gap in the cliffs. The pad is a little indistinct at times. The viewing point from the cliff rim south of the gap is easiest to reach. The view from that spot is particularly good and includes Tower Hill to the south. Next, return to Mount Rosea Track and walk south 1.1 km to a ford and small

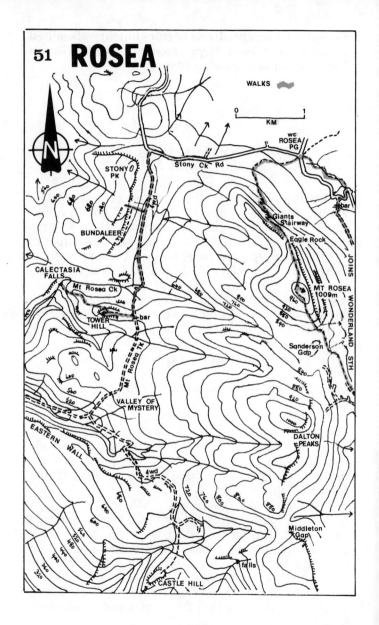

51 ROSEA

WALKS

N

0   KM   1

wc
ROSEA
PG

Stony Ck Rd

STONY
Pk

4wd

bar

Giants
Stairway

Eagle Rock

BUNDALEER

JOINS WONDERLAND STH

CALECTASIA
FALLS

Mt Rosea Ck

MT ROSEA
1009m

TOWER
HILL   bar

Mt Rosea Tk

Sanderson
Gap

VALLEY OF
MYSTERY

EASTERN
WALL

DALTON
PEAKS

4wd

Middleton
Gap

falls

CASTLE HILL

260

camp area just to the right of the road, then walk a further 500 m up to the road crest just east of Tower Hill. A small pad leads off west on the crest. Take it, and within 500 m reach Tower Hill rock stack. There are several awkward spots to scale on the way.

Unless one is a rock climber it is best not to try and climb the rock stack. Superb views to the Victoria Valley and Moora Moora Reservoir are to be had. The Western Wall looms in the south. Each of these can be fully appreciated from the rock stack base. just 100 m before reaching the rock stack, and just before the final short sharp ascent to the ridge, a fork foot pad leads off west to Calectasia Falls. Follow it for 750 m west-north-west, initially descending steeply, then gradually, to arrive at the falls. The rest of the day's walk involves climbing back up the foot pad to the Mount Rosea Track, then returning along that minor road.

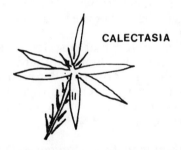

CALECTASIA

8 km; 3½ hours; walk last reviewed April 1988; 'A' grade, easy walk; all on tracks; features rock stacks and Calectasia Falls; water for lunch at falls; walk suited to any time of the year but best in spring; *Maps: Vicmap 1:25,000 Halls Gap Special or 1:25,000 Moora Moora* refers as does Map 51, page 260.

77   MOUNT ROSEA PICNIC GROUND-MOUNT ROSEA

Mount Rosea at 1,009 m above sea level is one of the highest points in the Halls Gap area. Much of the mountain, like the rest of the Grampians, is sandstone, but a volcanic intrusion exists at the so called Grand Stairway. The sandstone is well weathered and the resulting escarpment rim permits wonderful views.

Start a walk at the Mount Rosea Picnic Ground, where a track to Mount Rosea 2.8 km away leads off south-west from the road junction. It is a steady climb all the way. As the pad is followed, pass the Grand Stairway, Eagle Point and The Gate of the East Wind. These names are somehow very fitting for such a rocky place. The last part of the climb, after attaining the escarpment rim, is up a sloping, rock-strewn plateau. At the summit there is virtually a 360° view and the rugged beauty of the Grampians can be fully appreciated.

It should be noted that just 150 m short of the summit cairn there is a foot pad that leads off south. It leads all the way down to Borough Huts in the valley in the opposite direction, so avoid it and return to the Picnic Ground by simply retracing the route up to Mount Rosea.

5.6 km; 2¼ hours; walk last reviewed April 1988; 'B' grade walk; medium standard; all on tracks; carry water for lunch; features views; suited to any season; *Maps: Vicmap 1:25,000 Halls Gap Special* refers as does Map 51, page 260.

In the Grampians a very interesting walk can be
undertaken from Mount Rosea Picnic Area. A good
track scales the cliff face of Mount Rosea via the Grand
Stairway to the cliff rim. The pad then leads up
gradually through very eroded sandstone rocks to
a summit cairn and superb views (See walk 77 for
directions to the summit.) Just 150 m short of the
summit, another pad leads off south. After lunch
descend this pad southwards. It leads to Borough
Huts in the Fyans Creek Valley, but turn left where
it first meets and crosses a jeep track on a spur
2 km from Mount Rosea, and follow the jeep track.

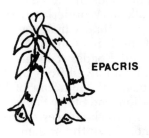

EPACRIS

Continue generally north on this jeep track, known
as Burma Track, in lovely forest. Eventually, after
skirting round the headwaters of Sawpit Creek and
the eastern flanks of Mount Rosea, meet Silverband
Road. Turn right and go 200 m down to Delleys Dell
to join a ferny foot pad up the valley of Dairy Creek
back to Mount Rosea Picnic Ground.

**10km; 5 hours; walk last reviewed April 1988; 'B'
grade, medium walk; all on tracks; features Mount
Rosea summit views; carry water for lunch as water
scarce throughout circuit; walk suited to any time
of the year** *Maps: Vicmap 1:25,000 Halls Gap Special*
refers as does map 53, page 271.

In the Grampians National Park, one of the better walks from Wonderland Turntable must surely be to climb up to Boroka Lookout. The climb is relatively long and involves an ascent of about 400 m. The track rises constantly over about 4 km, giving an average gradient of about one in ten. The reward at the top is a superb view east out over the Halls Gap area and to such distant places as the Major Mitchell Plateau, Lake Fyans, Lake Lonsdale and Lake Bellfield, plus Chatauqua Peak closer by. Wonderland and the Mount William Range dominate the scene. There are picnic facilities at the lookout, so lunch could be eaten while you rest and look at the view.

Start the walk at Wonderland Turntable beside Stony Creek rather than where the track crosses the intersection of the Halls Gap to Mount Victory and short Wonderland Roads. A lovely streamside foot track can then be followed from the turntable down Stony Creek, past the Guardian of the Canyon, an odd rock formation, and Stony Falls. Some 500 m from the turntable, the track crosses to the west bank for the second time. Leave the stream at this point and climb to the Mount Victory Road-Wonderland Turntable Road intersection, 250 m further on. Cross the junction to the start of the main Boroka Lookout track.

The climb which follows will take some people a lot longer than others. The really fit might take only an hour and a quarter. Initially the pad leads along a short flattish section then goes uphill. The route is through fairly open timber and there are good views from a number of points. The Mount Difficult Range escarpment is scaled in the process, so the route is often rocky and beautiful. The lookout is serviced by road, but it is a far more enjoyable experience to walk to it. Lunch at the lookout should be most pleasant because of the views and facilities. For the return walk, simply retrace the route. The descent will take even fit walkers close to an hour. It is better not to rush such a nice walk.

PULTENAEA

9 km; 4 hours; walk last reviewed April 1988; 'B' grade, easy walk; all on tracks; features Boroka Lookout; no water for lunch along route; walk suited to any time of year but best in spring; *Maps: Vicmap 1:25,000 Halls Gap Special* refers as does Map 52, page 267.

80   SUNDIAL TURNTABLE-SUNDIAL PEAK

Geologists tell us that approximately twenty million years ago the Grampians Ranges formed a promontory jutting out into the sea which then covered the surrounding countryside.

This easy walk suggestion that crosses some slopes and then virtually level country enables one to appreciate the forces of nature in geological creation on a grand scale.

The track starts at Sundial Turntable picnic ground which can be easily reached from Halls Gap via Wonderland, Silverband and Sundial Roads. Two features of the area illustrating the theory of its geological history are the sandstone cliffs at places such as Sundial Peak and the coastal vegetation which tells its own story.

As the track leads south, first through open forest, you see numerous heaths, grass trees, banksias, native pines and other plants typical of many areas, but as you approach the upper part of the 'dip slope' and scarp area you will see a different type of banksia, the *Banksia Integrifolia*. They are also known as Coast Banksias and can be recognized by their leaves which are dark green on one side and white on the other. The flowers are cylindrical and pale yellow. As you reach Sundial Peak numerous Coast Banksias will be seen on the rocky bluff area. The track is very easy to follow, but just before reaching Sundial Peak a track leads off steeply downhill westwards to Delley's Dell, Silverband Falls and the Bellfield settlement, and this track should be ignored. The last few hundred metres sees the main track dropping down around the western side of the headland then climbing up onto Sundial Peak itself.

At the peak there are truly magnificent views over Lake Bellfield and Halls Gap. It would be a good place for lunch, but there is no water supply, so come prepared. Retrace the outward route after lunch back to Sundial Turntable.

3.5 km; 1½ hours; walk last reviewed April 1988; 'B' grade; easy walk; all on tracks; carry water; walk suited to any season; *Maps: Vicmap 1:25,000 Halls Gap Special* refers as does Map 53, page 271.

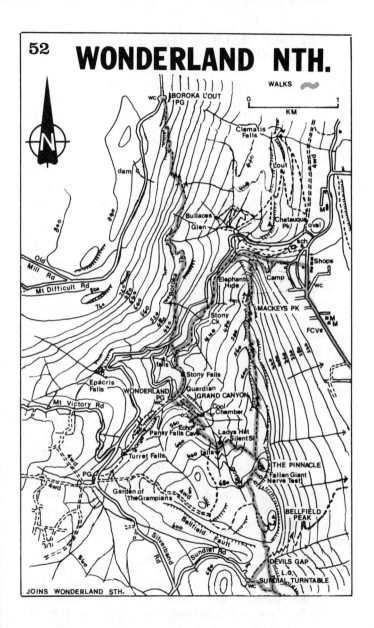

WONDERLAND NTH.

WALKS

0   KM   1

N

wc BOROKA L'OUT
PG

Clematis
Falls

dam

l'out

4wd

Buliaces
Glen

Chatauqua
Pk

oval

Old
Mill Rd

Mt Difficult Rd

sch

Shops

Camp

wc

Elephants
Hide

MACKEYS PK

Stony
Ck

FCVs

falls

Stony Falls

Epacris
Falls

WONDERLAND
PG

Guardian
GRAND CANYON

Mt Victory Rd

Cool
Chamber

Echo

Pansy Falls Cave

Ladys Hat
Silent St

THE PINNACLE

4wd

Turret Falls

falls

Fallen Giant
Nerve Test)

PG

4wd

Garden of
TheGrampians

4wd

BELLFIELD
PEAK

Bellfield Fault

Silverband
Rd

Sundial Rd

DEVILS GAP
l.o.

SUNDIAL TURNTABLE
wc

81   SUNDIAL TURNTABLE-LAKEVIEW
LOOKOUT-THE PINNACLE

The Pinnacle is perhaps the best cliff rim view in
Wonderland. The view includes Halls Gap and the
Fyans Creek Valley. There are three walking tracks
converging on The Pinnacle Lookout and the easiest
approach is from the south at Sundial Turntable via
Devils Gap. There are picnic facilities at the turntable.
Another excellent lookout named Lakeview can be
visited by adding a very short detour from the direct
route to The Pinnacle. The majority of the walk route
is close to the Wonderland Escarpment rim.

From the turntable head east 600 m along the foot
track to Lakeview to see the view of Bellfield Lake
and the Mount William Range across Fyans Creek
Valley. About 200 m short of the lookout, a track leads
north-west to Devils Gap, 600 m from Lakeview. Take
this track. A second rim view exists about midway
between Lakeview and Devils Gap. At the gap which
is the Bellfield geological fault line, pass tracks off
left and right and climb the 60 m high faultline pad
via a few hairpin bends, then follow the pad
northwards. About 600 m from Devils Gap, the track
divides temporarily. Take either track but, if using
the easternmost (right) track, ignore a fork off right
to Bellfield Peak a few metres from its start. In this
area much of the walking is along bare ribs of
sandstone across reasonably level terrain. Shortly
after the two tracks rejoin, another pad off left to
Stony Creek should be passed, and within a few more
metres a saddle should be met immediately south
of The Pinnacle area. Another pad veers off west at
this saddle for 100 m to a small gorge and water
supply. The gorge is worthy of a quick look. Next,
scale some sandstone rocks and walk north-east to
the Nerve Test 100 m away. The Nerve Test is
"reasonably" safe if the nerves are steady. Just
50 m north-east of it is The Fallen Giant, a huge slab
of sandstone which has fractured away from the cliff

rim. North again 100 m is The Pinnacle Lookout. It is enclosed with fencing for safety and affords an excellent panorama to Halls Gap and the Fyans Valley.

To return to Sundial Turntable, retrace the same route back as far as Devils Gap. It is then only 500 m of flat walking, via the right fork trail from the Gap south-west back to the turntable.

4.5 km; 2¼ hours; walk last reviewed April 1988; 'A' grade; family walk; all on tracks; carry water; walk suited to any season; *Maps: Vicmap 1:25,000 Halls Gap Special* refers as do Maps 52 and 53, pages 267 and 271.

HOVEA

82   WONDERLAND-THE PINNACLE

This walk features the pick of Wonderland's geological interest and scenery. Wear sturdy footwear as the way is frequently across rock. The route is one of the most popular with visitors to the Grampians and has the advantage of proximity to the main Halls Gap tourist area.

From the shops walk to the rear of the camp area opposite so as to reach the north-west end. From there follow a good foot track west up the valley of Stony Creek. Almost as soon as you enter bushland, diverge right at a fork so as to remain near to Stony Creek. The alternative track is the return route. About 1 km from the shops, amid lovely ferny bushland, cross the creek at a spot known as Venus Baths then continue upstream as the track leads south-west, initially past the base of massive Elephants Hide (a rock face adjacent to the east side of the valley). Some 2.4 km from the walk start, cross a foot bridge at track intersections then head on upstream on the east bank for the short rocky distance to Stony Falls. Re-cross the stream at the small falls and climb a short distance on a ridge to reach the main Wonderland car park and picnic area. Lunch is suggested using the picnic facilities, 3 km from the walk start.

Next, cross Stony Creek and immediately diverge left so as to walk into the Grand Canyon rather than the alternative canyon by-pass track. The canyon is one of the most fascinating features in the Grampians. You need to scale a couple of short ladders at the top end of the Canyon to gain the tops and to link with the by-pass track. Walk on up south-eastwards, past numerous rock features including the Cool Chamber, Echo Cave, Ladies Hat and Silent Street. Avoid a right fork track between Echo Cave and Ladies Hat. The hat formation is just past a small waterfall and near where the track leaves the more forested slopes to cross fairly open rocky slopes. At Silent Street short ladders need be negotiated to enter and leave this remarkable long ravine. Soon after ascending from Silent Street the main feature of this walk—The Pinnacle—should be reached. It is on the rim of the huge Wonderland Escarpment. Halls Gap is in view over the rim, as is much of the Fyans Creek Valley. The lookout is about 1.5 km from the Wonderland Turntable car park and lunch spot.

Next, wander south 100 m to the edge of the cliff to see The Fallen Giant, a massive slab of sandstone fractured off the cliff rim. Another 50 m south is the Nerve Test. It is a most curious wind-eroded feature.

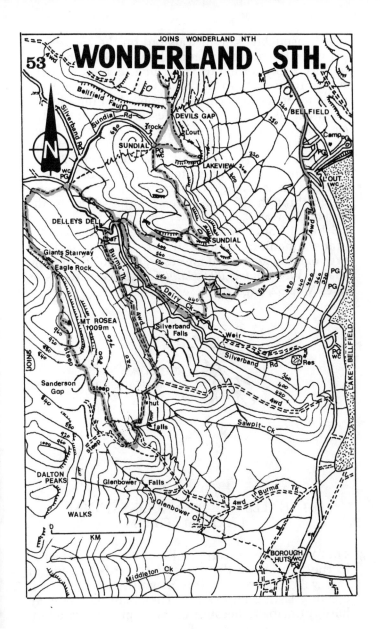

53 WONDERLAND STH.

BELLFIELD

Bellfield Fault

Silverband Rd

Sundial Rd

Trock

DEVILS GAP

L'out

Camp PG

SUNDIAL

wc

LAKEVIEW

L'OUT wc

DELLEYS DELL

SUNDIAL

Giants Stairway

Eagle Rock

Burma Tk

Dairy Ck

PG

PG

MT ROSEA 1009m

steep

Silverband Falls

Weir

Sanderson Gap

steep

Silverband Rd

Res

PG wc

hut

falls

Sawpit Ck

LAKE BELLFIELD

steep

DALTON PEAKS

Glenbower Falls

WALKS

Glenbower Ck

4wd

Burma Tk

0   1
KM

BOROUGH HUTS wc PG

Middleton Ck

It is 'reasonably' safe to walk out on the Nerve Test provided the nerves are good. Head back up the track in very rocky terrain to The Pinnacle, then start the return route back to the Halls Gap shops. The track to be taken leads northwards from The Pinnacle and soon begins the long steep descent adjacent to the east facing cliffs base. Several zig zags need negotiating. A short side track off left to Mackeys Peak could be avoided, and at a spot some 2.6 km from The Pinnacle the Stony Creek foot track is rejoined. It is then necessary to simply head east down through the camp area for the 400 m to the end of the walk.

7.5 km; 4 hours; walk last reviewed April 1988; 'A' grade; medium walk all on tracks; features Wonderland geological interest; suited to any season; *Maps: Vicmap 1:25,000 Halls Gap Special* refers as does Map 52, page 267.

ASTROLOMA
FLAME HEATH

83   HALLS GAP-PINNACLE-SUNDIAL-LAKE BELLFIELD

The Wonderland escarpment and views, plus koalas in the trees along the roadside towards the end of the walk, ensure that this magnificent circuit will create a lasting impression. The circuit is relatively hard, principally because of its length, but is all on foot tracks and roads. Carry some water for lunch on the tops.

From the Halls Gap shops go to the north-west corner and rear of the camp ground. The start of good foot tracks should then be met. Take the left fork pad and immediately start the climb up the Wonderland Escarpment to The Pinnacle Lookout on the cliff rim. Excellent views of Halls Gap are the main attraction at The Pinnacle. See the Fallen Giant and the Nerve Test within 150 m of the lookout southwards, then head off south along the tops on a good track. The route is rather rocky at times. Continue south past Bellfield Peak and down to Devils Gap. Diverge left to keep near the escarpment rim and to see Lakeview Lookout, then double back and walk the short distance to Sundial Turntable Picnic area. It would be a good lunch spot.

Next walk across fairly flat country to Sundial Lookout, again on the escarpment rim. The view here is of Lake Bellfield and the Fyans Creek valley. Double back several hundred metres to the track junction; turn left (south) down the track into a gully, then, once the track divides in the gully, sidle around the southern slopes of Sundial Peak eastwards for 1 km to another track junction. Veer left down a spur until Lake Bellfield dam wall is reached. Lastly, follow the main road back into Halls Gap. Much of this latter section has a foot pad alongside the road. You should see koalas in the trees along the roadside as you near Halls Gap.

16.8 km; 7 hours; walk last reviewed April 1988; 'A' grade, hard walk; all on tracks and roads; features Wonderland cliffs; carry water; walk suited to any season; *Maps: Vicmap 1:25,000 Halls Gap Special* refers as do Maps 52 and 53, pages 267 and 271.

Dairy Creek is one of the most beautiful ferny places in western Victoria. It is a good example of a wet sclerophyll forest type vegetation in a relatively dry region. It has flourished at this spot in the Grampians because of the deep shaded valley which descends the southern edge of the Wonderland escarpment. The creek cascades over Silverband Falls in a long silvery thread about 35 m high. There is a foot track right along the creek which allows a good appreciation of the ferns and falls, and Sundial Peak is situated high on the escarpment north of the falls. A most satisfying walk circuit can be taken which includes each of these highlights. A convenient car park is at Silverband Falls. View the falls first; they

LEPTOSPERMUM

are best appreciated from below although the access track to their base is steep. Next, follow a foot track upstream above the falls. The track leads through a host of different types of ferns and crosses and re-crosses the stream for 1.6 km to Delleys Dell at an old quarry site. Just where the track reaches the quarry, another track leads off east (right). Follow it up through open forest and via some zig zags for 1.4 km to another junction high on the range slopes. Turn left (north) steeply up 200 m distance to the rangetop Sundial Track. Just 300 m east (right) is Sundial Peak Lookout and its spectacular view.

Take the short return trip and perhaps have lunch at the lookout. There is no water supply for lunch. The lookout view is particularly good of Lake Bellfield some 400 m below. Retrace the 200 m sharp descent south off the range then turn left. Head south-east around the southern steep flanks of Sundial Peak and down 1 km towards Bellfield. At this point avoid the Bellfield track off left as the spur crest is crossed, and start the descent via southern wooded slopes for 1.5 km directly back to Silverband Falls. The headwaters of a small tributary of Dairy Creek harbour more ferns and provide real interest during this latter section of the walk.

6.5 km; 3 hours; walk last reviewed April 1988; 'B' grade, easy walk; all on tracks; features ferns and views; suited to any season; carry water for lunch; *Maps: Vicmap 1:25,000 Halls Gap Special* refers as does Map 53, page 271.

85   MOUNT WILLIAM FULL ASCENT

In undertaking this long walk, participants should be aware that severe weather conditions and snow can be experienced on the peak at virtually any time of the year. Warm clothing is a necessity. The summit is the highest in all Western Victoria. The mountain was named by the explorer, Major Thomas Mitchell. After climbing it he spent a freezing night on the tops and named the ranges after the Scottish Grampians.

The height of the summit is such that much of the Grampians and surrounding district can be

Mt William Road

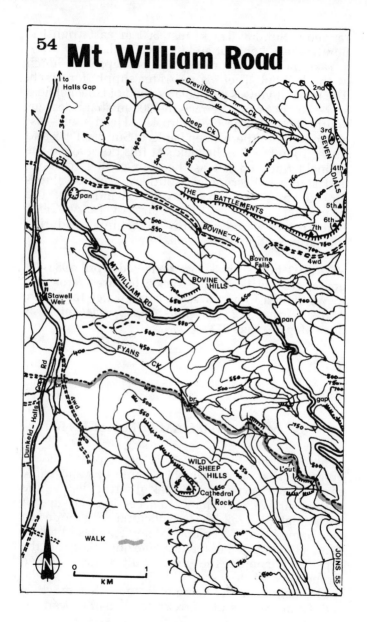

viewed. Even the road to the top permits quite spectacular scenery.

Some 3.3 km south along the Grampians Tourist Road (Halls Gap to Dunkeld Road) from the Mount William Road turnoff, a track leads off east. Take it, to start a most enjoyable climb up through the Fyans Creek Valley to Mount William, which is 1167 m above sea level. A total of some 750 m must be climbed. During the ascent the change in vegetation is quite noticeable. In the valley, the trees are sturdy, snow gums are present as altitude is gained and near the peak the vegetation is stunted sub-alpine in type. Near the walk start Grasstree Creek is crossed and near its east bank an old jeep track is intersected. The good pad then leads eastwards, crosses Fyans Creek, then begins a long ascent past bluffs and views of the Wild Sheep Hills to eventually reach the Mount William Road. It is then necessary to climb up the sealed road to the summit.

Initially the road climb is stiff and there are four hairpin bends. There is a very rough shortcut pad from the third hairpin bend, which bypasses the fourth hairpin bend, and some may like to use it. The vegetation beside the shortcut is quite varied and interesting. The top has very high towers on it. It is a worthwhile manoeuvre to walk well eastwards on the summit to get the best views to the east. **Note** that National Park plans include an intention to provide toilets at Mount William Turntable and to construct a walking track to the peak top although a low priority is designated to this improvement. Return to the valley using the same routing.

16.5 km; 7 hours; walk last reviewed April 1988; 'A' grade; hard walk; all on tracks and road; features views; no water for lunch or on higher slopes; walk suited to any season; *Maps: Vicmap 1:25,000 Mount William* refers as do Maps 54 and 55, pages 276 and 278.

A favourite walk in the Grampians is to climb Mount William from the western side. This alternative involves climbing the peak from the east side. It is a more beautiful approach but shorter and steeper.

Features of the walk include sub-alpine vegetation and views from cliff rims. Water can be scarce for most of the route. The tops can be bitterly cold at times so go prepared with warm clothing.

From Bomjinna Picnic Ground beside Mitchell Road, first use the flatter section of the good foot track, westwards. The pad leads up a valley. In forest it crosses a couple of small streambeds, then at a spot about 2 km from the start, the route turns south and rises 440 m spectacularly through the cliffs near Mount William. It emerges from forest at the Mount William Road turntable 3.5 km from the walk start. The 1,167 m high summit can then be approached by walking up the sealed roadway from the turntable. The road route to the top involves passing a gate, then an initial steep ascent. There are four hairpin bends. There is a rough pad from the third hairpin bend which bypasses the fourth hairpin bend if desired. The shortcut leads among quite varied sub-

**PULTENAEA
SUB ALPINA**

alpine vegetation. The summit, named after King William, is the highest in all Western Victoria and has some very high towers on it. It is worthwhile to walk well eastwards on the summit to obtain the best views eastwards. Both from the summit approach road and from the top, views are particularly good westwards to the Serra Range and other Grampians ranges.

After lunch on the top, a retrace of the road and foot track is suggested to conclude the day.

12 km; 5 hours; walk last reviewed April 1988; 'A' grade; hard walk; all on tracks and road; features views; carry water; walk suited to any season *Maps: Vicmap 1:25,000 Mount William* **refers as do Maps 54 and 55, pages 276 and 278.**

HOVEA

87 MOUNT ABRUPT

At the southern end of the Grampians is a rugged peak aptly named Mount Abrupt by explorer Major Mitchell. The summit is 825 m above sea level and affords superb views north along the Serra Range and south to Dunkeld town.

A graded track to the summit begins at the Mount Abrupt Tourist Road 7 km north of the Glenelg Highway, Dunkeld. The slopes are wooded and the rocky tops exposed, featuring low, sub-alpine

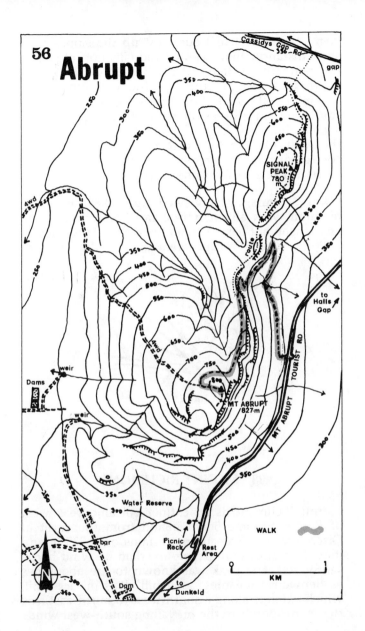

Cassidys Gap Rd

gap

550

600

650

700

SIGNAL
PEAK
780
m

450

650

route

350

to
Halls
Gap

250

300

350

400

4wd

250

350

400

450

500

550

600

650

700

750

800

weir

Dams

weir

MT ABRUPT
827 m

MT ABRUPT TOURIST RD

200

500

450

400

350

Water Reserve

350

300

WALK

bar

Picnic
Rock

Rest
Area

N

350

300

350

KM

Dam

to
Dunkeld

vegetation. The pad leads west up the slopes for a short distance, then ascends gradually north towards the ramparts of Signal Peak. It then doubles back south and ascends through the escarpment rim 1.8 km from the walk start. Another 1.2 km of walking south on the tops sees the summit trig attained after a final short, sharp pinch. This final pinch is from the west. On the tops care is needed to navigate correctly using small rock cairns as a guide in places. To return, retrace the same pad.

6 km; 3 hours; last reviewed April 1988; 'B' grade; medium walk all on tracks; carry water; suited to any season but best to avoid hot days; *Maps: Vicmap 1:25,000 Mount Abrupt* refers as does Map 56, page 281.

HAKEA

88   MOUNT RICHMOND

Mount Richmond is an extinct volcanic peak west of Portland, some 5 km inland from the coast at Discovery Bay. The summit attains only 225 m and its volcanic soils are largely overlain by wind-borne sandy soil. The peak was known to the aborigines as Benwerrin meaning 'long hill'. It is in fact a hill which extends along a south-west to north-east axis that corresponds to the prevailing south-west winds off the sea, which have thus extended the former length of the hill with sand.

Vegetation on the south-west side of the hill is typically heavily salt-pruned; in comparison, on the north-east and east sides it is of the cool and damp type. The vegetation extremes have resulted in a park being established to preserve some 450 species of wildflowers and many orchids. A number of walking tracks have been established and these link to jeep tracks and the main access road to facilitate excellent easy walking. Kangaroos, wallabies, koalas, emus and echidnas are common, as are many types of birds. A lookout tower has been erected on the summit adjacent to good picnic ground facilities.

While several walk alternatives exist, it is recommended that a circuit be followed. This includes the west side of the hill (West Walk) and the east

GREVILLEA
AQUIFOLIUM

side (Noels Walk). The lookout tower and picnic area are the suggested start and finish points. The lookout tower view is especially good towards Discovery Bay and the huge shifting sand dunes bordering the coast.

West Walk leads through the salt-pruned vegetation of banksias, hakeas, casuarinas (sheoaks), leptospermum (tea-tree), and xanthorrhoeas (grass trees), and the best wildflower spots.

Noels Walk leads through the more forested parts where stringy-bark trees and manna gum trees are common. You may well see koalas in the trees.

To start the walk, go just 150 m north of the lookout

283

tower and picnic area via the main access road then turn left onto West Walk. Head downhill, avoiding a left side track after 200 m, and continue to a spot 1.1 km from the road. You should then be on flats and at a jeep track. Turn right (north) and go 250 m to fork right onto the continuation of West Walk. After another 1.2 km of walking across the lower northern slopes of the hill, cross the main road and link onto Noels Walk. It descends to Telegraph Road within 850 m, meeting this jeep track at its intersection with Blackers Track. Head 250 m south-east on Telegraph Road then fork off south on the continuation of Noels Walk. An ascent through wooded country soon begins as the pad swings from south to west. Some 1.25 km after leaving Telegraph Road keep right at a track junction and walk westwards to regain the main road within 250 m. You need then to walk 200 m south on the main road to return to the lookout tower area.

5.5 km; 1¾ hours; last reviewed January 1987; 'C' grade; easy walk; all on tracks; carry water; walk suited to any season; *Maps: Vicmap 1:25,000 Dryden* refers as does Map 57, page 285.

89   BYADUK CAVES

In the Western District are a series of remarkable collapsed lava tunnels and caves which formed as a result of a 25 km long lava flow from Mount Napier, one of the many Western District extinct volcanoes. The lava tubes represent the hardened outer shell of the cooled lava after the molten interior flowed on down the Harman Valley. Some collapses enable access to tunnels and features; walkers can readily inspect most, although a torch is needed for a few

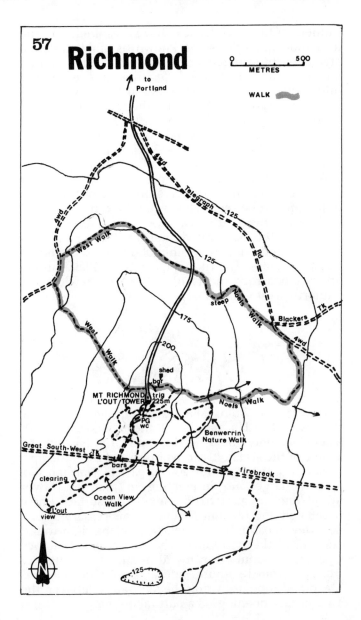

57 Richmond

0   500
METRES

WALK

to
Portland

4wd

Telegraph   125

West Walk

4wd

125

West   Walk

175

steep

Noels   Walk

Blackers   TK

4wd

200

shed

bgr

MT RICHMOND   trig
L'OUT TOWER   225m

Noels   Walk

PG
wc

Benwerrin
Nature Walk

Great South-West   TK

bars

firebreak

clearing

Ocean View
Walk

view   l'out

N

125

285

tunnels. Other collapses have resulted in the formation of depressions known as sinkholes. The area is of intense geological interest and is in a rich pastural district. Several features are especially interesting, including the arches at Bridge Cave and Shephards Cave together with the Flower Pot.

South of Hamilton, 18 km along the Macarthur Road at Byaduk North, you should turn east on a gravelled road to Byaduk Caves. It is 3.7 km along this side road to the road end and a small picnic area.

A track leads south across the lava flow for 150 m to Harman No. 1 Cave, the first of the series of features to be seen. This lava tube can be entered easily from the south-east side of a collapsed sector and can be penetrated north-west for 100 m underground. The entry sinkhole, 15 m in diameter, has steep sides. The tunnel has a typical lava tunnel arch-shaped roof and is 10 m to 15 m in width. At its north-west end is a large lava blister on the floor.

ACACIA
ROCK
WATTLE

Harman No. 2 Sinkhole is insignificant. It lies a few metres east of Harman No. 1 and is linked through a rockfall. One would need a rope for entry, but the whole of the sinkhole can be inspected from the lip.

Bridge Cave is about 200 m east of Harman No. 1. It is large and interesting in that it is over 100 m long and has two openings to the surface. Entry is difficult and to some extent is unnecessary as one can view most of the tunnels by walking right round the rim of the two holes. The westernmost surface opening is about 30 m by 20 m and the best entry point is from its south side at a rockfall, but it is steep and rope use would be advisable. Between the two surface openings is a natural bridge.

Church Cave lies 300 m south-south-east of Bridge Cave and is really interesting for entry. A long bracken-filled canal is central to the complex. At the north end of the canal it is easy to enter a large underground chamber from the east side. Within the chamber is a bat colony and from the chamber a 100 m long lava tube can be followed north. At the south end of the bracken-filled canal, entry from the east side is again easy and one can walk south through a 50 m long tunnel to emerge at another open canal sector. It is possible to climb out of this canal midway along its east side, but scaling is a bit awkward and some may prefer to return through the tunnel for exit.

The Basin lies 50 m south again and is a depression some 6 m by 6 m. It marks a collapsed section of a lava tunnel and is midway between Church Cave and The Flower Pot.

The Flower Pot is at the western end of a 30 m long complex extending eastwards. It has no direct entry, but can be reached underground. It has a 12 m diameter surface opening, and a 12 m diameter intact block sits on the lava tunnel floor below like a flower pot with ferns in it. Bathtub Sinkhole, 50 m east, provides access to the Flower Pot. A steep descent into the access tunnel is made from the western end of the Bathtub. The Bathtub about 50 m by 30 m has no special attractions. An almost completely clogged tunnel leads off its east end.

Tunnel Sinkhole, 50 m east of the Bathtub is entered from its north side and one can enter Shepherds Cave from it. The cave has three chambers, but the third chamber requires negotiation of a very low entry. A fine arch exists at the eastern end of the Tunnel Sinkhole, and it can be followed east into a large bracken-filled canal. Exit from this canal is possible in several places.

Turk Cave is at the eastern end of the canal and is also easily entered. It has a broad entry chamber, then an inner chamber featuring good roof stalactites.

BYADUK CAVES

(HARMANS VALLEY)

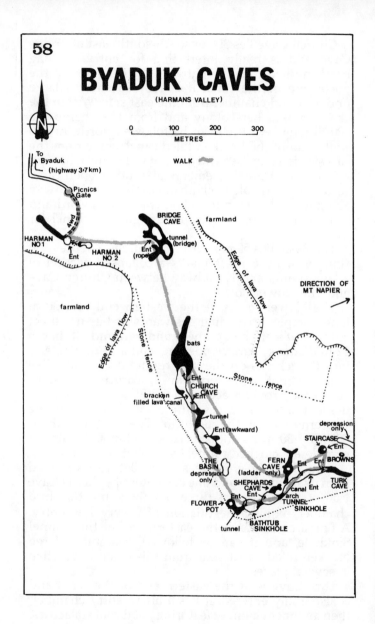

METRES

0   100   200   300

WALK

To Byaduk (highway 3·7 km)

Picnics Gate

4wd

HARMAN NO 1
Ent

HARMAN NO 2

BRIDGE CAVE

farmland

tunnel (bridge)

Ent (rope)

Edge of lava flow

DIRECTION OF MT NAPIER

farmland

Edge of lava flow

Stone fence

bats

Stone fence

Ent

CHURCH CAVE

bracken filled lava canal

Ent

tunnel

Ent (awkward)

depression only

STAIRCASE

Ent

BROWNS

THE BASIN
depression only

FERN CAVE
(ladder only)

Ent

Ent

TURK CAVE

SHEPHARDS CAVE

Ent   Ent

canal   Ent

arch

FLOWER POT

Ent

TUNNEL SINKHOLE

tunnel

BATHTUB SINKHOLE

A 1 m high sector of tunnel links the two chambers.

Staircase Cave is just north of the entry of Turk Cave. It has a 3 m diameter entry, easily negotiated to reach its 15 m diameter cave. There are several 30 cm high stairs on the east side of the cave.

Fern Cave lies just north of the Tunnel Sinkhole canal. It is mainly an underground lava tube system with very difficult access. A long ladder would be the only means of access through its 10 m diameter surface opening, which opening is fern-filled.

After seeing each of these features you need to retrace the route back to Harman No. 1 Cave area. There is stone fencing along both northern and southern flanks of the caves system. The stone fences are of lava rock from the lava flow. Mount Napier, the source of all the lava, can be seen eastwards.

3 km; 2 hours; last reviewed January 1987; 'B' grade; easy walk; across grassland and in lava tunnels; features places of volcanic interest; no water available for lunch; walk suited to any season; *Maps: Vicmap 1:25,000 Byaduk* refers as does Map 58, page 288.

90   LAKE SURPRISE

Mount Eccles and nearby Mount Napier volcanic parks together contain perhaps the most diverse representation of volcanic features in south-eastern Australia. At Mount Eccles there is an unusual volcanic maar flooded by a lake known as Lake Surprise. The district is mainly manna gum woodland and the rocky lava-formed terrain is inhabited by koalas, gliders, bandicoots, bush rats and tiger cats, plus many reptiles. The geological interest, together with that of the flora and fauna, therefore ensure excellent walking opportunities. A large variety of birds can be seen in the park.

Walk number 91 in this book aims to guide participants to a host of features in the Mount Eccles area, whereas this shorter walk suggestion aims to highlight beautiful, quiet Lake Surprise in the volcanic crater. The lake fills three linked craters along a volcanic fissure. The craters are said to have erupted about 6500 years ago. There is a shoreline circuit walking track of the lake. Before setting out on the walk it could be worthwhile to read the track notes of walk number 91 in order to gain a better appreciation of the park as a whole. Mount Eccles is 8 km west of Macarthur, a wool growing town in the Western District. In commencing the walk you should ignore the crater rim circuit track and descend via many steps from the picnic area, near the north end of the lake, to the water's edge. The distance is only about 200 metres.

The walk entails simply following the 1.6 km long lake shore track right around the lake back to the foot of the steps, then climbing back to the picnic area and lookout. Walking anti-clockwise around the lake is probably preferable so that the lightly wooded crater cliffs are seen to best advantage.

Evidently the water in the lake represents seepage from the surrounding plains and the water level corresponds with the ground water table of the district. There is no stream entering or leaving the crater. Usually the water is a dark green colour, so it and the adjacent vegetation create an atmosphere of tranquility and coolness. White cockatoos sometimes screech and break the peace, but their white feathers make a splendid contrast against the green lake water.

2 km; 1 hour; last reviewed January 1987; 'B' grade; easy walk; all on tracks; features volcanic interest; drinking water available; walk suited to any season; *Maps: Vicmap 1:25,000 Eccles* refers as does Map 59, page 291.

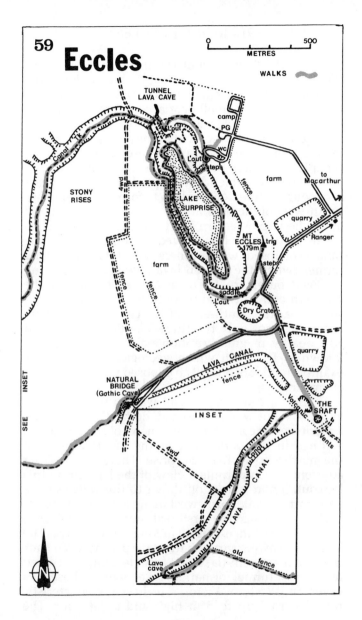

59 **Eccles**

WALKS

0   500
METRES

TUNNEL
LAVA CAVE

camp

PG

wc

L'out

L'out

steps

Canal

STONY
RISES

4wd

fence

farm

to
Macarthur

LAKE
SURPRISE

farm

quarry

MT
ECCLES
179m

trig

Ranger

steps

fence

saddle

L'out

Dry Crater

LAVA CANAL

quarry

NATURAL
BRIDGE
(Gothic Cave)

fence

Volcanic

THE
SHAFT

SEE INSET

Vents

INSET

4wd

Canal   Tk

LAVA CANAL

fence

Lava
cave

old   fence

4wd

N

291

Mount Eccles 8 km west of Macarthur in the Western District is a woodland National Park containing the most interesting Mount Eccles extinct volcano. The mount itself is a small scoria cone created by the prevailing south-west wind as it blew scoria north-east from the volcanic vents. The vents are, in fact, three craters along a fissure. These craters are now occupied by water and known as Lake Surprise.

The volcano, which last erupted about 6500 years ago, poured out extensive lava to form the stony rises south-west of the peak and to contribute to the build up of the large Western District volcanic plain. Lava canals exist where lava flowed from the vents. Some canals collapsed, whilst others were retained as long tunnels when the molten lava flowed away leaving a cooled outer crust. The main canal starts at the northern end and swings south-west. Another canal starts near the south-east of the complex. The main fissure has not only the three lake-filled craters but also nearby magma eruption points, including one known as The Shaft which, geologically, is a superb example (and rare one) of an exposed volcanic magma chamber.

There is a 2 km long circuit walk of the main vent and lake, but walkers would do well to be more adventuresome and try to see many of the geological features in the park. Start at the picnic ground at the north end of Lake Surprise. There is a lookout adjacent which permits a view of the lake. From this lookout, ignore tracks off down to the water's edge and start to walk north-west along a crater rim track.

Once walking, the first real surprise is within a very short distance. It is 60 m long Tunnel Cave. The lava once flowing through this cave probably ran back into the main vent (lake bed area) leaving the cooled outer crust tunnel formation. Like many of these lava caves in Western Victoria it has a characteristic rounded roof up to 5 m high and a flat floor. The cave is located just where the track starts to descend below the cliff rim after passing another lookout.

The track then descends across the main northern lava canal floor and up to the west rim of the crater system. A cross track is intersected on the canal floor. You should then follow the crater rim track on past adjacent farmland and to the south end of the crater. There are good vantage points for viewing the crater

Hovea

lake as you progress. At the south end, cross a saddle between the main crater and a nearby dry, smaller crater, then climb north to the summit of Mount Eccles itself for a distant view from its trig point.

Next, head south-east back down the slopes to the saddle, down sixty steps and to a roadway. Once on this road see Dry Crater and walk south past two scoria quarry entrance roads off left and to a fence aligned north-south adjacent to the west side of the quarries. Follow this fence south for a total of some 500 m and you should see the start of the southern sector canal and the geological oddity known as The Shaft. It is on a 10 m spatter cone. Be careful not to get too close to the 3 m diameter opening as it is approximately 30 m deep and therefore quite dangerous. Technically though, for those experienced in rock and cave climbing only, and with proper ropes, it could be descended so that one is in the actual magma chamber of the volcano.

After viewing The Shaft return the 500 m to the roadway and turn left. Head west to the end of the road where Gothic Cave (Natural Bridge) exists. It is part of the southern lava canal, but the canal has not collapsed at this spot. The 30 m long resulting cave is best entered from the western side.

A minor foot track leads off west from the cave area into forested stony rises. After some 1.2 km it reaches the rim of the main northern canal. A stone fence lies beside the track for the latter half of this distance to the main canal. Once at the rim, the pad turns south. Follow it along the rim for 200 m to another lava cave entrance and then descend the track into the canal. A rough pad should then be followed north along the floor of this large canal until after a jeep track is crossed and the north end of the Lake Surprise vent system is regained. From this point on, retrace the route to the picnic area. Koalas are often seen in the manna gums in this latter locality.

8 km; 3 hours; last reviewed January 1987; 'A' grade; easy walk; all on tracks and roads; features volcanic interest; drinking water available only at picnic area at start of walk; walk suited to any season; *Maps: Vicmap 1:25,000 Eccles* refers as does Map 59, page 291.

92   PORT FAIRY

In 1810 Captain James Wishart and his crew of two anchored the cutter *Fairy* in the river later named the Moyne River to collect fresh water, and named the spot Port Fairy. Thereafter, Tasmanian whalers used the area and built huts along the river bank. A whaling station was soon established. This marked the start of settlement, and by 1839 a store was opened and the settlement was called Belfast. The rich volcanic soil of the surrounding country attracted further settlers, including overlanders, so by the 1850s the town flourished as a busy port handling up to twenty ships per day. Many significant stone buildings were erected and to this day Belfast (renamed Port Fairy in 1885) holds a particular charm. In the early days, two settlers, Hutton and Powling objected to the neglect of tree planting by the town municipal authorities, so presented and planted many Norfolk Island Pines which to this day are a feature of the town.

PELICANS

Other attractions in the locality were noted right from the earliest days of white settlement. We are told that the settlers spent their leisure time with picnics at Tower Hill extinct volcano, Mount Rouse extinct volcano, Lady Julia Percy Island and with shooting at Yambuk. Immediately adjacent to the river mouth is Griffiths Island where a lighthouse of local bluestone was built and where there is a Muttonbird rookery. Also adjacent to the river mouth is Battery Hill where a fort and powder magazine were built. An historical walk round Port Fairy is thus worthwhile. It is suggested that transport be left beside the Princes Highway at a spot where the highway turns at right angles from north-south aligned Albert Street into east-west aligned Cox Street. This spot is actually on the town outskirts.

Initially walk east towards the town centre for one block on Cox Street. Turn left (north) into William Street to see an interesting bluestone house on the east side halfway along the block, then turn right into Bank Street. Go east and then just past Grant Street on the left is the Drill Hall (1874) once used as a garrison. Across the street at the corner of James Street is the Caledonian Hotel (1844), then north on James Street is a former school building and

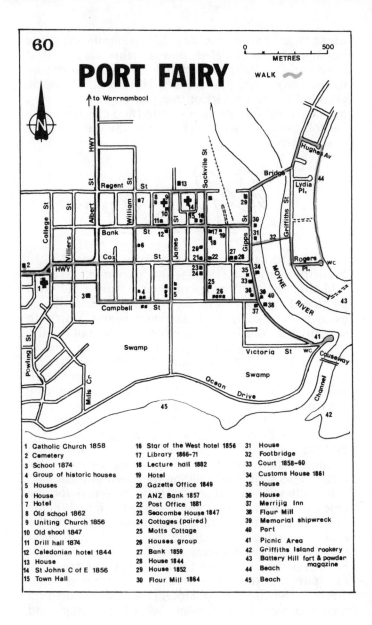

60
PORT FAIRY

WALK

to Warrnambool

1	Catholic Church 1858
2	Cemetery
3	School 1874
4	Group of historic houses
5	Houses
6	House
7	Hotel
8	Old school 1862
9	Uniting Church 1856
10	Old shool 1847
11	Drill hall 1874
12	Caledonian hotel 1844
13	House
14	St Johns C of E 1856
15	Town Hall
16	Star of the West hotel 1856
17	Library 1866–71
18	Lecture hall 1882
19	Hotel
20	Gazette Office 1849
21	ANZ Bank 1857
22	Post Office 1881
23	Seacombe House 1847
24	Cottages (paired)
25	Motts Cottage
26	Houses group
27	Bank 1859
28	House 1844
29	House 1852
30	Flour Mill 1864
31	House
32	Footbridge
33	Court 1858–60
34	Customs House 1861
35	House
36	House
37	Merrijig Inn
38	Flour Mill
39	Memorial shipwreck
40	Port
41	Picnic Area
42	Griffiths Island rookery
43	Battery Hill fort & powder magazine
44	Beach
45	Beach

Methodist Church (1856). Turn right into Regent Street where there is a large historic home on the north side of Regent Street and St Johns Anglican Church (1856) on the south side. It is worthwhile entering this fine church if it is open.

At the next corner, turn south on Sackville Street. The Oddfellows Hall is on the left, whilst at the corner of Bank Street is the Star of the West Hotel which was the Cobb and Co coaching station. Next door and just west on Bank Street are the Borough Chambers and a visitors centre. Sackville Street has the main commercial area, and as you proceed south along it from Bank Street, you pass a Lecture Hall (1881-82) and a Library (1866-71), both on the left. The library was the Mechanics Institute. On the right, midway along the block is the historic Port Fairy Gazette office, and at Cox Street intersection is the Post Office (1880), the A.N.Z. Bank (1857) and Seacombe House which was the Stag Inn (1841). Next door, still on Sackville Street, are paired cottages of note, and on the left further south is Motts Cottage. Turn east on Campbell Street to see four interesting houses on the left, then walk to Gipps Street intersection. The Merrijig Inn (1842) is on one corner, a bluestone house is on the other corner and across Gipps Street is a park, the river waterfront with a variety of boats, a memorial to a wrecked ship, an old flour mill ruin and also a picnic ground not far south along the river. Lunch is suggested at this picnic area.

Back along Gipps Street, head north from Campbell Street to see a Customs House and a Court House, the oldest house in Victoria, and the lovely line of Norfolk Island Pines along the street. Just past Cox Street, turn right along a foot path which leads to a footbridge over the Moyne River at a most picturesque spot. Once across the river, walk south on Griffiths Street a short distance to Rogers Place, then proceed east to the beach front nearby. The beach can be followed north a short distance to the

Surf Life Saving Club, then left via Hughes Avenue back to Griffiths Street. Just south, recross the river on a road bridge to see 'Riversdale' a large home (1852). Go south on Gipps Street one block, turn right into Bank Street at a flour mill site by the river (1864).

MUTTON BIRD

Walk west on Bank Street for four blocks, then south on James Street for two blocks to see a number of historic houses in James Street between Cox and Campbell Streets intersections. Head west on Campbell Street for four blocks past more historic houses to reach the Consolidated School (1874) at Albert Street. Just north, turn west into Powling Street to see St Patricks Church (1858) at the west end of the street, then turn right to reach the Princes Highway. West again along the highway for a short distance should see you at the historic cemetery where there is much to learn of the town and its people's history by browsing around. Finally, walk back east along the highway to the Albert Street corner to end the walk.

5.5 km; 2½ hours; last reviewed January 1987; 'B' grade; easy walk; all on streets; features historic port; lunch water available at riverside picnic area; walk suited to any season; *Map:* 60, page 296.

93 TOWER HILL

Tower Hill at the 275 km peg along the Princes Highway, west of Melbourne, is a large extinct volcanic caldera nearly 3 km in diameter with many spatter cones of scoria and a number of secondary craters within it. It is at the western end of a line (or fissure) of some thirty volcanoes between the Colac district and Port Fairy. It is close to the coast, amid very fertile plains and has been managed to create a most remarkable State Game Reserve. The volcano is said to have last erupted about 7000 years ago. The caldera contains a large area of water from the ground water table and the lakes within the crater were, in fact, largely dry until about 1946 and again in 1967-8. Their level fluctuates with variations in the ground water table. The caldera also has perimeter cliffs of layered ash accumulated by successive eruptions of ash. The prevailing south-westerly wind caused most ash to accumulate on the north-east side of the volcano so the cliffs are highest on that side. The fertility of the area and the scoria deposits induced indescriminate development for commercial purposes during the last century. However, since 1961 there has been a transformation leading to development of a State Game Reserve for tourists.

Over 250,000 trees have been planted since 1960. This is said to have caused a big build up in bird species so that today about 160 species occur, including many water birds. The trees and shrubs planted are mainly black wattles, blackwood, sheoaks, tea-tree, swamp gum and manna gum. Many animals have been introduced so that echidnas, wombats, emus, kangaroos, wallabies, native cats, koalas and possums can be seen. A Natural History Centre has been erected in the centre of the caldera, breeding pens have been established to foster more wildlife and many kilometres of tracks have been installed, including a nature trail. A brochure is available about the nature walk from the centre.

This walk suggestion is to include the nature trail together with a climb to the 98 m high summit of Tower Hill itself. The walk should begin at the Natural History Centre 1.5 km north of the park entrance from the Princes Highway. There are picnic facilities

SPRING

at the spot and an inspection of the Natural History Centre would be most informative before setting off. The Centre's roof is like a volcanic cone.

At first walk west down the grassy slopes from the centre to adjacent Wagon Bay, a secondary crater filled with ground-table water which is fenced off to assist the breeding of geese. Old quarry wagon remains are to be seen on the southern shore. Walk north-west along a track past the crater to see a small scoria quarry at the north end of Wagon Bay lake, then continue north-west. The track leads through restored wattle stands. Pass a track off left and then climb to the lip of a pronounced crater just northwards. This fairly deep crater is thought to be the scene of the most recent volcanic activity in the district. A track leads right around the crater lip and it should be followed for most of the circuit until at the south-east side. Next walk up to a small hill crest south-eastwards and the end of the jeep track. Walk south-east on the ridge crest down a short foot track amid eucalypts to join another jeep track. It in turn should be followed to a viewpoint on a crest nearby. The best views are of the Fairly Island sector of the caldera and to the caldera rim escarpments north-eastwards.

Just before this viewpoint, a jeep track leads off south and you should double back from the lookout to take this jeep track. It shortly leads to a water supply tank on a hill. A foot track then descends from near the tank southwards back to the Natural History Centre. Once at the centre, a pad should be taken south and parallel to the display centre access road so that Tower Hill summit foot track is reached within 250 m. Steps need to be scaled as you then climb west up past White Eye Crater and on to the summit itself some 400 m from the road.

A first class view of the reserve is then available and the coast can be seen also. About 150 m short of the summit is a foot track north down a gully to Wagon Bay. Take it, and once at Wagon Bay walk up the grassy slopes to the display centre to end the walk.

3.5 km; 1½ hours; last reviewed January 1987; 'A' grade; family walk; all on tracks; features volcanic craters and cones; water for lunch at natural history centre picnic area; walk suited to any season; *Maps: Vicmap 1:25,000 Koroit* refers as does Map 61, page 302.

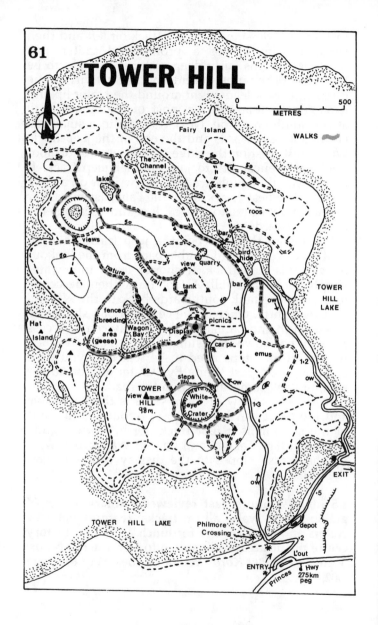

61

TOWER HILL

0 ——————— 500
METRES

Fairy Island

WALKS ～

The Channel

lake

crater

views

roos

nature trail

view quarry

bird hide

TOWER
HILL
LAKE

tank

fenced
breeding
area
(geese)

Wagon
Bay

Hat
Island

wc

picnics

display

car pk.

emus

steps

TOWER
view HILL
98 m.

White-
eye
Crater

view

EXIT

TOWER HILL LAKE

Philmore
Crossing

depot

L'out

ENTRY

Princes Hwy
275km
peg

302

At the 275 km peg along the Princes Highway, west of Melbourne, is Tower Hill. It is an extinct volcanic caldera 3 km in diameter and containing lakes, subsidiary peaks and craters. We are told the volcano last erupted some 7000 years ago. It is one of a number of impressive Western District volcanoes and is the westernmost of a string of volcanoes along a fissure stretching from near Colac. Tower Hill has been developed intensively as a State Game Reserve during the last 20-25 years and today supports over 250,000 planted trees, hundreds of introduced animals and many bird species that had not been seen in the district for decades. There is a Natural History Centre, picnic facilities and many walking tracks. A walk of great natural and especially volcanic interest is suggested, starting from the display centre. The centre is in the middle of the caldera and reached by a 1.5 km long access road north from the Princes Highway.

Head off west down grassy slopes to adjacent Wagon Bay after viewing the displays in the centre. The bay is a former crater inundated by the water from the ground water table, as are each of the lakes within the caldera. A fence round the bay and nearby slopes provides a breeding area for wildlife, particularly geese and waterbirds. Walk round the south side of Wagon Bay past an old quarry wagon ruin, then fork right three times keeping near the enclosure fence to join a jeep track nature trail north of Wagon Bay. Turn left and walk through areas renowned for wattles to reach the southern rim of a fairly deep crater. This is at a spot where tracks cross. The crater usually contains a small lake. Head round this crater rim and on north to a 'T' intersection in a small valley. Fork right to continue for 200 m east, then right a second time to head south-east past a tiny crater swamp inhabited by frogs. As you progress you join a jeep track along the western margins of what is known as The Channel, but a track off right needs to be avoided not long before The Channel is reached.

In walking south-east along the jeep track near The Channel, a causeway to Fairy Island is passed and soon after a bird hide is also passed. Water birds

**BLUE
WREN**

are common in this locality. About 120 m south of the hide, meet the park access road, turn left along the road and leave it after just 100 m to climb south up a spur via an initially obscured minor jeep track. Emus are common in this sector. The track is very grassy, but can be followed south, then south-west, to meet the main access road again. During this undulating grassy section a cross track needs to be avoided, as should a right fork track also.

Walk across the sealed access road and climb up and round the southern lip of White Eye Crater so that Tower Hill summit track is reached north-west of White Eye Crater. Views are excellent throughout this part of the walk. There are three tracks off left from the White Eye Crater rim as you progress towards Tower Hill summit track. Tower Hill, 98 m above sea level, should then be reached after a walk just 150 m west. The summit view includes most of the game reserve and extends to the caldera walls and the coast.

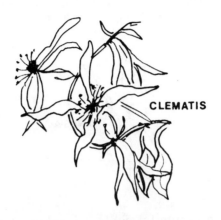

CLEMATIS

Retrace the 150 m, then turn left down a steep gully track to Wagon Bay. It is then only a short walk up grassy slopes back to the Natural History Centre.

4.5 km; 1¾ hours; last reviewed January 1987; 'A' grade; family walk; all on tracks and roads; features volcanic interest; water for lunch at Natural History Centre picnic area, walk suited to any season; *Maps: Vicmap 1:25,000 Koroit* refers as does Map 61, page 302.

95   PORT CAMPBELL NATIONAL PARK

A really fine National Park confronts Bass Strait south-east of Warrnambool. During wild weather, huge seas create a spectacle seldom rivalled. The best time to visit the area is when the winds are really whipping up the seas, and when the day is sunny. The Great

Ocean Road runs parallel to the coast, with side roads to points of interest. It is suggested that walkers use some of the roads as well as walking along the cliff tops, keeping as near as possible to the rim views, but not too close *as the edges are often crumbly.*

BANKSIA

See such wonderful sights as London Bridge, Loch Ard Gorge and the Twelve Apostles and many other features. Do not rush. Sit and wonder, photograph these massive sandstone formations, watch the waves crash and at sunset revisit the cliff tops for an awe-inspiring view. A two day's walk is recommended, with an overnight camp at the Port Campbell camping ground, but a transport shuttle would be needed.

Start at Peterborough, at the eastern end of the bridge over Curdies Inlet and walk onto the beach, then head east to see the Crown of Thorns, The Grotto, London Bridge, The Arch, Two Mile Bay and Port Campbell, *but note that a rifle range exists just west of Two Mile Bay, and if red flags are flying as an approach is made, head north to the Great Ocean road to by-pass the range, then return to the cliff tops down the Two Mile Bay road.* The camp area is right in the tiny town by the inlet and has all amenities. A direct track leads from Two Mile Bay Lookout to the camp.

On the second day go east again to even more beautiful sights. See Sentinal Rock, the Sherbrooke River mouth beach, Broken Head, Thunder Cave,

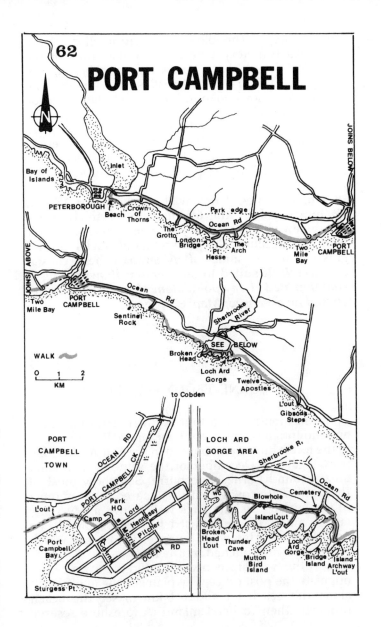

PORT CAMPBELL

62

N

JOINS BELOW

Bay of
Islands

Inlet

PETERBOROUGH

Beach
Crown
of
Thorns

Park edge

Ocean Rd

The
Grotto
London
Bridge

Pt
Hesse

The
Arch

Two
Mile
Bay

PORT
CAMPBELL

JOINS ABOVE

Two
Mile Bay

PORT
CAMPBELL

Ocean

Rd

Sentinel
Rock

Sherbrooke
River

SEE BELOW

Broken
Head

Loch Ard
Gorge

Twelve
Apostles

L'out

Gibsons
Steps

WALK

0   1   2
KM

to Cobden

PORT

CAMPBELL

TOWN

OCEAN RD

PORT CAMPBELL CK

L'out

Camp

Park
HQ

Lord

Hennessy

Pitcher

Mom

Curdie

OCEAN RD

Port
Campbell
Bay

Sturgess Pt.

LOCH ARD
GORGE AREA

Sherbrooke R.

Ocean Rd

Cemetery

WC

Blowhole

Island L'out

Broken
Head
L'out

Thunder
Cave

Mutton
Bird
Island

Loch
Ard
Gorge

Bridge
Island

Island
Archway
L'out

Survey Gorge, The Blowhole, Mutton Bird Island, Loch Ard cemetery wherein lie the victims of the Loch Ard wreck, Loch Ard Gorge and beach, The Haystack, The Twelve Apostles and finally The Twelve Apostles Lookout. Lunch each day could be at any point along the way, but water needs to be carried. The Sherbrooke River has, however, a good water supply, as does Port Campbell itself. There is a toilet block at the mouth of the Sherbrooke River (plus those at Port Campbell and Peterborough).

28 km; 11 hours; 2 day walk, each day of 13 km, 4½ hours and 15 km, 6½ hours respectively; walk last reviewed January 1987; 'A' grade, easy, overnight walk; much along cliff rims without tracks and on grass; features some of Australia's best coastal scenery; walk suited to any season; *if swimming is contemplated at any point along the coast, great care should be exercised; Map:* 62, page 307.

96 LORNE-TEDDYS LOOKOUT

Lorne has long been a tourist town featuring beach and mountain scenery, but February, 1983, saw much of the forest hinterland burned in the Ash Wednesday fires. Again in December of the same year, further areas around Lorne were burnt. Somehow most of the immediate town area was spared, as was most of the famous Erskine Falls walk. Now, a few years later, most of the district has regained its magnificence. This walk however is in areas which were largely untouched by the fires.

Start the walk at the beachfront in the town centre opposite the post office. The plan is to head off north along the beach for about 1 km to see the beach properly, then to head inland. A foreshore reserve exists between the beach and the Erskine River which flows almost parallel to the beach. There is a roadway from the main street of Lorne out through the reserve and a camp area, and you could use the roadway to go back onto the main street after seeing the beach. Turn left at the Main Street and walk south 500 m almost back to the post office. Turn right up steep, William Street for two street blocks then go left on Otway Street. Views improve as you climb to the top of a ridge and the junction of nearby George Street. George Street leads south-east up the ridge crest. By following this street to its end you should reach Teddys Lookout, but on the way there are excellent coastal views. Just 50 m beyond the Teddys Lookout car park, by way of a good foot track, is an excellent vantage point and suitable spot for a lunch break. There are views not only of the coast and Great Ocean Road far below but also of the lower reaches of the St George River. Teddys Lookout is about 4.5 km from the walk start and at an altitude of 120 m.

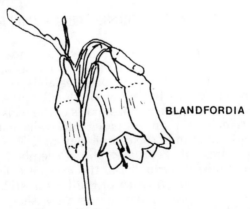

BLANDFORDIA

After lunch descend the foot track steeply down a spur from the lookout so as to reach the Great Ocean Road just near the mouth of the St George River and some 400 m distant. You should then turn left and follow the Great Ocean Road and coast back into town to complete a circuit. However the town's jetty is passed and is worthy of inspection, and there is a park area fronting Loutitt Bay for much of the distance; consequently the park can be crossed and the busy road avoided. The distance from the mouth of the St George River back into town is about 2.5 km.

7 km; 2½ hours; last reviewed February 1988; 'B' grade; family walk; all on tracks, roads and beaches; features beaches and Teddys Lookout view; carry water for lunch; bus transport along Great Ocean Road between Geelong and Apollo Bay available for access to walk start if desired; walk suited to any season, but best in summer *Maps: Vicmap 1:25,000 Lorne* **refers as does Map 63, page 317.**

97   ERSKINE FALLS-LORNE-CORA LYNN FALLS

For decades Lorne has been renowned as a walkers' resort and it is clear that the district is still as popular as ever. New tracks have been established more recently to add to the network already present. It is now feasible to see the best parts of the walk areas and to include them in a circuit walk with an overnight camp in Lorne camping ground. The tragic Otways fires of February and December, 1983, somehow missed virtually all the Erskine Falls area tracks, and while evidence of the fires is still to be seen in some places, damage is very slight. It is suggested that transport be left at the Erskine Falls car park after arrangements have been made for the overnight camp in the town. It would then not be necessary to carry a heavy pack for the two-day walk. The overnight stop would then be at the beach and thus could be most attractive, especially for summer-time swimming. Lorne is set on the coast and has a magnificent back-drop of steep mountains clad in forest. There are also wonderful gorges and waterfalls.

From the Erskine Falls car park there is an excellent foot track right down the valley of the Erskine River to the sea, and this track should be taken for most of the first day's walking. Initially the track leads very steeply down from the car park to the river, just downstream from the base of Erskine Falls. It can be slippery, but the descent is very short and it takes only five minutes to walk down the pad, then up the riverside a little to the falls base. The falls are one of the bigger falls in Victoria in respect of height. They are set in a particularly attractive area of eucalypts and ferns and a fair volume of water flows over them for much of the year.

BORONIA

Follow the track downstream along the north bank to pass pretty Straw Falls. These falls are more like a large cascade or 'weeping rock'. Further down stream is another cascade, but a much smaller one, then the track crosses to the south bank and tends to contour along slopes above the river. Splitters Falls can be clearly seen on a tributary, north across the valley, and they too are quite high and beautiful. Tall eucalypts frame the view of the falls. A side track to these falls exists but the view from the main track should be adequate for most people.

It is about 2.5 km from Erskine Falls car park to the turnoff to Splitters Falls. The pad should be followed on downstream mainly on the south bank until more small falls are passed, then on the north bank until some 6.7 km from Erskine Falls. At this point about 1 km short of the Great Ocean Road is a bridge and a rock overhang known as the Sanctuary. Next, the Little Erskine River confluence is passed and massive cascades can be seen in the broad bed of the stream near the confluence. At this point the track is high up southern slopes from the river after having crossed to the south bank on the bridge. There is, in fact, also a minor pad on the north bank from the bridge past the Sanctuary and to the head of the cascades, but it is better to keep to the main pad by using the bridge. As the Great Ocean Road is neared a quarry can be seen across the river, then a camping ground is entered. It, or another camp area across the Ocean Road, could be your overnight stop. The camp across the road is nearer to the beach front.

On the second day of your walk the distance to be covered is greater than the 8 km of the first day, so start early. First walk the beach until level with the Surf Life Saving Club, then cross the Great Ocean Road and head up Bay Street to the top of the hill to turn left into George Street. Walk up George Street and on south to the Teddys Lookout car park some 2.5 km from camp. At this point, and indeed while on George Street, you should have excellent coastal views. Follow a small steep foot track down south-west from Teddys Lookout so that you overlook the Great Ocean Road and the St George River mouth.

On reaching the riverside 500 m away, head upstream on a good foot track rather than to go towards the beach. The track is the former route of an old timber tramway. Once the coast is left the vegetation reverts from coastal types to eucalypt forest and ferns. Avoid minor side pads off right uphill from the river, and follow the river to a crossing. Just 300 m later, return to the north bank again using a bridge. At a point about 2 km from the Great Ocean

Road area pass some lovely rock pools including Mirror Pool then meet a road at Allenvale. Cross the road at the car park there and diverge off left onto a good foot track which leads to Phantom Falls.

Allenvale farm is on a bend in the river and the track crosses a bridge and skirts the farm clearing before it leads on past a berry farm. The Allenvale farm area is most attractively set and lovely basket willows adorn the river bank. For about 1.5 km the track follows the south bank of the St George River. There are rapids and broad sloping rock to be seen. You then cross to the north bank and within 200 m turn left (west) at a track junction. Next take a detour for 400 m to see 10 m high Phantom Falls before returning to the track junction to head towards Cora Lynn car park.

It is just 300 m along a very ferny pad to Cora Lynn car park. This car park is at a gate and road giving access to the Allen Dam watershed. From Cora

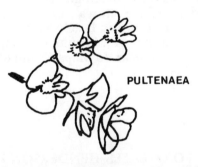

PULTENAEA

Lynn car park follow a 3.5 km long streamside walking track to Cora Lynn Falls. The route follows Cora Lynn Creek all the way and includes some twenty crossings. As the falls are neared special care needs to be taken on slippery, wet rocks. At times it could be very hard to avoid wet feet. The route is particularly lush with ferns and the falls are quite superb. They cascade over many 'steps' of bare rounded rock descending perhaps 50 m all told. The track then climbs via hairpin bends, up a side gully and then past Cora Lynn Falls. Next avoid a track off right steeply uphill, and within some 500 m from the base of the falls Cora Lynn Creek is again met at the confluence with Parkinson Creek. Two walking pads diverge from the confluence. Take the right fork and head up Parkinson Creek valley where an old jeep track is joined. This track leads to a ridge top after crossing Parkinson Creek and ascending eastwards. The Lorne to Erskine Falls Road leads along the ridge top and Blanket Leaf Picnic Ground is reached where the road and ridge are climbed, some 2 km from the base of Cora Lynn Falls. Turn left on the road and follow it 2.5 km, then turn right onto the sealed Erskine Falls Road. Finally, descend Erskine Falls Road 1.5 km back to the car park and walk end.

25 km; first day, 8 km, second day, 17 km; walk times; 3 hours and 5 hours; walk last reviewed February 1988; 'A' grade, easy, overnight walk; all on tracks, roads and beach; features nine waterfalls and cascades, fine forests and beach; walk suited to any time of the year, but best in summer; *Maps: Vicmap 1:25,000 Lorne* refers as do Maps 63 and 64, page 317 and 320.

98   SHEOAK FALLS-HENDERSON FALLS-PHANTOM FALLS

There is a very beautiful walk circuit near Lorne which includes six waterfalls plus some rapids, a small canyon and a stretch of coast, yet the total distance is only 14.5 km. The mouth of the St George River is a good place to commence the circuit. It is about 2.5 km on the Apollo Bay side of Lorne along the Great Ocean Road.

Start off by walking along the side of the Great
Ocean Road for 2 km following the cliff tops away
from Lorne to the mouth of Sheoak Creek which is
the first main gully entering the sea beyond St George
River. The stretch of coast is rocky and wild and a
delight at any time. A foot track leads inland next
to the western bank of Sheoak Creek and should be

SWALLOW

followed upstream for 500 m to 8 m high Sheoak Falls.
The latter 200 m is via a side track to the falls base,
while an upper (left) fork track rises above the head
of the falls then, at a stream bend, crosses to the
opposite bank to provide access to a lesser waterfall,
but one which features an adjacent large rock
overhang known as Swallow Cave. As the name
implies, swallows nest in the crevices of the overhang.
In flood time (rarely) the stream can be a bit difficult
to cross at this spot and great care should be taken
if wading is contemplated. By this stage the fairly
open coastal area has already been left and forest
walking ensues.

Follow the good foot track on upstream along the
north bank until about 1.5 km from the Great Ocean
Road. The river must then be crossed three times
on bridges and ferns make the spot quite pretty. A
small waterfall must be passed and after two further
bridges are crossed, a large picnic area and the
suggested lunch spot should be reached. The spot
is 3.2 km from the coast and 5.4 km from the walk
start. It is a heavily forested spot. On the north side

315

of the cleared area of the picnic ground is another foot track which leads down and across Sheoak Creek. Follow it, after lunch, and within 300 m, reach the forest road which services the picnic area from Lorne. Opposite, two trails diverge off the road. Take the right hand track which ascends up around a spur, crosses Sharps Road (a minor forest road) within a few metres, then sidles westwards towards Henderson Falls, Wonwondah Falls and The Canyon. Continue along this good track until a right fork pad leads down about 50 m to small chute-like 6 m high Wonwondah Falls at a point about 1.5 km from the picnic area.

Return up the 50 m and continue west 300 m to a track junction. Then fork left to walk 600 m, return, to lovely veil-like Henderson Falls, 12 m high and set amid excellent tree and ground ferns. Back at the track junction, fork left and soon climb gradually up a gully, over a small saddle, down across another gully and up into the unusual start of what is known as The Canyon. The formation appears to be a collapsed natural tunnel. The pad leads through the canyon then climbs out its opposite end via a 'porthole'. Not far on, an old jeep track should be reached at a spot about 1.6 km from the Henderson Falls Track turnoff. Walk on down the jeep track for 1 km to reach the St George River at the head of 10 m high Phantom Falls. Descend the foot track to the falls base, then follow the St George River downstream 400 m. Turn right at a track fork to continue downstream 1.6 km, passing the river bed's broad sloping rocks and rapids set near a cliff line and adorned with a few lovely basket willows. A berry farm is passed, then at adjacent Allenvale farm, which is on a bend in the stream, look for a prominent foot bridge over the river about 100 m across the farm's grassy slopes. The bridge leads south, then a short track leads up to the Lorne to Allenvale Road. Cross the road as soon as it is reached to enter a rough car park area on the east side of the river near a

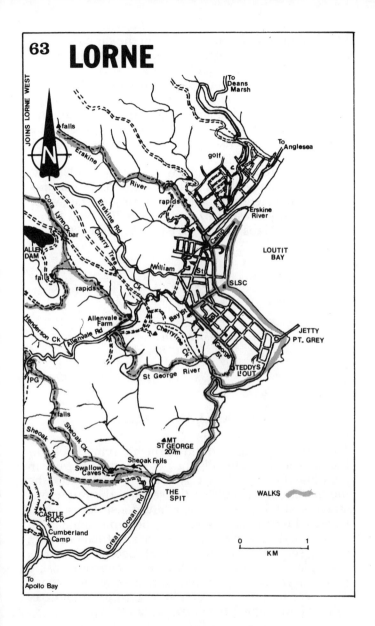

JOINS LORNE WEST

To Deans Marsh

To Anglesea

falls

Erskine River

golf c

rapids

Erskine River

Camp

LOUTIT BAY

Cora Lynn Ck bar

ALLEN DAM

falls

Cherry Tree Ck

Erskine Rd

William St

SLSC

rapids

Allenvale Farm

Allenvale Rd

Henderson Ck

Bay St

Cherrytree Ck

George St

JETTY PT. GREY

TEDDYS L'OUT

St George River

PG

falls

Sheoak Ck

MT ST GEORGE 207m

Swallow Caves

Sheoak Falls

WALKS

THE SPIT

CASTLE ROCK

Cumberland Camp

Great Ocean Rd

0   1
KM

To Apollo Bay

road bridge. A foot track leads from the car park down along the river's east bank for 2 km, back to the river's mouth and the walk's end.

The route is partly along an old tramway alignment and, like most of the day's walk, is within eucalypt forest. A good bridge is crossed along the way and three minor tracks off uphill to the left should be ignored in favour of keeping near the stream.

14.5 km; 5 hours; last reviewed February 1988; 'A' grade; medium walk; all on tracks and roads; features waterfalls; water for lunch from picnic area tap; walk suited to any season; _Maps: Vicmap 1:25,000 Lorne_ refers as do Maps 63 and 64, pages 317 and 320.

GUM
NUTS

99   KALIMNA FALLS

The Otway Ranges around Lorne are remarkable for the number of waterfalls they contain and the ocean coastline in the district is quite magnificent. The mountains dip steeply to the sea and the numerous streams are all lined with really dense forests and ferns, while the ridges tend to be more open with many good viewing points, especially those looking out to sea. The mouth of the St George River is a good place to commence a circuit walk encompassing four waterfalls, a ridge top walk and a stretch of coast. The river mouth is about 2.5 km on the Apollo Bay side of Lorne along the Great Ocean Road.

A foot track leads inland on the Lorne side of the bridge over the river and, within a few metres, is joined on the right by a track from Lorne via Teddy's Lookout. Head upstream and fork left as several minor tracks lead off to the right after about 300 m of walking and remain near the river as the main track swings west. Cross to the south bank at a ford after about another 400 m, then upstream a further 300 m cross a bridge to rejoin the north bank. Fairly dense forest is prevalent throughout the area once the coast is left. Continue upstream near the river to reach Allenvale (2 km from the walk start) at a spot where a road crosses to the west bank of the river. Walk west along the roadway for 1.2 km then keep left where Sharp Road branches off. After 200 m three foot tracks join the road. Head onto the track leading west towards Kalimna Falls just before the road descends to a picnic area beside Sheoak Creek (Sheoak Picnic Ground). The pad continues along the north bank of the creek for 1.5 km following the route of an old timber tramway and sleepers and box cuttings are still to be seen. The area is quite ferny.

Wander along the track westwards, past a cascade and on to a bridge across the creek. Another foot track from the picnic area then joins in on the south bank. Head upstream on the pad for 1.3 km, then fork right 200 m down to Lower Kalimna Falls. Undercutting by the stream permits walking behind the 7 m high falls, making quite an attractive setting. Lunch is suggested at the spot, 6.4 km from the walk start.

Retrace the 200 m to the main track then head upstream past an intersecting minor jeep track and to a foot track off left within 400 m of joining the main foot track from Lower Kalimna Falls. Keep right and walk on up the south side of the valley for 700 m to reach Upper Kalimna Falls. These falls are about 15 m high and set amid many tree and ground ferns.

Retrace the 700 m to the ridgetop track turnoff right,

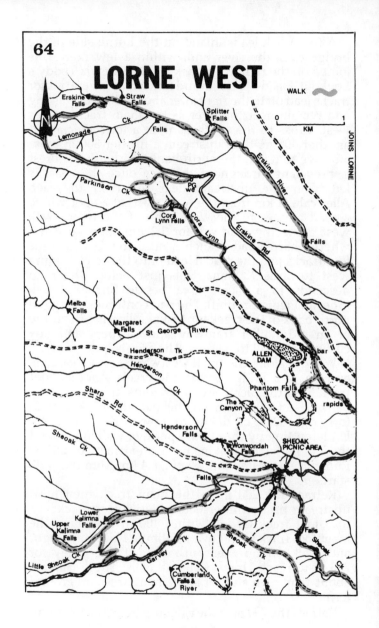

LORNE WEST

WALK

0   KM   1

JOINS LORNE

Erskine Falls
Straw Falls
Splitter Falls
Ck
Falls
Lemonade
Erskine River

Parkinson Ck
PG we
Cora Lynn Falls
Cora Lynn
Ck
Erskine Rd
Falls

Melba Falls
Margaret Falls
St George River
bar
ALLEN DAM

Henderson Tk
Henderson Ck
Phantom Falls
rapids

Sharp Rd
The Canyon

Sheoak Ck
Henderson Falls
Wonwondah Falls
SHEOAK PICNIC AREA

Falls

Lower Kalimna Falls
Upper Kalimna Falls
Little Sheoak Ck
Garvey Tk
Tk
Sheoak Tk
Falls
Sheoak Ck

Cumberland Falls & River

Snow Gums at Millers Hut near Mt Wellington

Victoria Range, Grampians National Park

London Bridge, Port Campbell National Park

then descend it across the valley of Little Sheoak Creek and up to Garvey Track, a forestry road on the next ridge south some 500 m. Turn left and follow the road east-north-east 1.6 km to a barrier and minor jeep track leading off right, uphill. Ignore a foot track to Cumberland River at the spot. Climb the jeep track onto ridge tops and follow it as it swings south-east along the tops. Walk for 2.8 km, avoiding a left fork lesser track at the 700 m stage and a right fork track to Castle Rock at the 1.7 km stage. The last section of the distance involves a fairly sustained descent down east to a saddle.

On the saddle, turn left (north) down a 150 m long foot track. It joins onto another foot track which runs parallel to and high above Sheoak Creek. Turn right, downhill, so that within another 150 m a track off left is met. Use it to cross the creek and see Swallow Caves and falls just upstream then retrace the route to continue down the valley. The pad follows high above the south bank of the stream, from the falls down to the coast 500 m away. Sheoak Falls can be clearly seen from the distance during this descent, but if wishing to go to their base it is necessary to walk a 200 m long side track which doubles back from a point about midway to the coast. These falls are some 8 m high.

Once at the coast, turn left and follow the Great Ocean Road along the cliff tops for 2 km back to the mouth of the St George River. The coastal walking permits wonderful seascapes to finish the day's circuit.

16.2 km; 5½ hours; last reviewed February 1988; 'A' grade; medium walk; all on tracks and roads; features waterfalls; water for lunch from stream, walk suited to any season; *Maps: Vicmap 1:25,000 Lorne* refers as do Maps 63 and 64, pages 317 and 320.

NORTH EASTERN REGION

100 FRASER NATIONAL PARK-COOK POINT

Fraser National Park is a paradise for water craft and water skiers. It is also a place to be sure of seeing Great Grey Kangaroos at close proximity. This walk suggestion starts from a grassy area where kangaroos abound at the north-west tip of Coller Bay, 2 km along the north fork of the main access road of the National Park and where there is a barrier closing off a minor road up Keg Spur.

First, walk eastwards along the lake shoreline road for 1.2 km to the road end and toilet block, then wander along a well graded contouring foot track not far above water level for 2.75 km to the Cook Point area. The pad actually cuts across the neck of the point and as it does so, Blowhard Spur jeep track leads off west uphill. At this point leave the main tracks and walk east onto the long low Cook Point which juts right out into Lake Eildon. There are excellent views across the lake and many boats are usually in the vicinity. Swimming is a possibility if the weather is warm, and the tip of the point would be an excellent place to have lunch before retracing your outward route back to the walk starting point.

8 km; 3 hours; last reviewed January 1987; 'B' grade, family walk; all on tracks; features Lake Eildon; water for lunch from lake usually suitable for drinking; walk suited to any season; *Maps: Vicmap 1:25,000 Coller Bay* refers as does Map 65, page 325.

101 CANDLEBARK GULLY-
FRASER NATIONAL PARK

Candlebark Gully has a nature trail established in it at Devil Cove, Fraser National Park near Eildon. It is a most interesting track and really helps one to appreciate the delicate balance of nature, to learn the names of many plants and trees and to see kangaroos.

A leaflet is available from the Park Ranger. It lists nineteen points of interest along the track and describes in great detail matters of interest at each of the points. The leaflet is obtainable at the Ranger's office, or at the Park's entry control when it is manned during the more popular summer months.

FLAME
ROBIN

The track is not quite 2 km long and has no steep grades. You should make a point of walking very slowly and reading the appropriate part of the leaflet fully at every point of interest. You will be amazed how accurate this leaflet is. For example, it states that at Point 8 it will be obvious, very shortly, why Kangaroo Ridge is so named. Despite the fact that kangaroos have the ability to move from area to area, sure enough, there are the kangaroos on the small ridge, illustrating just how animal habitats (like plant habitats) are well defined and often in a delicate state of balance.

For access to Candlebark Gully travel north for

1 km along the north fork of the main park access road which divides at the park entry control post. The track is right beside Lake Eildon and, as such, is close to all tourist facilities including excellent camping and boating facilities. Tame rosella parrots and noisy mina birds can usually be seen in the camp areas near the trail.

2 km; 1 hour; last reviewed January 1987; 'C' grade, family walk; all on tracks; features nature trail; walk suited to any time of the year; *Maps: Vicmap 1:25,000 Coller Bay* refers as does Map 65, page 325.

102 FRASER NATIONAL PARK-
BLOWHARD SPUR

Just north of Eildon is Fraser National Park, a paradise for water craft and water skiers. It is also one of the best places in Victoria to get close to great grey kangaroos and tame rosella parrots.

A pleasant walk begins at Keg Spur turn-off at the north-west tip of Devil Cove, 2 km along the north fork of the park access road. This spot has large grassy slopes and is one of the best places to see the kangaroos.

From the Keg Spur barrier follow the lakeshore road east to its end 1.2 km away, as the first leg of a very pleasant walk circuit. From the road end there is a good contouring foot pad along steep lakeside slopes for 2.75 km to the neck of long, low Cook Point. Walk to the point for good views, a good lunch spot and perhaps a swim. Many boats can usually be seen in the area.

Next, climb westwards up a jeep track on the crest of a spur until you look down all over Eildon Reservoir. The climb is steep, 2.25 km long, and is

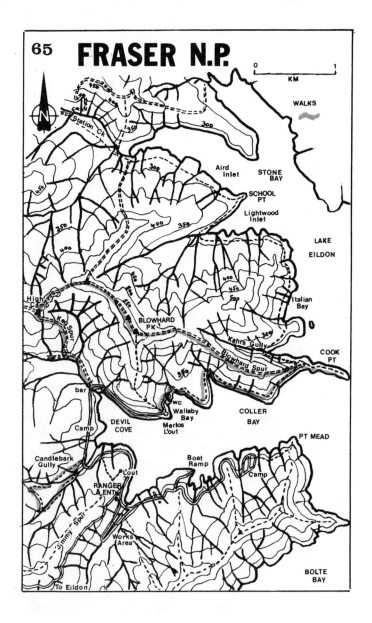

known as Blowhard Spur. Near the top, Mount Buller can be seen away to the east. In fact, many snow-capped peaks may be seen in winter. From the top of Blowhard there is a minor foot pad off south leading steeply down to the lake shoreline road at Merlo's Lookout, but better to pass the turnoff and walk on north-west a while. Walk 1 km north-west on a jeep track to another knob, crossing a saddle in the process. Another jeep track joins in from the right on the knob and there are further good views in the area. Next, turn south-west on the jeep track to descend across another saddle and on up to High Camp 800 m away, at a point where another jeep track joins in from the right. It is a track from Skyline Road on the western edge of the park. Again the junction is on a knob with a clear summit and good views. From the knob, head down Keg Spur south-east 800 m on a very steep section of jeep track to reach a road junction on creek flats. The flats are very grassy, a haven for kangaroos and an excellent spot to see wattles in bloom in winter and spring. Turn left, and walk the final 600 m along the road to complete the walk circuit at the Keg Spur barrier.

9.5 km; 3½ hours; walk last reviewed January 1987; 'B' grade, medium walk; all on tracks; features views, kangaroos and rosellas; water for lunch from lake; walk best suited to winter and spring; *Maps: Vicmap 1:25,000 Coller Bay* refers as does Map 65, page 325.

103   BINDAREE-THE BLUFF-HELICOPTER SPUR

Into the mountains east of Mansfield is the beautiful Howqua River valley and an historic cattleman's hut known as Bindaree Hut. The hut is on the bank of the river not far from the ramparts of The Bluff and

Square Head Jinny. Sturdy forests, river and cliffs make an excellent area for walking. A two-day walk from the hut to the tops and return via precipitous Helicopter Spur is suggested. Access to Bindaree from Mansfield is via Mirimbah, the Stirling Circuit Road (Stirling Ring Road), then south 9.8 km to the Howqua River. Bindaree Hut is then 1.7 km west along the Pikes Flat Road and the hut area is well suited to

HIBBERTIA

camping if desired. However the walk could start from where the Howqua is first met near another hut on the south bank. There is a ford 250 m west of where the river is first reached, and Sixteen Mile Road (a minor forestry road) leads off from the ford towards the tops. As with all high country walks snow is possible, even in mid summer, so walkers need to be well prepared. Helicopter Spur is exceedingly rugged and not suited to other than experienced walkers. Exposure on one bluff renders the route quite unsuited to those sensitive to negotiating cliff sections, even though the rock work is not of a standard comparable with rock climbing as such.

After crossing the ford at the river, head generally south-west up via five hairpin bends on Sixteen Mile Road. Over a 6.7 km distance the road rises from about 800 m elevation to about 1200 m at a saddle just north-west of the cliffs of Square Head Jinny. The route is within forest and the road walk is relatively uninteresting compared to what is in store. The road leads on for 5.1 km more, contouring across the headwaters of Sixteen Mile Creek and its tributaries to gain another saddle and road intersection. There are fire dams above and below the intersection. Turn left up a track southwards for 400 m to where a road runs parallel on the right side. Diverge left at this road and climb steeply on a rough track so as to attain the tops and Bluff Hut at 1500 m elevation. This section is 1.6 km long. There is spring water just short of the hut near some tea-tree.

The Bluff Hut area was once a delightful little grassy saddle with a rustic and historic cattleman's hut in it. The serenity has been marred by four-wheel drive access. Horseriders and thoughtless tin shanty extensions have spoiled the hut. A good track leads south-west from the hut towards The Bluff and into more pleasant surroundings.

The suggestion is to take an afternoon return walk to The Bluff from the hut and to have a late lunch beside the walking track on the slopes of Mount Eadley Stoney. The locality is well endowed with alpine herbage and is right at the treeline so there are good views. It is 4.5 km each way to The Bluff and the good track extends right to the summit rock cairn. The cliffs on the northern face of The Bluff and Mount Eadley Stoney are some of the best in Victoria. The track to the summit lies across the slopes of Mount Eadley Stoney, then crosses a saddle and thereafter it remains near the northern crest of the slopes of The Bluff. The summit of The Bluff is 1720 m above sea level and from it can be seen Lake Eildon westwards, Mount McDonald southwards and Mount Buller northwards. The Bluff has a south sloping 'dip slope', mostly tree covered on its lower reaches, but well above the treeline near the summit.

Back at Bluff Hut, collect water for the evening camp and head off east up the jeep track along the tops until a suitable camp area is reached. Within 1 km there are superb spots to camp.

Next day, continue along the jeep track east in

excellent alpine surroundings, passing over the northern shoulder of fairly inconspicuous Mount Lovick and on to Lovicks Hut which is in a fairly deep saddle 6 km from Bluff Hut. Some 4.5 km east of Bluff Hut the jeep track veers off right and leads via a roundabout southern route through alpine ash trees to Lovicks Hut, approaching Lovicks from the south. Lovicks is another old cattleman's hut steeped in the history of the high country.

From Lovicks Hut follow the jeep track north-north-east and climb to emerge on the top of spectacular Helicopter Spur 1.8 km away. The spur crest is grassy and fairly flat where the jeep track joins it. You should leave the jeep track and turn back west down the open spur top, then consider lunch within the next 300 m to 400 m while on the tops and before difficult terrain is encountered.

The very steep spur must next be descended north-westwards. There are three areas of rocky bluffs on the spur, the uppermost area having two cliff sections in close proximity. The first and third bluff areas require care, but are readily negotiable by remaining on the very crest of the spur, even though at first appearance the way may seem awkward. The second bluff area, however, requires very careful descent. There is a defined foot track right down the spur but, at this second bluff, people have obviously attempted to locate easier alternatives and have formed pads in several directions. The only reasonably safe route is to keep to the east side of the bluff and to use good handholds of rock to negotiate a rock gully. Take extreme care if the rock is at all wet. Some walkers may feel safer if they carry a length of rope to lower packs. About 1.5 km down the spur, the rocks discontinue and the route is down a defined spur crest for a further 1 km. The track then swings north onto a fairly flat spur top within forest, turns further to the north-east and tends to disperse in scrub. A jeep track contours the eastern slopes of this spur and the track leads to join the jeep track within several hundred metres. Once on the jeep track, turn left and descend back to a ford at the Howqua River 2 km away. Cross the ford, turn left and within 200 m the walk circuit is ended.

36 km; 11½ hours walking spread over two days of 23.8 km; 7½ hours and 12.2 km, 4 hours; walk last reviewed March 1987; 'A' grade, medium, overnight, Alpine walk; all on tracks and jeep tracks; features The Bluff and Helicopter Spur; camp water from Bluff Hut vicinity, carry water for lunches; two fords of Howqua River to be negotiated usually about 50 cm deep; bad exposure on bluffs on Helicopter Spur; walk not suited to snow season; *Maps: National Mapping 1:100,000 Howitt and 1:100,000 Mansfield* refers as do Maps 67 and 68, pages 336 and 340.

HELICHRYSUM

104   BINDAREE-THE BLUFF-MOUNT HOWITT

The Bluff and Mount Howitt are two of the better climbing mountains in the Victorian Alps, both being quite high and characteristically alpine, and each having special attractions. The Bluff is noted for its huge escarpments while Mount Howitt provides some of the state's best mountain scenery. The two peaks are linked by a high level range which provides superb walking. This walk recommendation includes both peaks and the linking range, the lovely Howqua River Valley and the spectacular descent of the Howitt Spur. The walk begins and ends at Bindaree, on the banks of the Howqua River. To reach it, travel via Mansfield, Mirimbah, Stirling Circuit Road, then 9.8 km south to the Howqua River. *Being an alpine walk, ensure you take warm and waterproof clothing.*

To start the walk, go 250 m west and ford the river, then climb generally south-west on Sixteen Mile Road, a minor forestry road, via five hairpin bends, then over a saddle below the cliffs of Square Head Jinny and up through the headwaters of Sixteen Mile Creek, until a crossroad is met at two fire dams 11.8 km from the Howqua River ford. Turn left (south) and climb up a track for 400 m to where a road temporarily abuts on the right side. Next diverge right onto this road, south-west, and climb steeply up to and around a hairpin bend so as to attain the tops and Bluff Hut at 1500 m elevation. This section is 1.6 km long. The hut area is often frequented by four-wheel drive vehicles and horseriders, so this former most pleasant camp area should now be avoided and camp established 500 m to 1 km east among the snow gums. Lunch (late) is suggested at the camp and an afternoon side trip taken to The Bluff.

A good track leads south-west from Bluff Hut towards The Bluff, initially through snow gums. It is 4.5 km each way to the summit cairn by good foot track. It sidles across the slopes of Mount Eadley Stoney and across a saddle, then remains near the crest of the northern cliffs of The Bluff. The cliffs are among the best in Victoria. Views from the summit cairn at 1720 m elevation include Lake Eildon, Mount McDonald and Mount Buller. Extensive alpine grass, herbs and many wildflowers are a feature of the upper slopes of The Bluff, much of which is above the tree

331

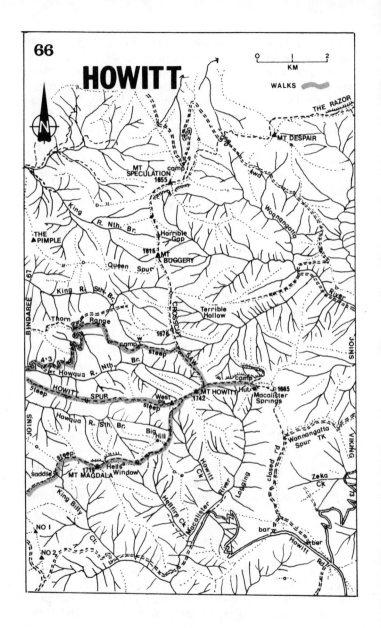

HOWITT

66

WALKS

0   1   2
KM

N

THE RAZOR

MT DESPAIR

MT
SPECULATION
1655

camp

4wd

King
R. Nth. Br.

Wonnangatta

Horrible
Gap

THE
PIMPLE

1816
MT
BUGGERY

Queen Spur

King R. Sth. Br.

River

CROSSCUT SAW

Terrible
Hollow

JOINS

BINDAREE 67

Thorn   Range

1676

camp
W.

steep

4.3

Howqua R. Nth. Br.

HOWITT   SPUR

West
Pk.

camp

MT HOWITT   Hut
1742

Macalister
Springs

1665

Steep

steep

Howqua R. Sth. Br.

Big
Hill

Wonnangatta
Spur TK

VIKING

JOINS

steep

1719
MT MAGDALA

Hell's
Window

Howitt
Ck.

Lodging

closed rd

Zeka
Ck.

saddle

King Billy

Macalister River

NO 1

Ck.

Hellfire Ck.

bar

Howitt

Rd.

NO 2

line. The general direction of the whole of the 4.5 km is south-west.

On the second day, set off east among snow gums and ideal alpine walking surroundings. The minor road to be followed skirts cliff tops and scales several high points. It leads over the northern shoulder of Mount Lovick, then starts a descent to Lovick's Hut, a cattleman's hut which is 6 km from Bluff Hut. It is situated among big sturdy snow gums in a low saddle of the range top. The jeep track reaches the hut via a roundabout southern route among woolly-butt forest and approaches the hut from the south.

From Lovick's Hut follow the jeep track north-north-east, then climb up to the top of Helicopter Spur, 1.8 km from Lovick's. Next climb east 1.5 km to meet the Great Dividing Range. The jeep track then swings south along the range top, but the intention is to head to the left on the long distance Alpine Track, which foot track leads off after the jeep track turns south. Follow the Alpine Track east down into a saddle, then climb steeply up to lofty Mount Magdala. The views west become very good during the steep ascent. The summit is well above the tree line and features huge cliffs on its north face. Just east of the top is a cleft known as Hell's Window and it must be passed next as the Alpine Track is followed further eastwards downhill. Then a small hill is passed by sidling along its north side and you need to ascend, swinging north over Big Hill in lovely alpine garden surroundings. Next climb on to the giant of the district—Mount Howitt, which is 1742 m high, is completely treeless and gives a superb view in all directions, especially east to the Viking and the Razor and north along the Crosscut Saw. Mount Howitt is 7.5 km from where the Alpine Track was joined. To finish a most memorable day, walk east down a well-defined foot pad for 2.5 km through a saddle and up slightly among snow gums to Macalister Springs camp and hut. The spot is particularly good for camping, but the spring water should be boiled before drinking despite its appearance.

On the third day, return to the summit of Mount Howitt, then proceed to the top of the Howitt Spur by walking west-north-west to a high knob and following markers and the good pad. The pad marks the top of the Alpine Track Access route from the Howqua River Valley, while the knob marks the top of the Howitt Spur, one of the most magnificent spurs imaginable. The views west and the vegetation are unforgettable. Descend through this garden setting, noting Hell's Window and Mount Magdala to the left, then enter sturdy woollybutt forest.

ALPINE TRACK

Continue on westwards until a steep descent brings you to a ford 8.2 km from Macalister Springs. Cross the stream and head to the right for 100 m past hut ruins and onto a logging road on the south bank of the Howqua River. Follow this road, west downstream, directly back to Bindaree by keeping near the river. There are three bridge crossings of the Howqua River as you walk this 3.8 km long last sector. Some very beautiful sturdy forest exists in this remote valley.

54 km; 19¼ hours walking, spread over three days of 24.5 km 8¼ hours, 17.5 km, 6½ hours and 12 km 4½ hours; walk last reviewed March 1987; 'A' grade, hard, overnight, Alpine walk; all on tracks; features

The Bluff and Mount Howitt alpine scenery; walk suited to warmer months only; camp water for first night needs to be carried from Bluff Hut and for second night needs to be boiled at Macalister Springs, carry water for lunch each day; *Maps: National Mapping 1:100,000 Howitt and 1:100,000 Mansfield* refers as do Maps 66, 67 and 68, pages 332, 336 and 340.

105   EIGHT MILE-THE BLUFF-SIXTEEN MILE

In the Upper Howqua River valley there are many lightly timbered and grassy clearings. Such places as Sheepyard Flat, Ritchies, Pikes Flat and Bindaree are all well known to bushwalkers and trout fishermen. The flats usually support plenty of raspberries, blackberries and wild roses, indicating the presence of old farms and cattlemen in days gone by. Old cattle pads still remain, as do some of the cattlemens' huts. This walk includes lengthy stretches on old pads with the surrounding mountains giving a finishing touch to ideal walking. Access to the area is via the Mount Buller Road from Mansfield to the Howqua Track turnoff 2 km east of the Merrijig hotel, then along Howqua Track past Sheepyard Flat to the site of former Eight Mile Hut 11.2 km from Sheepyard Flat bridge. At this point a partly obscured turnoff exists on the left side of the logging road, and a road leads for 500 m down to a ford across Eight Mile Creek. The side road is a bit rough but still negotiable to conventional vehicles, likewise the ford in normal conditions. On the east bank of the ford is a grassy clearing where the Eight Mile Hut once stood. The spot is ideal for camping if desired.

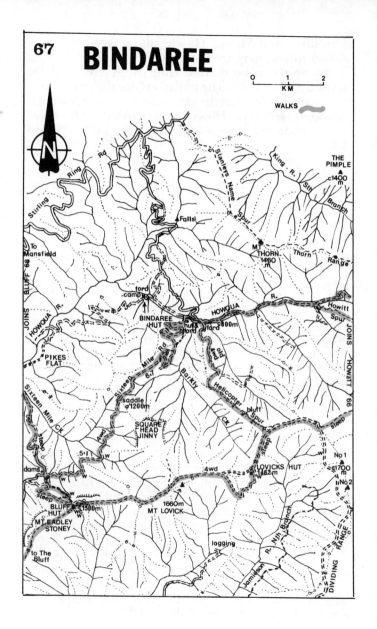

67 BINDAREE

WALKS

0 1 2
KM

N

THE PIMPLE
c1400 m

Stirling Rd

Ring Rd

To Mansfield

Stanleys Name Spur

King R. Sth Branch

Falls

MT THORN 1460 m

Thorn Range

ford camp

BINDAREE HUT

HOWQUA R.

800m

Howitt Spur

JOINS HOWITT 66

hut & ford

ford

old 4wd

JOINS BLUFF 68

HOWQUA R.

PIKES FLAT

Sixteen Mile Rd

6.1

Barkly

Helicopter Spur

bluff

Ck

saddle 1200m

SQUARE HEAD JINNY

steep

steep

steep

No 1 c1700 m

Sixteen Mile Ck

5.1

4wd

LOVICKS HUT 1462 m

No 2

dams

W

steep

1660m MT LOVICK

BLUFF HUT c1500m

MT EADLEY STONEY

logging

Jamieson R. Nth Branch

DIVIDING RANGE

to The Bluff

The walk plan is to climb to the summit of The Bluff from the Howqua River then return by a different routing along the river valley the next day. The tops are subject to snow at any time of the year so warm clothing may be needed and the safety of the walk under prevailing conditions should be carefully considered before setting off. The circuit involves a very long but rewarding climb on the first day.

Start walking from the east bank of Eight Mile Creek at the ford and head up a jeep track south-east onto a spur. An early start is essential.

You need to fork right to keep to the spur crest 300 m after starting out. The left fork marks the Alpine Access Track and the return route. The spur is covered with open forest and continues south-east. You need to climb the spur crest jeep and foot track for 4.2 km after passing the Alpine Access Track and in the process you gain 700 m elevation to attain 1250 m on Rocky Ridge. The middle reaches of the Eight Mile Spur are relatively flat with steep inclines at the start and at the top. The track climbs further on the Rocky Ridge and reaches 1424 m within another 1 km, so over all, much climbing is needed.

Views towards Mount Buller and The Bluff are excellent once on Rocky Ridge, although in the main the track lies just a few metres down the southern slopes of the ridge so that to appreciate northerly views to Mount Buller one needs to leave the track, perhaps for lunch on grassy tops at the crest. The track swings north-east along Rocky Ridge and after 2 km (of which the latter 1 km includes some descent), the track leaves the tops and heads south-east into Bluff Saddle via grassy lightly timbered slopes for 400 m. Bluff Road passes through the saddle and should then be reached. The last 100 m to the road is along an old jeep track. Walk east up Bluff Road for 900 m to the Bluff Walking Track car park. From this point onwards, the main ascent of The Bluff starts. The track leads south-east and soon it rises steeply

up the rocky snow gum-covered ramparts of The
Bluff. Your climb becomes steeper and steeper until
hands need to be used to assist climbing. About
2 km from Bluff Saddle, cliffs on The Bluff are reached,
but the track enables relatively easy negotiation
considering the gradient of nearly forty-five degrees.
Once at the cliff tops the route is east 400 m to a
rock cairn which marks the summit of The Bluff
1720 m above sea level. The mountain has a treeless

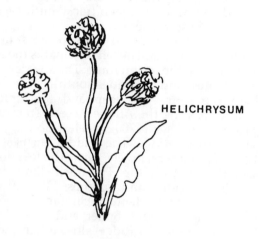

HELICHRYSUM

top, so views are broad and include Eildon Reservoir
to the west, Mount Buller to the north and Mount
McDonald to the south. The main feature is to the
north where north-facing cliffs are some of the biggest
in Victoria. Just east of The Bluff is Mount Eadley
Stoney which also features high cliffs.

The suggested route next is to go to Bluff Hut
4.5 km north-east via the tops. The first section
involves keeping near the northern cliff rim of The
Bluff on a good track and to descend to a saddle
between The Bluff and Mount Eadley Stoney. The
track then sidles across the southern slopes of Mount
Eadley Stoney without attaining its summit. This
whole area is an alpine paradise of wildflowers in

December and January and views are superb. Bluff Hut and the former alpine meadow immediately about it have been spoiled by four wheel drive access, horseriders and hut extensions.

Walkers are advised to proceed to the water supply, (50 m down the track northwards to the right of a thicket of tea-tree) before heading off east 500 m to 1 km to find a camp spot for the night on the tops. The hut is at 1500 m elevation and the tops nearby have lovely snow gums and perfect camping possibilities.

On the second day, head down the steep track north from Bluff Hut, past the water supply. After 800 m there is a road bend off left. Avoid this roadway and descend north for 400 m to a road intersection and two fire dams. Continue across the intersection and down the road north, round the western slopes of a knob at first, then down a steep spur to the junction of Sixteen Mile Creek and the Howqua River. During this 4 km long descent 475 m elevation is lost, to bring you to 725 m above sea level at the confluence.

The Alpine Access Track passes the streams' confluence and after a break, perhaps for morning tea, you should follow the track west downstream. The foot track actually branches off the road just short of the confluence during the approach descent so that a short retrace of walking is needed. This former cattleman's pad remains on the south side of the river valley all the way to Eight Mile Hut site and the end of the walk—all you need do is follow it west for the 9.5 km involved. At times the track is right by the banks of the Howqua River and at other times it is high up the slopes. Some 3.5 km from the confluence, on river flats, is Ritchies Hut, one of the historic huts of the district. It is set beside Fourteen Mile Creek and the Howqua and would be a most enjoyable spot for lunch. Overall the river valley walk section descends 175 m in elevation, but the track rises and drops many times to that the descent is

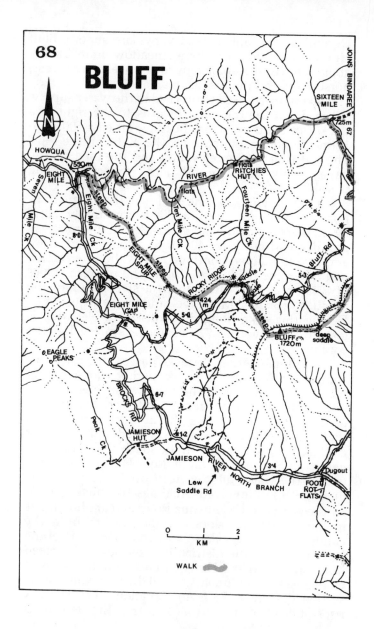

68

BLUFF

N

JOINS BINDAREE

SIXTEEN MILE

725m 67

HOWQUA

590m

EIGHT MILE

Seven Mile Ck

Eight Mile Ck

8·0

steep

EIGHT MILE SPUR

steep

RIVER

flats

RITCHIES HUT

flats

Ten Mile Ck

Fourteen Mile Ck

BLUFF Rd

5·3

ROCKY RIDGE

1424 m

saddle

EIGHT MILE GAP

5·4

steep

EAGLE PEAKS

BLUFF 1720m

deep saddle

Brooks Rd

Peak Ck

6·7

JAMIESON HUT

1·2

JAMIESON RIVER NORTH BRANCH

3·4

Dugout

FOOT ROT FLATS

Low Saddle Rd

0   1   2
KM

WALK

largely unnoticeable. Several idyllic river flats are passed and each has good camping possibilities. In November the valley is renowned for wonderful displays of Prostanthera (purple mint bush) flowers. The last 300 m is a retrace of the previous day's walk.

PROSTANTHERA

30 km; 12 hours walking time spread over two days of 14.2 km, 7½ hours and 15.8 km, 4½ hours; walk last reviewed March 1987; 'A' grade, hard overnight Alpine walk; all on tracks and roads; features The Bluff; water for camp from Bluff Hut area, no water for lunch first day and Howqua River water for second day; walk not suited to snow season; *Maps: National Mapping 1:100,000 Howitt and 1:100,000 Mansfield* refer as do Maps 67 and 68, pages 336 and 340.

The Upper Howqua River descends from some of Victoria's choicest alpine country and an access track leads up through the river valley to the long distance Alpine Track in the high country. A spectacular round walk, especially good in summer, can be taken from the foot of the Howitt Spur by the river to the tops and return. Access to the area is via Mansfield, Mirimbah, Stirling Circuit Road, then south on Bindaree Road for 9.8 km to the Howqua River, and east on a minor riverside road for 3.8 km to the base of the Howitt Spur via three bridges. There is a clearing and in it the ruins of a hut. The spot is at 880 m elevation, just before a fourth bridge.

RANUNCULUS

Commence walking up the road continuation on the north bank of the river. The road rises to the crest of the Thorn Range within 4.3 km, then descends into the Upper King River catchment where logging has taken place. Walk the road as far as the range crest, avoiding a right fork minor side road after 1 km then, at the saddle, turn right (east) up another jeep track. Within a few metres it begins to cross the ridge and descend. At the road high point, go right onto a foot track so as to follow the very ridge crest. By this stage most of the tall forest areas have been passed and snow gums start to predominate. A foot track then leads right along the ridge at first east, then south-east, then east again and down into a saddle where there is a small but good camping area. Lunch is suggested in this locality as water is available just north, down the slopes. The spot is about 2.5 km from where the logging road was left and is right at the foot of the main steep climb onto the spectacular Crosscut Saw.

The highlight of the day comes after lunch as you ascend among snow gums and rocks on a reasonable pad to reach the treeless crest of the main divide. Views become superb and, while 300 m of elevation is gained, the distance is only about 1.3 km. The latter section is particularly attractive, being like an alpine meadow; then at the crest, the striking Viking and Razor dominate the view east.

The Alpine Track leads right along the tops. From this point, leave the Thorn Range (also known as Stanleys Name Spur) and follow the main track south-east near 'the blade' of the Crosscut Saw. The next 1.5 km perhaps form one of the most beautiful tracks in Victoria. Views, alpine flowers and rocks, a few snow gums and looming Mount Howitt (1724 m) will no doubt entice walkers to linger.

Where the Crosscut Saw joins on to Mount Howitt, diverge left onto a track leading east down to Macalister Springs 1.5 km away. The descent route is most delightful and The Springs area would be a good afternoon tea spot. Vallego Gantner Hut is at The Springs, as is an excellent camping area with a good view of The Terrible Hollow. *The water from Macalister Springs (the start of the Macalister River) needs boiling, however.*

Next, walk west back up the track and to the summit of Mount Howitt for a view of most of Victoria's alpine area. It provides an unobstructed view as the tree line is substantially lower. Proceed south-west to a knob 2.5 km from Macalister Springs which knob marks the very top of the Howitt Spur. *A few markers will assist if fog prevails.* Join the spur and start the really wonderful descent down the Alpine Track Access through magnificent alpine

MOUNTAIN VIOLET

garden conditions. Rocks and tremendous vistas, and fascinating Hells Window to the left, create an unforgettable experience. About 1 km down the spur and 3.5 km out from Macalister Springs, sturdy forest is entered. Continue west on the good track, sometimes in snow gums, sometimes in almost rain forest, and often past view points until a final sharp descent brings you back to the walk starting point just across a ford. Track markers should make navigation quite easy. The distance from the top of the spur to the end of the walk is 8 km.

19 km; 7 hours; walk last reviewed March 1987; 'A' grade, hard Alpine walk; all on tracks; features some of the best of Victoria's alpine scenery; suited only to warmer months; creek water available for lunch, but carry water also; *Maps: National Mapping 1:100,000 Howitt* refers as does Map 66, page 332.

In north-eastern Victoria is the massive lofty granite plateau of Mount Buffalo, 1000 m higher than the surrounding countryside and flanked by huge rock faces and cliffs. The plateau was one of the earliest National Parks to be declared in the State of Victoria. This was in recognition of its outstanding attractions. In consequence, the Mount Buffalo Chalet has long been a retreat for walkers and tourists. The Chalet is set most impressively at the plateau escarpment rim. Behind it, on the plateau, is one of the best *easy walks* in Victoria. This walk includes the well known landmark known as The Monolith.

STYPANDRA

It is suggested that walkers first view the Pulpit Rock and Bents Lookout area at the escarpment rim in front of the Chalet, and then head off on the circuit plateau walk. Bents Lookout is directly in front of the Chalet, and Pulpit Rock is 500 m distant north-west along the Buffalo Gorge and falls rim track. The view is of the Ovens River Valley over 1000 m below and the falls plunge over most incredible rock faces, often frequented by rock climbers.

From the Chalet follow a road east down past picnic facilities to the road end near tennis courts and the escarpment. A broad foot track should then be followed past the left side of the tennis courts so as to see further viewpoints on the way to the Underground River. A descent southwards brings you to Eurobin Creek 800 m from the Chalet. The creek flows under granite boulders, hence the name 'Underground River'. Alpine ash forest covers the gully area and is most attractive. A climb up some hairpin bends and across spur slopes brings one to the View Point Track off left within 700 m. Turn right and proceed 400 m to reach the minor road which connects the chalet with the Lake Catani camp area. The dam wall of Lake Catani is just upstream and a footbridge across Eurobin Creek is just below the dam. Take this footbridge and the track which leads along the lake shore for 1 km to link with the main Horn Road which is the principal road on the plateau. Turn left and within 100 m turn right up a minor jeep track which angles back north-west from the Horn Road. This jeep track should be climbed via a hairpin bend and a spur until it becomes a foot track and gives access to Lake View. The climb is steep, but short in that you gain 150 m elevation over a distance of 800 m.

Lake View is a lookout point from granite boulders on a hilltop. The view point reveals much of the plateau area, including the view across towards The Monolith, your next goal.

About 50 m short of Lake View Lookout Point the foot track continues down the northern slopes for 800 m back to the Horn Road. Leave the forested slopes temporarily at this point and walk the road 200 m to the left so as to reach a small saddle. At this spot, opposite the National Park offices, is another foot track off right back into the forest. Take this track which climbs up via a hairpin bend and some steps to a saddle 800 m away, then turn right for the 200 m return walk to The Monolith. A ladder provides access to the top of this remarkable granite tor.

Back on the main track, continue 200 m, avoid a track joining in from the right, pass over a small saddle

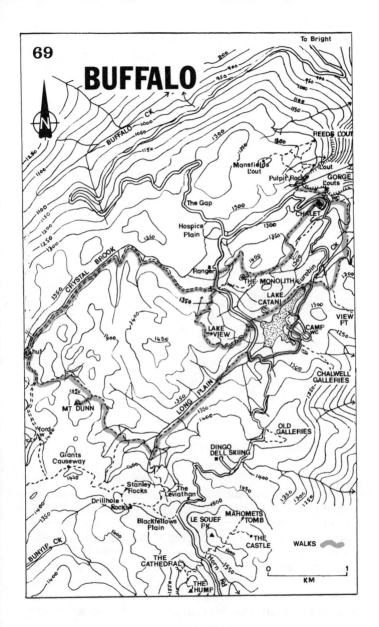

69

BUFFALO

and walk down to another track junction 700 m north-east. Veer left and climb onto a small ridge, then follow the track north-east past a horse yard and stables and on to the Chalet another 700 m distant.

8.2 km; 3 hours; last reviewed March 1988; 'A' grade, easy Alpine walk; all on tracks; features views and granite tors; carry water for lunch at Lake View; walk suited to any season except winter and early spring; *Maps: Vicmap 1:25,000 Eurobin* **refers as does Map 69, page 347.**

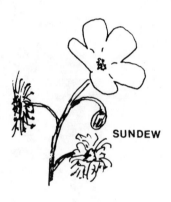

SUNDEW

108   MOUNT BUFFALO PLATEAU-MOUNT DUNN

Mount Buffalo National Park features a massive granite-capped plateau rising abruptly to 1720 m which is dissected by geological fault lines. Streams flow along the faults mostly in a north-easterly direction, then cascade off the plateau rim. One stream, Crystal Brook, leaves the rim at Buffalo Gorge via waterfalls 240 m high. Huge granite escarpments permit wonderful views of the surrounding river valleys and nearby high country, while granite tors and tiny alpine plains on the plateau make the whole park a walkers paradise each summer, especially when the alpine flowers bloom. Snow usually prevents winter walking and the plateau camp ground closes each winter too. Numerous day walks are possible and one of the best includes a circuit passing the Buffalo Chalet and the Lake Catani camp ground, so could be joined at either point. For the purposes of these notes, the circuit starts and ends at Lake Catani camp.

From the camp ground, first head west 600 m along the camp access road which leads near the south shore of Lake Catani to link with the main Horn Road. By walking 200 m down Horn Road to the right, you should cross a stream and reach a foot track off left up the Long Plain. This track leads south-west up Eurobin Creek for 1.7 km, initially for 500 m on the north bank then on the south bank of the stream. As the name implies the walk is via a long plain, but a plain which is alpine in character. It is very narrow and features interesting alpine plants. At its western end you should fork right at a track junction and climb north-west towards Mount Dunn in a forested area. Within 500 m you need to fork right again and continue to climb to a saddle 800 m distant and immediately north of Mount Dunn.

FERN

A 900 m long return trip up the peak is recommended. You need to ascend 80 m including by way of some ladders, and the panorama of the plateau from the boulder-capped summit makes every metre worthwhile. Once back at the saddle, head north-west out onto an alpine meadow and a suitable lunch spot beside a tiny stream. Some 900 m from the Mount Dunn turn-off, the pad reaches a fire access road after crossing a low saddle. Turn right along this minor road and within 500 m reach a hut and car park at the end of minor Reservoir Road. The spot is just downstream from the dam wall of the small Devils Couch reservoir. The hut is open and could be used for shelter if required.

Next follow The Reservoir Road north-east 300 m, pass a left fork fire access road (and barrier at a bridge), then continue out to The Horn Road 3.1 km from the reservoir hut area. This valley walk is close to Crystal Brook and is through interesting alpine plant-community areas.

At Horn Road turn left and proceed just 150 m along the road northwards, crossing a minor gully. The National Park Ranger's office is adjacent and a track leads up 500 m east, swings south for 300 m

KUNZEA

via some steps, then forks. Take the right fork side trip for 200 m, return, to the Monolith. This feature is a remarkable, vertically sited, granite tor with a lookout built on top of it. It provides one of the Buffalo Plateau's best views of the plateau itself as opposed to plateau rim views. A ladder facilitates access to the lookout.

Next head off east again towards the Buffalo Chalet. After 200 m, avoid a track joining in from the right and 700 m further east turn north uphill, avoiding a track off east (ahead). Climb onto a small ridge, follow the track east past a horse yard and stables and continue to the Buffalo Chalet 700 m away. Head down the main chalet entry steps, cross the road in front of the chalet and reach the plateau rim at spectacular Bents Lookout.

This escarpment is one of Victoria's most scenic and it is worth while taking a 1 km return side trip to view the escarpment at several vantage points. Pulpit Rock, a famous landmark, could be the turn around point. To reach it, simply walk the cliff rim Gorge Track west, crossing Crystal Brook as you progress.

CELMISIA SNOW DAISY

Once back at the grand old Buffalo Chalet, follow a road east, down past picnic shelters, to its end near tennis courts and the escarpment.

Your next goal is the Underground River. To reach it the tennis court should be passed along its left side so as to see two viewpoints. A descent southwards follows to Eurobin Creek 800 m from the Chalet. The creek flows under granite boulders, hence the name 'Underground River'. The forest in this locality is particularly sturdy and there is quite a gully

351

formed by the creek as it nears the plateau edge. A climb up some hairpin bends, then across the end of a spur, brings one to the View Point Track junction within 700 m. Turn right and, within 400 m, reach the minor road which connects the chalet with the Lake Catani camp area. The dam wall of Lake Catani is just upstream and a bridge crosses Eurobin Creek

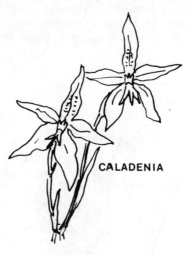

CALADENIA

at the junction. Lastly, follow the road south-west along the lake shore back into camp 800 m distant.

15.5 km; 5 hours; last reviewed March 1988; 'A' grade, medium Alpine walk; all on tracks and minor roads; features granite tors and escarpment views; water for lunch from stream near Devils Couch; suited to any season except winter and early spring; *Maps: Vicmap 1:25,000 Eurobin* refers as does Map 69, page 347.

Silent Street, Wonderland, Grampians National Park

Razorback and Mt Feathertop, Bogong National Park

Mt Bogong from Mt Feathertop, Bogong National Park

Bright, 77 km east of Wangaratta in the north-east of the State, is scenicly located at the foot of the Victorian Alps and is one of the State's most popular holiday towns. There are a number of fine walks round the town, along the Ovens River and through cool parks featuring magnificent deciduous trees. One of the most pleasant of walks is known as the Canyon Walk, which is adjacent to the river. It can be extended east of the main road bridge over the river to create

HARDENBERGIA

a most enjoyable 6 km route. Besides the main road bridge, there are three foot bridges, one at each end of the suggested route and one permitting short-cutting if desired.

The walk leaves Gavan Street (Ovens Highway) at the Pinewood Hotel corner via Back Porepunkah Road for just a couple of hundred metres to the Ovens River bridge. Remain on the south bank and head downstream on a good foot track between Riverside Avenue and the river. This track continues downstream for 1.5 km, crossing several small foot bridges over former mine sluicing channels and leading past several viewpoints of the river as it flows through a small 'canyon'. A suspension bridge then permits crossing to the north bank for a return walk on another pad 1.5 km long, which is closer to the river bank and gives a better appreciation of the canyon. Keep going east from the road bridge through a camping area and within 500 m meet another foot bridge over the river. Turn left away from the river so as to join Germantown Road almost immediately. A 1 km walk east along this quiet road brings you to a third foot bridge. Cross to the south bank and then you can follow the south bank foot track 1.5 km west back via parkland and camping areas to the Back Porepunkah Road *road* bridge and the walk end.

WARNING: Watch any children in your party whilst walking in the area of the sluicing channels.

6 km; 2 hours; last reviewed January 1987; 'B' grade; family walk; all on tracks; features Ovens River; water for lunch from river; walk suited to any season; bus transport to Bright available from Wangaratta; *Maps: Vicmap 1:25,000 Bright* **refers as does Map 70, page 355.**

110   BRIGHT-HUGGINS LOOKOUT

The popular tourist town of Bright in north-eastern Victoria is set beside the Ovens River and lies close to steep hillsides that offer various and most pleasant views of the town.

This walk suggestion is to visit Huggins Lookout south of the town, and also to undertake what is known as the Golf Links Walk north of the town, for good views from the north. The Ovens River needs to be crossed twice.

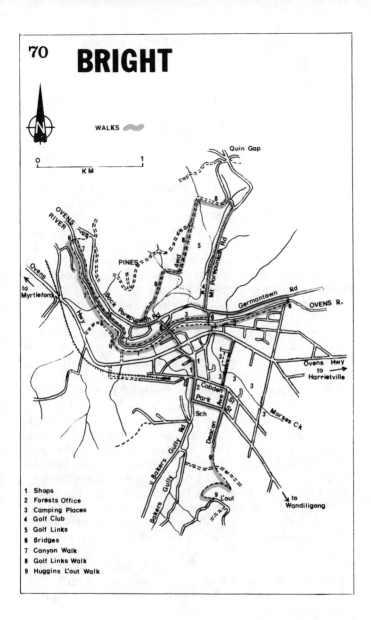

70 **BRIGHT**

WALKS

N

0   1
      K M

Quin Gap

OVENS RIVER

PINES

Ovens
to
Myrtleford

Back Porepunkah Rd

4wd

Mt Porepunkah Rd

5

Germantown Rd   OVENS R.

Hwy

Ovens Hwy
to
Harrietville

Cobden

Park   Ave

Morses Ck

Sch   Deacon St

Baker St

Baker's Gully Rd

9 L'out

to
Wandiligong

1 Shops
2 Forests Office
3 Camping Places
4 Golf Club
5 Golf Links
6 Bridges
7 Canyon Walk
8 Golf Links Walk
9 Huggins L'out Walk

355

Due to the foresight of earlier residents, many of the streets of Bright are lined with magnificent deciduous trees. Elms, poplars and scarlet oaks provide quite a spectacle in autumn and many other types of deciduous trees create interest throughout the year.

The circuit should start and end at the main shopping area in Ireland Street. At first, walk south up the street, which is lined with elms, maples, liquidambars and ash trees, to turn left onto Park Street for one block. Park Street has elms, Indian bean trees and golden ash. Turn right at Deacon Avenue and a graded walking track can then be followed south as it continues on from the nearby south end of Deacon Avenue. The track is short and rises steadily to Huggins Lookout. A jeep track is crossed as you ascend the northerly aspect slopes. These slopes have good wildflower displays in spring, including leopard orchids, but remember wildflowers are protected and should not be picked.

Huggins Lookout is at a hillside-contouring forestry road and permits views northwards towards the township. After viewing this excellent panorama you should retrace the short route down the foot track and back north on Deacon Avenue. However, after passing along hawthorn-lined Deacon Avenue to Park Street, you should continue north one more block to Cobden Street, cross the street and enter a park and camping area. You can then walk north through this camp to join Cherry Lane after crossing Morses Creek on a bridge. Just nearby Cherry Lane links to the Ovens Highway (Delany Street). At this point you should turn left to head west along the beautiful deciduous tree-lined highway which features elms, ash, pinoaks and scarlet oaks. Within one street block recross Morses Creek, then turn right into parkland bordering the Ovens River. A foot bridge lies immediately ahead and should be used to cross the river to its north bank. Lunch could be eaten in this area by the river.

Take the pad from the bridge and head north a few metres to join Germantown Road.

Turn left at the road, then almost immediately turn right up Mount Porepunkah Road past the town's golf club. A 1 km walk up this pleasant rural road and you are at Oregon Road junction. Turn left along

Hibbertia

this forest road at the northern edge of the golf links and continue along the perimeter of the links using a firebreak jeep track. Views of Bright township southwards are excellent in this locality.

The jeep track should be followed as it turns south and descends beside the golf links, and down to Back Porepunkah Road. As you descend ignore a forestry road, off right, leading into the adjoining forestry plantation area. There are also a couple of right angle bends to be taken during the descent. Once on Back Porepunkah Road you should turn left and continue the short distance to the second road off right which, actually, is still Back Porepunkah Road. It crosses the Ovens River and returns you to the Ovens Highway (Gavan Street). Anderson Street is almost directly opposite. Take it and within one block you are back at the shops of Ireland Street. Anderson Street is lined with Himalayan cedars, elms, horse chestnuts and liquidambar trees.

7 km; 3 hours; last reviewed January 1987; 'B' grade; family walk; all on tracks and roads; features views

of Bright; water for lunch at Ovens River; walk suited to any season; bus transport to Bright available from Wangaratta; *Maps: Vicmap 1:25,000 Bright* refers as does Map 70, page 355.

111   BEECHWORTH HISTORICAL RAMBLE

Historically, Beechworth is a most interesting town. It was founded in 1852 during the gold rush and over the next fourteen years gold produced totalled four million ounces. It had a population of 40,000 at one time, but now has only 3700 residents.

Unlike most other gold towns, Beechworth became a major centre on the old Sydney to Melbourne coach road and buildings for the administration of all north-east Victoria were erected solidly and elegantly as if to display the wealth of the district. Ned Kelly frequented Beechworth's hotels and both he and his mother were tried in its Court and placed in its gaol. Ned often raided in the district. The National Trust has seen fit to help restore some of the buildings and to foster museums. With so many places of historical interest, all set in such pleasant natural surroundings, the opportunity for a ramble is most appealing. To fully appreciate the atmosphere of the district it is advisable to stroll.

You need to observe the magnificent old trees planted in the 1850s and the numerous old houses, some with iron lace and real elegance; others are simply miners' cottages with wooden verandahs adjoining the footpath. Each one tells a slightly different story of success or failure in the quest for gold. You will enjoy Beechworth whether or not you usually prefer to walk in areas away from towns.

Using the detailed town map in this book follow this suggested route which includes the town and nearby natural attractions.

Go to Keystone Bridge, the historic granite bridge over Spring Creek at the south end of the town on the main Wangaratta Road. Small Newtown Falls and an old mining race cut in 1866 can be seen here. Then set off walking.

GAOL

Gorge Road leads off north along the west bank of Spring Creek, forks right after 100 m and descends gradually for 2.5 km to another bridge over Spring Creek at the head of Gorge Falls. The walk is on a minor road through pleasant lightly forested and granite boulder-strewn country at the edge of town. Several boulders, named for their odd shapes, are passed. Buddah Rock on the right and Sphinx Rock on the left are just two. Gorge Falls lie just downstream of the bridge and cascade for a total of 120 m into the valley that was once the Reids Creek Goldfield. Have a good look at the falls and perhaps have lunch in the area (but do not drink the polluted water), then continue up the road as it swings south. After 900 m of walking through native pine forest, the famous Beechworth Powder Magazine should be reached. It was built in 1859-1860 for storing gun powder and has been restored by the National Trust. It is one of over thirty buildings in the town classified by the Trust. Near the structure, a replica of a typical slab hut of the goldfields has been built for a caretaker.

Continue on through Gorge Reserve on asphalted Gorge Road north-east from the Magazine rather than heading towards town. After 1.3 km of forest walking through many more native pines, past more boulders and two view points, reach the main road to Wodonga called Sydney Road. Here at the junction is the famous Golden Horse Shoes monument commemorating the election of the first member to enter State Parliament from the district. An elated miner apparently shod his horse with golden shoes. Just a few metres to the right along Sydney Road, a road leads off left at right angles and leads to the Beechworth Cemetery within about 300 m. On the north-west side of the cemetery are two Chinese Burning Towers, with hundreds of Chinese graves behind them. The Chinese were a common sight on the gold fields.

Return to Sydney Road and follow it south-east towards town, but instead of turning south-west into town after 750 m continue 350 m, straight along the extension of Sydney Road called Junction Road and past the large old State Primary School, then cross High Street and walk 300 m to the shore of Lake Sambell. Turn right to reach the water's edge, then follow a road for 900 m around the western shore and out of the reserve onto Albert Road. The lake area is quite picturesque in autumn and appears to have been an old dredging area. Once at Albert Road, turn right and walk 450 m to the centre of town at the intersection of Ford Street.

Between High and Ford Streets there are good examples of Victorian era style signwriting, stone work, guttering and cast iron work. At Ford Street intersection, on the right, is the Post Office built in 1853, and on the left is the restored Bank of Victoria building housing a large gemstone and fluorescent

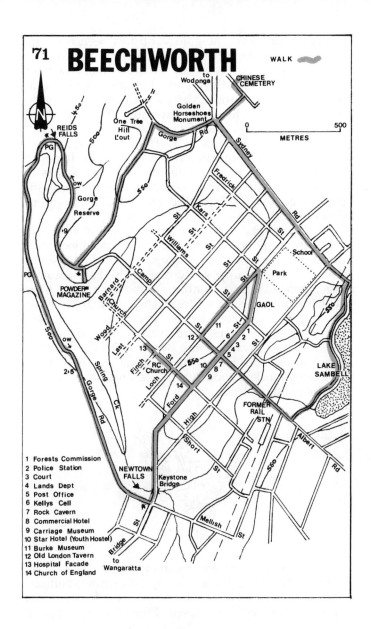

71 **BEECHWORTH**

WALK

to Wodonga

CHINESE CEMETERY

Golden Horseshoes Monument

One Tree Hill L'out

Gorge Rd

Sydney Rd

0 500
METRES

REIDS FALLS

PG

Fredrick St

Gorge Reserve

Kars St

Williams St

St

School

Camp

Park

POWDER MAGAZINE

Barnard

Church

GAOL

Wood

Last

11

6 St 7

St

12

13

5 4 3 2

Finch

RC Church

550

10

8

LAKE SAMBELL

Loch

9

Spring Ck

14

Gorge Rd

Ford

FORMER RAIL STN

2.5

High

Albert Rd

Short

NEWTOWN FALLS

Keystone Bridge

St

Mellish St

Bridge St

to Wangaratta

1 Forests Commission
2 Police Station
3 Court
4 Lands Dept
5 Post Office
6 Kellys Cell
7 Rock Cavern
8 Commercial Hotel
9 Carriage Museum
10 Star Hotel (Youth Hostel)
11 Burke Museum
12 Old London Tavern
13 Hospital Facade
14 Church of England

mineral collection. The gold vault has been restored and there is a magnificent chandelier on display.

Across Ford Street is the Westpac Bank (former Bank of New South Wales) building which also handled much of the district's gold behind its very thick walls and enclosed courtyard. The Post Office tower has slit windows facing each of the Westpac Bank and former Bank of Victoria buildings across the intersection, presumably for security during gold loading at the banks. The Westpac Bank has a decorative Coat of Arms showing the lion (Britain) positioned as if submissive and the colony more dominant.

Albert Street becomes Camp Street once across Ford Street. Follow Camp Street for one block and turn right into Loch Street to visit the Burke Museum (1856) which is supposedly one of the best country museums in Victoria. Continue along Loch Street over William Street to Kars Street, then turn back at an acute angle into Ford Street. This routing is to see some lovely old trees, gardens and a bandstand in the gardens. Next pass the Beechworth Gaol on the left, fronting Ford Street. The gaol was originally built as a wooden stockade which was replaced in 1859 by the present structure.

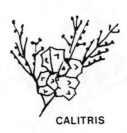

CALITRIS

Across William Street, on the left again, is a group of five granite buildings housing Government offices. At the north end of the group are two former Gold Wardens' offices. The present Police Station used to be the Sub-Treasury. The Court House still operates and the former Telegraph Office is at the south end of the line. Opposite is the Shire Hall which has a cell beneath the rear of it in which Ned Kelly was placed in 1870.

Across Camp Street on the right is the old Star Hotel which has been restored and is now used as a Youth Hostel. Opposite is Tanswells Commercial Hotel, restored at great cost, obviously. Take a look inside the dining room and at the century old cellar. Both are magnificent. Next door, the National Trust has set up a carriage Museum in an old Coach House and Stables built in 1859. Continue up Ford Street to Church Street and note the old churches on each corner as you turn right. The Anglican Church (1859) has a Norman Tower. In the next block is the Catholic Church and one further block on, still on the same side of Church Street, is the Goldfields Hospital facade. This old hospital was once the only one between Melbourne and Goulburn (NSW).

Return along these two blocks to Ford Street and turn right. It is then only 600 m down Ford Street back to Keystone Bridge and the end of the walk. If you can somehow freshen up, why not have dinner at Tanswells Hotel in the old atmosphere and put a most satisfying end to a memorable day.

10.5 km; 3½ hours; walk last reviewed January 1987; 'A' grade, easy walk; all on tracks and roads; features National Trust classified buildings; water not available for lunch at Spring Creek falls (water polluted); walk suited to any time of the year; *Map: Vicmap 1:25,000 Reids Creek* refers as does Map 71, page 361.

At 1986 m above sea level, Mount Bogong is Victoria's highest peak and one of the State's most beautiful mountains. Much of north-eastern Victoria can be seen from its top on a fine day and the view even includes Mount Kosciusko and Mount Jagungal in New South Wales. Several ascent routes provide magnificent walking, but the majority of people climb the northern spurs from Mountain Creek.

**ACAENA
BIDGEE WIDGEE**

In these days of 'fun and fitness' many athletes run up the northern spurs and down again to get fit and take only two or three hours. They take no precautions it seems, and in the author's view it is only a matter of time before tragedy occurs. Bogong is a peak requiring respect. A number of people have died on this mountain in the past, and sudden violent weather changes, plus blizzards, occur even in mid summer. There are steep slopes and cliffs surrounding much of the summit and it can be very difficult to locate descent spurs in fog and especially in blizzards. A snow pole line exists along the tops with subsidiary pole lines to the spurs, and these do assist greatly. When you climb Bogong, take no risks. Also, pick a fine day when the forecast is fine, and then you will be certain to have a wonderful experience. If the weather looks grim, forget the trip. You will not see much, anyway, due to mists and fog.

The best day trip to undertake is up the Eskdale Spur and down the Staircase Spur. Climbing is easier in the clockwise direction. Start the walk at the Mountain Creek picnic and camp area 10.6 km east of the Kiewa Valley Highway at Tawonga. The spot has good facilities and is at 600 m above sea level. It is at the junction of Trappers Gap Road. Eastwards from the camp area is a jeep track up the Mountain Creek Valley.

Head off up the jeep track east to the Walkers Intention Book near the first landmark, Sodawater Creek. This creek, 500 m from the walk start, is the first of many fords to be crossed. There are fords at every stream along the jeep track, but walkers can cross each stream on foot bridges adjacent to the fords. As you continue, Doorway Creek is crossed, then Mountain Creek is crossed four times. The base of the Staircase Spur is reached 1.8 km from the walk start. Keep on the jeep track and note the spur foot pad for the return section of the walk. The spot is at 660 m elevation and in mixed forest. A camp site is beside the stream at the junction.

Continue 4 km east on the jeep track as it rises towards Camp Creek Gap. More fords are passed, then the jeep track doubles back uphill to the left and zig-zags to the gap to meet Trappers Gap Track as it crosses the saddle. A foot pad short cuts the zig-zag and should be used to ascend directly to Camp Creek Gap some 600 m distance from the creek generally eastward. From the gap, southwards, the Eskdale Spur foot track forks off right and another Walker's Intention Book is at the track start. The gap is at 1120 m elevation and still within mixed forest. The track ahead soon ascends into snow gum country

365

and is very steep. About 1.2 km up from the gap, the track crosses a tiny stream after sidling a bit. Water is usually available, so that lunch could be eaten here by the stream although some may prefer to wait until reaching Michell Hut further south up the spur. The creek is at 1340 m and the Hut, 1.3 km on, is at 1620 m. The hut has tank water. It is a small hut which sleeps up to six persons.

About 500 m on up the spur track the tree line is met and a snow pole line marks the way. Granite Flat Spur Track joins in from the left right at the tree line at 1700 m elevation. The next 1 km up the pad is steep and exposed. Alpine grass and flowers

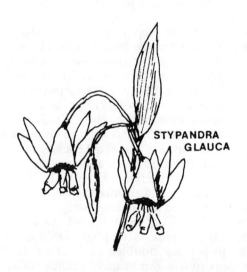

STYPANDRA
GLAUCA

plus views add interest. Then as the top of the Eskdale Spur is attained at 1960 m, the main pole line is met at pole number 1272. You should then turn right and follow the pole line foot track west. Within 200 m, at pole 1279, the top of the Staircase Spur is reached which marks your return route. However, first continue 300 m ahead to the final short climb to the prominent rock summit cairn of Mount Bogong. Once at the top it is best to wander about the rounded top so as to obtain the best views in each direction.

To descend the mountain return down the pole line track east for 300 m to pole 1279, then turn left down the Staircase Spur. The former site of Summit Hut is passed within 250 m, then a memorial to three skiers is passed. They died in a blizzard in 1943. The track is pronounced and poles indicate the way as you descend along the east side of the Twin Knolls, Castor and Pollux, then meet the tree line at 1720 m elevation and 1 km from the tops. Once among snow gums the spur track tends north-west, then after a steep descent it flattens out a bit. A second steep section is followed by a second flat section and the former Bivouac Hut site is then passed, 2.5 km down from the tops. The site is now used by some campers. A new hut lies 200 m north of the old hut site and it should be reached next. It has a stove and tank water, but no bunks. Just north of it, the spur pad begins to plunge even lower again. Some 3.3 km later, after descending from 1420 m through mixed forest, the Mountain Creek Track is rejoined at 660 m. It is then necessary to turn left and retrace 1.8 km along the jeep track to complete the walk at Mountain Creek picnic and camp area.

19 km; 7 hours; walk last reviewed March 1988; 'A' grade, hard, Alpine walk; all on tracks; features views and highest point in Victoria; suited to warmer months only; best to carry water for lunch, water plentiful for first 5.8 km only; *Map: Vicmap 1:25,000 Trappers Creek* refers as does Map 72, page 368.

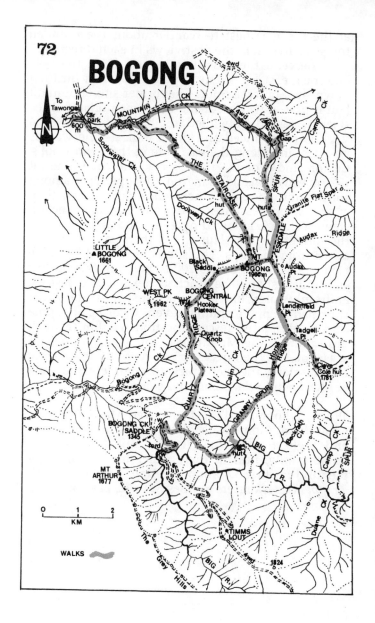

72

BOGONG

To Tawonga

N

Car park
600 m

MOUNTAIN
ford

CK

4wd

4wd

Gap

Camp Ck

Ck

Soda water Ck

THE STAIRCASE

hut

Duckwell Ck

huts

Granite Flat Spur

ESKDALE SPUR

Audax Ridge

LITTLE BOGONG
1661

Black Saddle

MT BOGONG
1986 m

Audax Pt

WEST PK
1962

BOGONG CENTRAL
1974

Hooker Plateau

Landsfield

QUARTZ RIDGE

Quartz Knob

Camp Ck

Horse Ridge

Tadgell Pt

w Cleve Cole hut
1781

Bogong Ck

GRANNY SPUR

Beckett Ck

T SPUR

Camp Ck

BOGONG CK SADDLE
1345

ford

BIG hut

MT ARTHUR
1677

Duane R.

Duane Ck

0   1   2
KM

WALKS

TIMMS LOU

4wd

1824

The Grey Hills

BIG R.

113   MOUNT BOGONG TWICE

Mount Bogong is Victoria's highest peak at 1986 m elevation, and as such a number of ascent routes have developed over the years. The majority of people climb the northern spurs, but the southern spurs are extremely attractive too, so that a walk crossing the peak from north to south, then back again next day, is most rewarding. *However in so doing, walkers must take account of the extreme exposure and violent weather changes that characterize the mountain. Warm and waterproof clothing to cope with blizzard conditions is essential even in mid summer.* The mountain has claimed many lives in the past, so take no risks. The summit has steep slopes and cliffs round much of its perimeter, so difficulty can be experienced in locating descent spurs in bad weather. Snow pole lines do cross the summit, however, and also the upper reaches of the spurs. This walk suggestion is to climb the Eskdale Spur, descend Quartz Knob, camp, then climb Grannys Spur and descend the Staircase Spur. *Walkers would do well to adhere to this route precisely, weather permitting, as climbing the Eskdale Spur is easier than The Staircase Spur, and descending Granny Spur requires expert navigation in trackless bush.*

Start the walk at the Mountain Creek picnic and camp area 10.6 km east of the Kiewa Valley Highway at Tawonga. The spot at Trappers Gap Road junction has full facilities for camping and picnics. It is 600 m above sea level and Mountain Creek jeep track leads off east from it. You enter the Bogong National Park immediately and a Walkers Intention Book is near Sodawater Creek, the first landmark as you set off. The jeep track leads east for 1.8 km to the foot track turnoff at the base of the Staircase Spur, and during this section's walk there are a number of stream fords. However, walkers *can* use foot bridges at each stream rather than get wet feet.

Pass Staircase Spur and head east on the jeep track as it rises towards Camp Creek Gap. Further fords can be avoided by using foot bridges. The latter section of jeep track, some 5.8 km from the walk start, climbs via a zig-zag and Trappers Gap Road crosses Camp Creek Gap where the jeep track meets the saddle at 1120 m elevation. Walkers should, however, by-pass the zig-zag to ascend directly to the gap 600 m distance eastwards from the first road hairpin. A ferny pad links the two spots.

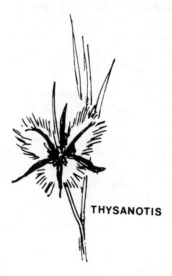

THYSANOTIS

Eskdale Spur Track then leads off steeply uphill south from the Camp Creek Gap. Another park Walkers Intention Book is located at the start of the foot track.

Soon the mixed forest of the Mountain Creek Valley is left and snow gums are reached as you climb steep Eskdale Spur. About 1.2 km from the gap, and after sidling a bit, the pad crosses a tiny stream. Water is usually available here for a lunch break at 1340 m elevation. Alternatively some may like to climb to 1620 m, 1.3 km on, to have lunch at Michell Hut. It has tank water and sleeps up to six persons.

Some 500 m further up the spur from the hut, the tree line is met and snow poles then indicate the route. Granite Flat Spur Track joins in from the left at the spot at 1700 m elevation. Continue up the track for another 1 km and the top of the spur will be attained at 1960 m. Alpine grass, flowers and views feature during the climb. At the top, snow pole number 1272 of the main summit pole line should be met. Turn right and within 200 m pass the top of the Staircase Spur Track at pole 1279. *The spot marks the descent point for the following day's walk.* Keep climbing west on the main pole line track and the large rock cairn on the peak summit is reached after just 300 m. Some wandering about the top is needed for the best views from the rounded summit. Most of north-east Victoria is in view on a fine day.

From the summit cairn, walk along the main pole line track 1 km west-south-west to cross Black Saddle, then another 1 km south-west to the Hooker Plateau area. The whole of this area is treeless, above 1900 m elevation, and very exposed. Another pole line then should be followed south to leave the tops and descend Quartz Knob. About 1 km south, the foot track steepens and the open tops change to exposed ridge walking. A few gnarled snow gums begin to appear, then the track descends into many snow gums. About 1.7 km from the Hooker Plateau tops, the track swings south-east after the snow pole line has ended. Within 600 m, it swings south again, then descends by way of several rocky knobs so as to meet a track junction after another 2 km. *The junction at 1430 m elevation marks the following day's return route via Cairn Creek.*

For the overnight camp, you should continue down the main right fork track, 400 m in distance, to a minor road just east of Bogong Creek Saddle. Turn left down the road and, after 1 km a hairpin bend, then a ford across the normally shallow Big River, will be reached. Camp on the east bank in a small cleared area at 1210 m elevation.

ANGUILLARIA

Next day, retrace 1.4 km of the previous day's walk, then continue east on the Cairn Creek Track. It sidles south-south-east along the southern slopes and onto a spur top, then, after 1.3 km, crosses the crest and degenerates. It, in fact, can be hard to follow at times. It sidles steeply down into a side gully 700 m to the confluence of the Big River and Cairn Creek at 1100 m elevation. Cross Cairn Creek at the confluence. Scrub and steep terrain make this section of the walk difficult and a compass should assist. Cairn Creek Hut is at the confluence and has two bunks.

Granny Spur is due north, but to attain it you need to diverge to the north-west for 500 m, then swing north-east and retain the spur crest. There is effectively no track. Once the crest of the spur is gained the climb is easier. Tall timber forms a dense canopy and scrub underneath is limited. Climb continually, keeping always to the highest ground. A faint foot pad should be pursued. After a knob is passed over, snow gum country is reached and walking becomes far easier. About 2.3 km from the Big River, the spur crest swings north-north-east and is then known as Horse Ridge. A second knob exists at the spot. A foot pad should become evident as Horse Ridge is climbed from about 1600 m elevation

372

up to its top at Tadgell Point at 1900 m elevation. Lunch could be considered in this locality. Snow grass slopes and a few snow gums extend over this 1.8 km stretch and make excellent walking conditions. Tadgell Point is on the Mount Bogong Plateau and the main summit snow pole line is rejoined. It is 2.5 km along the tops northwards, then west to Bogong's summit and a good track leads all the way. The pole line keeps to the very crest whilst the foot pad sidles slightly to the west of the tops for some of the distance. The whole of the distance is treeless and exposed. Watch the snow pole numbers and when back to number 1279, 300 m short of the summit, decide whether to take a second climb to the cairn. (Perhaps the weather prevented views the previous day).

To descend the mountain via Staircase Spur from pole 1279 requires care. The track is steep and exposed. The former site of Summit Hut is passed within 250 m, then a memorial to three skiers is passed. They died in a blizzard in 1943. Snow poles indicate the way as you descend and pass along the east side of Twin Knolls, Castor and Pollux to the tree line at 1720 m. It is 1 km from the tops to the tree line. Once among snow gums, the spur track tends north-west, then after a steep descent it flattens

BAUERA

out a bit. A second steep descent is followed by a second flat section and the former Bivouac Hut site is then passed. It is now used as a camp area and is 2.5 km from the tops. A new hut exists 200 m north and has stove and water tank, but no bunks.

A long descent follows once the new hut is passed. You descend from 1420 m at the hut down from snow gums into mixed forest and after 3.3 km rejoin the Mountain Creek jeep track at 660 m elevation. To finish the walk you need to then turn left and retrace the 1.8 km of jeep track walking undertaken the previous day.

38 km; 14 hours walking spread over two days of 18.5 km, 6 hours and 19.5 km, 8 hours; walk last reviewed March 1988; 'A' grade, hard, overnight, Alpine walk; jeep and foot tracks mostly, but about 3 km of trackless scrub and timber requiring good navigation; features Mount Bogong; camp water from Big River; carry water for lunches; walk suited to warmer months only; *Maps: Vicmap 1:25,000 Trappers Creek and 1:25,000 Nelse* refer as does Map 72, page 368.

114   THE TWINS

The mountains round Bright are undoubtedly the main attraction for the many holiday-makers who stay in the district every year. They see such places as Mount Hotham, Mount Buffalo and Falls Creek. In winter, snow is the attraction and in summer the alpine meadows provide superb walking. A number of relatively easy day walks are possible and one of the best of them is a little known route from Mount St Bernard to The Twins. Historic Mount St Bernard can be reached via Harrietville and up the Alpine

Way to the Dargo Road turnoff. The spot is just at the tree line at about 1500 m elevation. The walk is only short, but a steep climb is necesary in order to attain the 1703 m high summit of The Twins.

From the road junction a jeep track leads west uphill across the grassy eastern slopes of Mount St Bernard. These slopes are used as a ski run in winter. Follow the jeep track which skirts a southern shoulder of the small peak's summit. Soon the track undulates, basically south-west, down through snow gums to the low saddle 2 km away and at the eastern base of The Twins, which tower above. At this point leave the jeep track and follow the long distance walking track known as the Alpine Track. It zig-zags up the very steep slopes and is marked with yellow markers. Soon more open alpine grass slopes are reached with just a few interesting snow gums remaining and views become really good. About 1 km from the saddle, and after negotiating the zig-zags, the top of the easternmost Twin should be attained. It is above the tree line and grassy, and almost demands a rest to admire the view and alpine flora. Southwards, the Blue Rag Range dominates the scene, while to the north there are numerous well known peaks. Just 500 m west-north-west is the westernmost Twin which is slightly higher and has a trig point on its top. The walk between the two vantage points is easy and across open meadow. Views westward are the feature from the trig point, especially of Mount Buffalo, knobbly Mount Cobbler and the Mount Howitt—Crosscut Saw area. Beneath the main skyline can be seen the rugged outline of The Razor and The Viking to its left. Lunch on the summit is suggested.

Next head north-west down a minor jeep track amid snow gums for 1 km to where The Twins jeep track is rejoined. Turn right sharply to follow the jeep track as it contours round the northern slopes of The Twins among snow gums. After 2.5 km the saddle at the eastern base of The Twins should be regained

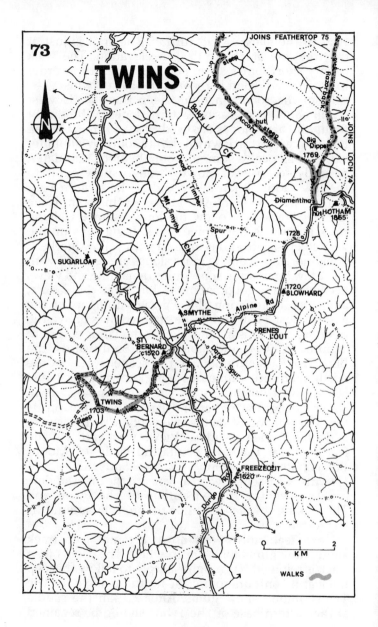

73

TWINS

JOINS FEATHERTOP 75

steep

Bon Accord Spur

Bakry

JOINS LOCH 74

2nd Razorback

hut steep

Big Dipper
1769

C'k

Dead Timber

Mt Smythe

Diamentina
hut

HOTHAM
1865

Spur

Ck

"Spur"

1728

SUGARLOAF

1720
BLOWHARD

SMYTHE

Alpine Rd

PRENES
L'OUT

ST
BERNARD
c1520

Dargo Spur

TWINS
1703

steep

steep

FREEZEOUT
1620

Dargo Rd

0   1   2
K M

WALKS

376

and then you need to retrace the route back to Mount
St Bernard to end the walk.

**9 km; 3¾ hours; last reviewed March 1988; 'A' grade,
medium Alpine walk; all on foot and jeep tracks
although alpine foot track on summit is minor and
of alpine meadow; features alpine views; no water
for lunch; not suited to winter walking as snowbound;
Map: National Mapping 1:100,000 Dargo refers as
does Map 73, page 376.**

115   MOUNT LOCH

Adjacent to the Mount Hotham ski area is Mount
Loch, one of the numerous larger peaks of north-
eastern Victoria. It attains 1875 m elevation and has
a large area above the tree line so that views are
uninhibited, especially those towards Mount
Feathertop. Mount Loch, however, can be reached
reasonably easily from the Hotham area road by way
of a high connecting ridge. But it must be realized
that this is essentially a summer walk as the whole
area is snowbound in winter and spring. Fog can be
a hazard at *any time* and due care needs to be taken
to guard against it. Fog and snow *can* occur
throughout the year.

Commence at the Mount Loch car park at
1800 m elevation on the Alpine Road just west of
Mount Hotham ski village. The Mount Loch jeep
track, the Alpine Walking Track and the Mount
Bogong Snowpole Line all lead north-east from the
car park. The pole line especially is excellent for
navigation purposes and each pole is numbered,
commencing at the car park with pole number one.
Initially, though, the numbered poles are interspersed
with a few un-numbered poles over the first 700 m

to a saddle and as a ski-lift is passed. Head from the saddle to the Charles Derrick Memorial Cairn near the top of a knob 1.4 km from the walk start. Pole 31 is at the spot.

FALCON

Descend again to Derrick Col 1740 m elevation and Pole 44, 2 km from the car park, then climb fairly steeply to Pole 60, either by way of the pole line pad, or the jeep track a bit west of the line. By now, 2.6 km from the start, views back at Mount Hotham are excellent and 1820 m elevation has been attained.

The jeep track turns north at the spot, whereas the poles lead south-south-east downhill across open snow grass slopes. Follow the poles (and Alpine Walking Track) gradually downhill, leaving the exposed tops and reaching Pole 90 at a tiny creek crossing suited for a lunch break. During the 1.4 km long descent views, both east and west, are excellent and on a clear day include even Mount Kosciusko in New South Wales.

At 1740 m elevation and just 200 m beyond the stream is the Charles Derrick memorial Refuge Hut at Pole 94. It is worth a short walk from the lunch spot before turning back. The whole locality is like an alpine garden with just sufficient snow gums to enhance the scene without blocking views.

After lunch return to Pole 60 by retracing the outward route, then take a side trip to Mount Loch summit. To include the summit you need only walk north on the jeep track for 600 m, then leave the

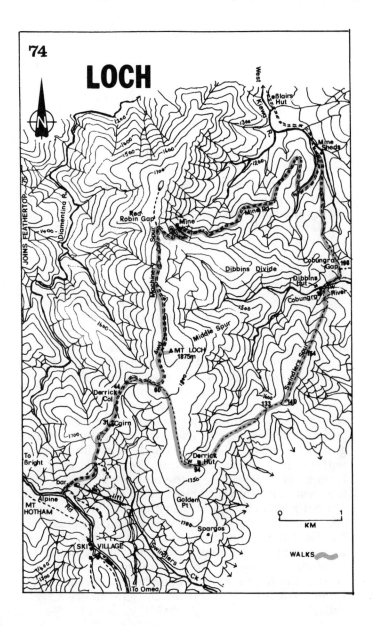

74

LOCH

N

JOINS FEATHERTOP—75

Diamentina R.

West Kiewa R.

Blairs Hut

Mine Sheds

1300

1200

Mine Rd

Red Robin Gap

Mine

1700

1600

1500

1400

Machiner Spur

Dibbins Divide

Cobungra Gap

198

Dibbins Hut

Cobungra River

1500

Middle Spur

▲ MT LOCH
1875m

60

Swindlers Spur

1754

133

149

1600

1700

Derrick Col

31 Cairn

1700

To Bright

Derrick W g Hut
94

bar

Alpine Rd

lift

1750

MT HOTHAM

Golden Pt

1700

SKI VILLAGE

Swindlers

Ck

1600

1500

Spargos

0   1
KM

WALKS

To Omeo

jeep track to cross snow grass for 200 m eastwards to the cairn and rocky top. This sector is very open and treeless. Again views are excellent, but especially so of Mount Feathertop.

The remainder of the walk involves just retracing the route to Pole 60 then retracing the pole line route to the car park at Pole No. 1.

10 km; 3 hours; last reviewed March 1988; 'A' grade medium Alpine walk; all but 400 m on tracks with remainder over snow grass; features views, water for lunch at Pole 90 on upper limits of Cobungra River; walk suited only to summer and warmer months such as March and April; *Map: Vicmap 1:25,000 Feathertop* refers as does Map 74, page 379.

116   MOUNT LOCH-DIBBINS

In walking and cross-country skiing circles one often hears the remark, 'Mount Feathertop is the only really alpine-looking peak on the Australian mainland'. It certainly seems that the statement is true, especially when one stands on top of Mount Loch and looks across the Diamentina River valley to The Razorback and Mount Feathertop. There are just enough snow gums to make the foreground very interesting without in any way blocking distant views. Late November to February is the alpine springtime and the best time to visit this area. Winter walking is normally out of the question, although it is wonderful for cross-country skiing if you are an experienced Nordic skier. A really good circuit walk can be undertaken in the area. It includes views not only of Mount Feathertop and The Razorback, but also of the Cobungra River valley, West Kiewa River valley, Bogong High Plains and Swindlers Creek valley.

Commence at the Mount Loch car park at 1800 m height on the Alpine Road, just west of Mount Hotham ski village. The Mount Loch jeep track, Alpine Walking Track and Mount Bogong Snowpole Line all lead north-east down from the car park. The pole line especially is excellent for navigation purposes and each pole is numbered, commencing at the car park with pole No. 1. The walk is not recommended in foggy weather as views are the main walk feature and good navigation is essential.

Walk down the jeep track past snow grass slopes and a few snow gums, then past a ski tow, off right, after 700 m, cross a small saddle and head up to Charles Derrick Memorial Cairn near the top of a knob 1.4 km from the car park. Snow pole No. 31 is at the spot, the poles having, basically, followed the jeep track. Descend again to Derrick Col at 1740 m and pole No. 44, 2 km from the car park, then start a fairly steep climb to pole No. 60, following the poles or the jeep track.

SPOTTED SUN ORCHID

By this time, 2.6 km out, views back to Mount Hotham are excellent and 1820 m height has been attained. The area is more open and the jeep track turns north at the spot whereas the snow poles lead south-south-east downhill across snow grass slopes. Follow the poles (and Alpine Walking Track) gradually downhill, leaving the tops and reaching pole No. 90 at a creek crossing on the north-eastern slopes. The stream is the extreme upper limits of the Cobungra River watershed and is a reliable drinking water supply. During the 1.4 km long descent, views both east and west are excellent. The pad and pole line swing east from the creek and Charles Derrick Memorial Hut is at pole No. 94 at 1740 m elevation, amid lovely snow gums. The hut is a very comfortable emergency shelter with a stove, but no bunks. It is in excellent condition and is 4.2 km from Mount Loch car park.

Continue on downhill, north-east along the pole line and Alpine Track. The route follows Swindlers Spur which remains high with good views and more fine snow gums. After 1.5 km at pole No. 133, a saddle should be crossed at 1620 m elevation, then onwards another 700 m are extremely good views to the right of pole No. 140. The view is of the Cobungra River valley and is from a fairly flat topped section of Swindlers Spur at 1680 m. At pole No. 154, 500 m on, the spur suddenly steepens and the pad and pole line route descends rapidly to the Cobungra River over a 1.4 km length, losing altitude to 1350 m and

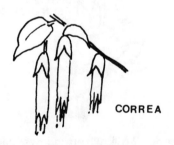

CORREA

leaving the snow gums. Dibbins Hut, re-furbished, but still an old rustic cattleman's hut, lies beside the river's south bank on grassy flats in an area ideal for camping. The hut is comfortable and is 8 km from the walk start. Camp is suggested here. Pole No. 187

is the nearest to the hut, the pole line passing just east of it.

Next day, cross the Cobungra River on a log at the pad and poles alignment, turn right along the north bank for 250 m on the pad across grassy slopes, and past some fencing, then turn north at pole No. 194. Leave the river and climb about 150 m in distance, rising about 30 m on the pad to low Cobungra Gap at pole No. 198. Leave the pole line at the gap in a wooded area and fork north-north-west onto another foot track. (The Alpine Track leads east up the pole line and is left at this point.) Head down towards Blairs Hut and Westons Hut through stands of alpine ash trees on the sidling pad. It soon joins the end of a jeep track and leads onto the crest of a spur, then after 1.65 km, meets the Red Robin Mine Battery at 1200 m elevation. Several small roads are

SASSAFRAS

near the battery in an area which has been logged in the past. Turn sharply back south-west at the battery to follow the east bank of the main creek in the area via a rough mine access road. A steady climb follows, up the roadway through alpine ash and into snow gums. The road initially crosses the creek at a sharp bend, then leads to the Red Robin gold mine at 1600 m elevation some 3.8 km up from the battery. At the mine the road zig-zags and attains Red Robin Gap 1700 m high and 500 m further. The Gap is on the magnificent Machinery Spur crest.

Turn south remaining on the spur crest jeep track as it rises to a point just 200 m west of the summit of Mount Loch 1.8 km south of Red Robin Gap. Excellent views exist right along Machinery Spur. The main feature is Mount Feathertop across the valley, whilst snow gums are very beautiful too. Leave the road for a short side trip to Mount Loch (like Mt Hotham and Higginbotham, named after an early State Governor) then return to the road and head on south for 600 m to rejoin the outward route at snow pole No. 60. This latter section is quite open and indeed exposed. Turn right along the pole line and finish the day's walk with a 2.6 km long retrace of the walk back to the Alpine Road at Mount Hotham.

19.5 km; 8 hours; spread over two days of 8 km and 11.5 km (3 hours and 5 hours) respectively; walk last reviewed March 1988; 'A' grade, medium, Alpine, overnight walk; all on tracks and roads; features Mount Loch views; water for lunch on day one near Derrick Hut and for overnight camp from the Cobungra River, but no water available for lunch on day two after leaving the Red Robin Battery area; walk best suited to summer and quite unsuited to winter and early spring; *Map: Vicmap 1:25,000 Feathertop* refers as does Map 74, page 379.

117   HARRIETVILLE-MOUNT FEATHERTOP

Mount Feathertop in the north-east of the State has long been a drawcard for walkers wanting a magnificent venue and a challenge. The traditional route of ascent of the mountain has been up the Bungalow Spur Track from Harrietville. Many walkers take an overnight trip staying the night at Federation Hut, but others prefer a hard one day walk with no need to carry the heavy pack. The peak is the second highest in Victoria at 1922 m and, as such, it is subject to violent and sudden weather changes, plus heavy snow in winter and spring. Naturally walkers need to take account of these factors. The reward for the day's climb is a view of much of north-eastern Victoria. The last 200 m elevation is above the tree line.

GREENHOOD ORCHID

Just north of Harrietville is a bridge over the East Branch of the Ovens River. A road leads off along the east bank from the bridge and it leads across the old Harrietville gold diggings for about 1 km to the start of the Bungalow Spur Track. This foot track follows up the south side of a small creek initially, crosses it onto a spur, then sidles on the spur back to recross the stream. This marks the start of a long climb, usually with no water available over much of the middle reaches of the climb ahead. So, if required, collect drinking water from the creek, then continue up the foot track as it rises onto the slopes of a spur which supports drier type vegetation than that nearer the creek. The track climbs to Wombat Gap about 5 km from the foot track start and some 650 m higher in elevation. At the gap the main Bungalow Spur is joined. The way is then south-east up into areas of woollybutt (alpine ash) trees via the southern slopes of the spur until the former site of the Old Feathertop Hut is reached, 2.5 km from Wombat Gap. There is a grassy clearing where the hut used to stand and snow gums become common just short of the locality. Water is available 200 m south down a side track so lunch is suggested in the clearing, at an altitude of 1600 m.

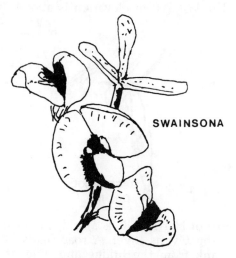

SWAINSONA

After lunch continue up south-east for 1.2 km to reach the tree line, Federation Hut and a grassy ridge at about 1720 m elevation. From the hut keep going up the foot track eastwards for 500 m to a saddle known as 'The Cross' where the Razorback Ridge Track joins in from the right via the western slopes of Molly Hill. At The Cross Feathertop can be seen fully for the first time. As the name implies there is a cross erected at the saddle attesting to the fact that people have lost their lives in this area. Great care needs to be taken to avoid bad weather and the summit ahead should *not* be attempted if fog is about.

To gain the summit 1.5 km distant, sidle north-east on Molly Hill to another saddle and avoid the North-West Spur Track off left as you proceed. It is then necessary to simply climb directly up the main southern spur to the top. The view from the top no doubt will cause you to linger, but remember not to cut the time too short for the later descent back to Harrietville, retracing the morning route.

21.4 km; 8 hours; walk last reviewed February 1987; 'A' grade hard Alpine walk; all on tracks; features Mount Feathertop; water for lunch from stream 200 m from Old Feathertop Hut site; walk not suited to winter or early spring as completely snowbound over upper reaches; *Maps: Vicmap 1:25,000 Harrietville and 1:25,000 Feathertop* **refer as does Map 75, page 389.**

STINKWOOD

118   THE RAZORBACK-MOUNT FEATHERTOP

Mount Feathertop is Victoria's second highest peak and perhaps the only peak that looks like a true alpine peak. From most directions, any climb is difficult. The Razorback Ridge however offers high level walking with views nearly all the way to Mount Feathertop. The district is heavily snow covered in winter and often in spring, but in summer provides some of Victoria's best walking. During any walk, great care must be exercised in foggy conditions, but in this walk *the final ascent of the peak should not be undertaken in fog.* Remember that in this area violent and sudden weather changes are frequent. Try this walk *in summer* from Diamentina Hut on the Alpine Road 1 km west of the summit of Mount Hotham. The Razorback Ridge route leads northwards and basically there is a good foot track that follows the ridge, although there are points where the pad contours the slopes rather than remaining on the crest. At first the track starts off north along a snow pole line.

ZEBRA   FINCHES

Within about 800 m of the start of the walk, the foot track divides and you should veer right rather than continue to follow the snow pole line over a hill and down the Bon Accord Spur. The main track immediately begins to sidle the eastern slopes down into a deep saddle known at the Big Dipper. It is about 2 km from the walk start. The track then sidles further to regain the tops gradually. About 7 km from the walk start and on the crest, the top of the Champion Spur is reached. The *National Mapping 1:100,000 Bogong Sheet* incorrectly shows a track joining onto the Razorback at this point. No track exists on Champion Spur. The ridge track temporarily turns east for about 500 m to wind through between the Twin Knobs area in a most pretty locality. Soon the track divides with one route leading round the eastern slopes of a knob at the top of the Diamentina Spur. Better to veer left and sidle more directly through snow gums down the west side of the knob. The tracks rejoin within about 400 m, then continue along the tops towards nearby Molly Hill. The route then

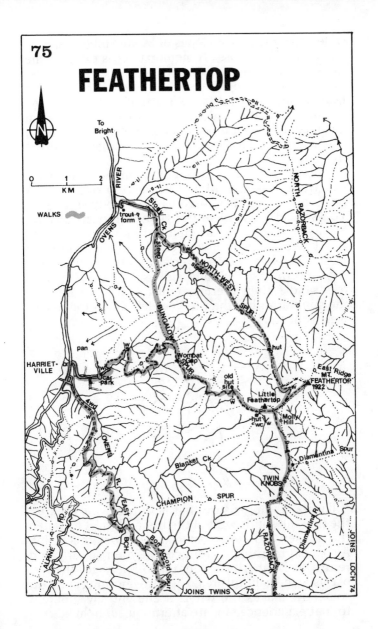

75

FEATHERTOP

N

To
Bright

0   1   2
KM

WALKS

OVENS RIVER

Story Ck

trout farm

NORTH RAZORBACK

steep

NORTH-WEST SPUR

BUNGALOW SPUR

W

pan

hut

HARRIET-VILLE

car park

Wombat SPUR

old hut site

W

East Ridge
MT. FEATHERTOP
1922

Little Feathertop

W

Molly Hill

hut wc w

4wd

OVENS R.

Blanket Ck

Diamentina Spur

CHAMPION SPUR

TWIN KNOBS

ALPINE RD.

EAST BCH.

Bor Accord Spur

RAZORBACK

Diamentina R.

JOINS LOCH 74

JOINS TWINS 73

389

sidles down the west slopes of Molly Hill to a saddle known as 'The Cross'. A memorial cross exists at the saddle giving due warning that lives have been lost on this mountain. This spot is some 10.5 km from Diamentina Hut and there is a track junction in the saddle. Turn left and descend west about 500 m distance to Federation Hut and camp site on a particularly lovely grassy section of ridge just at the tree line.

Once at camp it is strongly recommended that a side trip be taken to Mount Feathertop summit. The peak top is 2 km distant and 1922 m above sea level. You should allow plenty of time to return to camp *before dark*, but a late afternoon walk is preferable to watch the sun sink low over Mount Buffalo in the west. To reach the top, return to The Cross, then head north-east, initially sidling Molly Hill slopes to a saddle, then veering right up the spur crest to the summit rather than to veer left down the north-west spur track.

CALADENIA

Back at camp, ensure that at sunset you walk up the tiny hill south-west of the hut and toilet to watch the sunset. It is often spectacular from this point. Also, next morning it is suggested you rise early and return to Feathertop's summit to really get the feel of this wild beautiful area. The early morning sunlight somehow makes the whole scene entirely different to that experienced in late afternoon sunlight.

The rest of the day's activities involves retracing the Razorback Ridge route back to Diamentina Hut.

30 km; 12 hours (assuming two trips of 4 km each from camp to Mount Feathertop included); two day walk, each day 15 km, 6 hours; walk last reviewed February 1987; 'A' grade, easy, overnight, Alpine walk; features Mount Feathertop; no water for lunches, water for camp from a tank at the Federation Hut, from springs adjacent to the North-west spur track immediately west of Feathertop's summit or from a deep gully east of the hut; whole of walk on tracks; walk *not* suited to winter and early spring; *Maps: Vicmap 1:25,000 Harrietville and 1:25,000 Feathertop* refer as do Maps 73 and 75, pages 376 and 389.

119 BUNGALOW SPUR-MOUNT FEATHERTOP-NORTH WEST SPUR

Mount Feathertop is the favourite mountain for many Victorian Bushwalkers. It reaches 1922 metres, the state's second highest peak. It is always heavily snowbound in winter and usually has impressive cornices. But in summer the slopes are green and wildflower decked. There are five customary approach routes to the summit, but all start at widely separated spots and therefore to ascend by one route and to descend by another requires a transport shuttle. Few walkers seem to realize, however, that a walk circuit can be completed from the base of the traditional North-west Spur route. The Bungalow Spur actually starts near the North-west Spur. It is only the Bungalow Spur foot track that starts at Harrietville, and joins the spur well up the mountain. The lower reaches of the Bungalow Spur have a rough foot pad and the ascent is rather steep, but more gradual than the very steep North-west Spur track. *For this reason, and to facilitate navigation, it is strongly recommended that the circuit be completed in an anti-clockwise direction with an overnight stop in Federation Hut, or preferably camped on the open alpine grass outside the hut. Naturally winter walking is best left to the experts only, and even then an ice axe is usually essential as is full blizzard conditions gear. On a sunny day in winter sun glasses are essential to prevent snow blindness.*

TETRATHECA

Travel along the Ovens Valley Highway to a spot south of Bright which is 14.7 km south of the Tawonga Road turnoff and to a bridge across the Ovens River to the entrance to the Stony Creek Trout Farm and Deer Park.

To start the walk you need to bypass the trout farm. To do this, travel Stony Creek Road 200 m north, then go eastwards. Soon this roadway enters the trout farm and services a number of breeding ponds. You should however, walk the road straight east, passing through a gate.

After 1 km of walking, and by this time in forest, the route leaves the streamside flats and farm. A farm jeep track at the spot heads off up some slopes to the right, but you should walk the minor foot pad diverging off left up the slopes just where the jeep track leaves the flats. You should keep left of a fence bordering a clearing until 1.6 km from the walk start.

A gully should be crossed next, and only 10 m up the other side of the gully the pad starts to return to the streamside flats. Do not descend, but fork right up a wooded spur leading south. Light scrub exists, but a minor pad is recognizable heading up the spur crest. With further climbing the ascent becomes quite steep and the pad sometimes disappears due to thick scrub, then later reappears higher, but all that is needed is to keep to the highest ground. After 1.5 km of arduous climbing the gradient becomes easier, but is still persistent for a further 1 km. By this stage the hardest part of the ascent of the mountain is over, but there is still a long gradual climb ahead. Continue on south-south-east up a very gradual grade for 1 km still in forest to reach a small hilltop. Head over the hill on a foot pad keeping to the same general direction, then over a second more scrubby knob 200 m further on and walk down a 500 m long gradual, but somewhat scrubby, descent to Wombat Gap, keeping to the highest ground on the ridge.

Wombat Gap is where the main Bungalow Spur foot track from Harrietville reaches the spur crest from the right. Follow the well defined track next. It is well graded and soon leaves the Bungalow Spur crest to skirt up the southern slopes and to reach the Old Feathertop Hut site within another 2.5 km.

If required, water is available from a creek 200 m down from the track to the right (south) via a tiny pad. A small clearing on the spur in the area permits the first good distant views and snow gums are quite gnarled, old and beautiful. Lunch is suggested at the clearing even though camp is only 1.2 km further up the track.

Federation Hut, the recommended camp area, is right at the tree line and is set on a magnificent part of the spur. Tent pitching is preferable. If the weather is good walkers should make the effort to climb to the summit once camp is pitched, even though the climb thus far may have caused some tiredness. The top is still 2 km distant, but the weather changes very rapidly and by leaving the climb till the next morning weather may cause a complete lack of visibility.

To reach the summit, simply continue on up the foot track east 500 m to a saddle known as 'The Cross' where the Razorback Ridge track joins in from the right on the western slopes of Molly Hill. Feathertop comes into full view from the saddle and lies north-east 1.5 km away. Climb up on the pad avoiding the North-west Spur Track off left at a saddle after 500 m, then simply scale the summit spur to the 1922 m high bushwalker's paradise. The view includes much of North-East Victoria and is especially good of the Ovens Valley and south along the Razorback to Mount Hotham and Mount Loch. Return to camp, then at sunset do not miss walking about 200 m to the top of the small hill, just south-west of the hut, to watch the sun set over Mount Buffalo.

MUMC HUT

On the second day, climb to the summit either again—or for the first time if not achieved the previous evening—leaving packs at the North-west Spur Track turnoff. The second ascent is worthwhile in that morning light casts a different setting to the afternoon light. Next, head on down the North-west Spur Track as it sidles down across the very steep western slopes of the summit. *In winter, be warned deep snow makes the route very awkward and the track becomes quite indistinguishable.* The pad leads onto the prominent North-west Spur and out along a fairly flat stretch of the narrow spur to conspicuous M.U.M.C.

Hut, an igloo-shaped large, well kept hut. This hut is some 3.5 km from Federation Hut. M.U.M.C. Hut has water laid on and as such could be a good early lunch spot before leaving the heights.

From the hut the pad leads north-west down the spur crest gradually for about 2.5 km, then makes a dramatic 2 km long descent to Stony Creek. The whole distance from the hut is within trees. In the middle reaches the track is overhung by a fair amount of scrub. Stony Creek is crossed on logs and a good water supply exists at the crossing so, if lunch was not eaten at the hut, the creek would be a good alternative. The pad then climbs a little, then descends again to skirt the stream's northern slopes for 1.2 km to another log crossing. It then crosses a blackberry and raspberry infested flat and rises up to rejoin the previous day's outward route after 400 m. It is then a 1.6 km retrace to the walk's end.

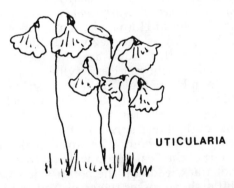

UTICULARIA

27.6 km; 11 hours, spread over two days of 14.1 km, 6½ hours and 13.5 km, 4½ hours respectively; last reviewed February 1987; 'A' grade, overnight, medium, Alpine walk; mostly on good tracks, but scrub on pronounced lower Bungalow Spur; features Mount Feathertop views; water for camp from hut tank, from in a deep gully east of Federation hut, otherwise it is available from springs beside the

North-west Spur Track on the slopes immediately west
of Mount Feathertop's summit; walk suited best to
summertime with winter and early spring walking
not advised; *Maps: Vicmap 1:25,000 Harrietville,
1:25,000 Feathertop and 1:25,000 Freeburgh* refer as
does Map 75, page 389.

120 BUNGALOW SPUR-MOUNT FEATHERTOP-
BON ACCORD SPUR

Mount Feathertop is Victoria's second highest peak
at 1922 m. It is located in the North-east of the State.
Its summit is well above the tree line, so views are
superb. The peak is beautifully shaped and it excels
all others in mainland Australia in likeness to a true
alpine peak. *However, it can be dangerous in winter and
is renowned for violent weather changes even in summer.*
It is linked to Mount Hotham by a magnificent high-
level ridge known as the Razorback Ridge. Mount
Feathertop and this ridge are the focus for the
following walk, starting at Harrietville.

Just north of Harrietville in the Ovens River valley
is a bridge over the Ovens River East Branch where
a road leads off from the north end of the bridge
and heads south, then east, across the old Harrietville
gold dredgings for about 1 km to a small car park
and the start of the Feathertop walking track.

The foot track leads up the south side of a small
creek a little, then crosses the creek and commences
a long climb on the well graded route. *Collect some
drinking water at the creek as usually there is no water
available in the middle reaches of the long climb ahead.* At
first the track remains not far from the stream amid
damp vegetation, but then it recrosses the creek, and
rises onto the slopes of a spur which is covered with
drier forest. It then ascends the spur to Wombat Gap
about 6 km from the walk start and 650 m higher.

The way is then south-east of the main Bungalow Spur. Stands of woollybutt trees are prevalent as Wombat Gap is left and the well graded track sidles the southern slopes of the Bungalow Spur to reach the former site of the Old Feathertop Hut 2.5 km from Wombat Gap. Snow gum country is reached just before the clearing marking the old hut site. Water is available 200 m south down a short track from the clearing and the spot would be good for a lunch break. By this stage you have climbed a further 360 m in elevation to reach 1600 m above sea level.

Next, continue up south-east for 1.2 km to reach the tree line, Federation Hut and the suggested camp site for the night on a grassy ridge top. Usually, tent pitching is preferable to using the hut.

SNOWGUM

If the weather is good, walkers should make the effort to climb to the summit of Mount Feathertop once camp is organized, even though the climb thus far may have caused some tiredness. The crest is still 2 km distant and 200 m higher, but the weather changes very rapidly and by leaving the climb till next morning, weather may spoil visibility. Additionally the distance to be covered the following day is considerably longer than that of day one, so it is best not to overstretch matters on the second day.

To reach the summit, continue on up the foot track

east 500 m to a saddle known as 'The Cross' where the Razorback Ridge track joins in on the right from the western slopes of Molly Hill. Feathertop comes into full view from this saddle. Head north-east on the continuing track, sidling Molly Hill for 500 m, then avoid the North-west Spur track off left in favour of ascending the main summit spur. The view from the top includes much of north-eastern Victoria. Return to camp after a good look round, then at sunset do not miss walking about 200 m to the top of a small hill behind the hut and toilet block in order to watch the sunset over Mount Buffalo.

On the second day rise early especially if you failed to include the summit deviation the previous evening and wish to include it before heading off along the Razorback Ridge. You need first to return to 'The Cross' then turn south to sidle the western slopes of Molly Hill to gain the crest of the Razorback. About 1.5 km from 'The Cross', the track splits with one track passing along each side of High Knob which is the top of the Diamentina Spur. The most direct route of the two to take is the right fork western slopes pad.

After the two tracks rejoin, the way continues along the crest of the Razorback through a very beautiful area known at the 'Twin Knobs'. The pad winds through between knobs and gullies of rock on the crest then it turns west briefly to meet the top of the Champion Spur about 3.5 km from 'The Cross'. The *National Mapping 1:100,000 Bogong Map Sheet* incorrectly shows a track joining in from the Champion Spur at this point. The route ahead is south along the tops, into snow gums and downhill a bit, but still on the ridge crest. Then the track sidles down the eastern slopes amid alpine grassland and into the Big Dipper (a deep saddle), 5 km from the Champion Spur.

At the saddle the main track begins to rise up the eastern slopes of the ridge again, but you should head south-west steeply uphill out of the saddle to remain on the crest. The climb is 500 m distance directly onto the top of the Bon Accord Spur and to a point 1769 m above sea level. A snow pole line from Diamentina Hut passes over this knob and down the upper sector of the Bon Accord Spur. The spot is about 1.5 km out from Diamentina Hut and the Alpine Road to Mount Hotham.

Descend west following the snow pole line initially and within 500 m the alpine meadows are left as you enter snow gums. The track remains right on the spur, passes an old hut ruin within another 500 m, descends steeply in scrubby country, then descends further through fine stands of alpine ash trees to reach Bon Accord Hut. The hut is about 2.5 km from the top of the Bon Accord Spur, has tank water and is situated on a flat sector of the spur crest. Lunch is suggested at the hut amid the alpine ash forest. The hut is old, with four bunks.

To continue, head on north-west along the foot track which maintains a relatively flat and gentle gradient for some 2 km as it bypasses some high points on the spur. The track then begins a very steep descent and by way of subsidiary spurs and zig-zags reaches the confluence of Washington Creek and the Ovens River East branch. The confluence is only 620 m above sea level and some 7 km from Bon Accord Hut. A log bridge provides access to the west bank of the Ovens River. The track then rises up the grassy and lightly forested slopes from the river and leads basically north-north-west for about 2.8 km as an old mining track before it becomes a jeep track.

There are still old mine workings to be seen. At times the foot track is well above the river level as it sidles round a number of spurs. Once on the jeep track section, it is 1.2 km further to Dickenson Creek and the boundary of the Bogong National Park. The jeep track then follows near the river bank for 1 km past the Feathertop Chalet and onto the Main Street of Harrietville. There are remains of an old powder magazine on the right just as the main street is neared.

To complete the walk you then need to walk down the main street past the hotel and milk bar to the Ovens River bridge 600 m distant. Immediately across the bridge on the right is the Bungalow Track access road upon which the walk commenced the previous day.

38.5 km; 14 hours, walking spread over two days of 14 km, 6 hours and 24.5 km, 8 hours; walk last reviewed February 1987; 'A' grade, hard, overnight, Alpine walk; all on tracks and roads; features Mount Feathertop and Razorback Ridge; Camp water at hut tank, or from deep gully due east of Federation Hut, otherwise from springs beside the North-west Spur track immediately west of Mount Feathertop, water for lunch, first day, from stream near Old Feathertop Hut site and water for lunch on second day from tank at Bon Accord Hut; walk not suited to winter or early spring; _Maps: Vicmap 1:25,000 Harrietville and 1:25,000 Feathertop_ refer as do Maps 73 and 75, pages 376 and 389.

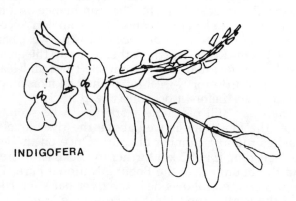

INDIGOFERA

INDEX TO MAPS